IMAGES of America

FRANKLIN COUNTY

To my grandparents Wallace Walker and Elizabeth Clara Muchmore Page

IMAGES
of America

FRANKLIN COUNTY

Lola Shropshire

ARCADIA
PUBLISHING

ISBN 978-0-7385-0882-5

Published by Arcadia Publishing
Charleston, South Carolina

Printed in the United States of America

Library of Congress Catalog Card Number: 00-101203

For all general information contact Arcadia Publishing at:
Telephone 843-853-2070
Fax 843-853-0044
E-Mail sales@arcadiapublishing.com
For customer service and orders:
Toll-Free 1-888-313-2665

Visit us on the Internet at www.arcadiapublishing.com

Sources

Sadler Hiram Burrow's unpublished *Writings, Letters, Papers and Documents*, George Henry's unpublished Masters Theses, *History of Franklin County*; Sue White and Virginia McPhail, books *1800 Census Index, Register of Births and Marriage Records*; Historian Norman Powell, *A History of Ozark*; T. Moore's *Diary*; Goodspeeds *History of Franklin County;* Franklin County Historical Society, *Historical Society Observers;* Ferguson and Atkinson, *Historic Arkansas*; Virginia Muchmore Canady, *History of Altus, 100 years, 1888–1998*; Mary Maude Gallagher, *100 Years of St. Mary's Church, Altus and Its Mission*; *The Spectator*; *Arkansas River Valley Handbook,* published in 1887; Sharon Bass, *For the Trees*; Janice Holt Giles, *The Kinta Years;* Hazel Presson, *The Story of Arkansas*; C.H. McKennon, *Iron Men*; Glenn Shirley, *"Bud" Ledbetter, The Fourth Guardsman*; numerous articles of the *Fort Smith Times Record*.

CONTENTS

ACKNOWLEDGMENTS

Thank you to the following: Bob Burrow for sharing the collection of negatives, writings, papers, and documents of his father, Sadler Hiram Burrow; Fuji Film Studios Color Processing, Bentonville, for printing the negatives of the Burrow Collection; Historian Norman Powell for sharing his photo collection and information, and wife Latane Andrews Powell's photos and memories; Grace Mason Watts and Coy Watts for photo images they collected and preserved; Harry Blackman for information and sharing his postcard collection; the staff's help and photos of the Fort Smith Public Library Collection; Ann Sayers for her help; Louise Zolliecoffer and her son, Robert, for photos and information; Pat Hewitt for information; Bedford Camera and Video for developing and printing photos; Shirley Parker Demere for information; Mark Coker's help and Tena Coker's encouragement; Lynn Riebow for the loan of his equipment; Chester Cowen for his help; Edith Page Wright for sharing photos and memories; Dollis Page Rickard for sharing photos and memories; David Rickard for sharing memories of Altus and coal-mining and for Sally Rickard; Billy and Tommy Leverette for sharing memories of coal-mining; Ronnie and Sherrill Adams Cox for photos and history; Jimmy Jacobs for being mayor and for family photos and memories of Altus; Ozark Librarian Nancy Smith for great help and encouragement; Paul Post for family photos and information; Attorney Gary Udouj for photos, and information of the Udouj and Wiederkehr Families; John and Julie Northrip for encouragement; Elizabeth Muchmore Page and Wallace Page for taking many photos and preserving them, and for their historical narratives; Alice Warren Muchmore for photographing, printing, and preserving family photos; Father Hilary Filiatreau for the use of St. Mary's Catholic Church Photo Collection; Sister Madeline Clifton for sharing photos, and memories; Jo Eveld and *The Spectator* for publishing an old photo; Sheriff Kenneth Ross for unlocking my car; Chris Ewing for information; Mary Belle Ervin, of *Belle Museum and Chapel*, for sharing photos and for the preservation work of she and her husband Delbert Ervin; Isaac Bollinger for sharing a photo and information; Charlie Hiatt for sharing photos and stories, and his wife M.J. Hiatt; Sister Irene Verkamp for sharing photos and history; Karla and Lee Rozell who shared postcards; Dr. Larry Pillstrom for sharing photos and information; Mark and Beverly Jane Hamm Roloff for family photos and memories; Author Janice Holt Giles's daughter, Libby Moore Hancock, for use of photos; U.S.Forest Service Archeologist Mike Dryden for use of Forest Service photos and information; U.S. Forest Service Public Affairs Specialist Tracy Powers, Russellville, for photos and information; Greg Miller, U.S. Corps of Engineers, Ozark Field Office, for sharing photos, information, and for contacting the U.S. Corps of Engineers, Little Rock Office, for me. For those whom I've forgotten, I'm sorry and thank you.

INTRODUCTION

Franklin County was created from a portion of Crawford County by an act of the state legislature on December 19, 1837. The Arkansas River divides the territory into two parts. One-third lies to the south of the river, which is predominantly agricultural, and two thirds is on the north side of the river. Franklin County enjoys graceful and vastly productive prairie lands. Due to the difficulty of early crossings of the Arkansas River, county seats were established in Ozark in North Franklin County and in Charleston in South Franklin County.

Northern Franklin County is remote, mysterious, and beautiful. It not only has similar farmlands to South Franklin County, but has the grandeur of the Ozark Mountains. The Ozarks' combination of fertile soil and mild climate produces fruit, wine vineyards, precious stones, coal, granite, marble, and wood forests. The most notable aspect of Franklin County, though, is the decent and honorable people who live there.

A big thank you to those who contributed in any way to the publication of this book, if only in the form of encouragement. I'm pleased, as I hope you are, that many beloved friends and family live once again in the pages of this book.

I did not use many wonderful photos due to lack of information of the subject, or I was already using one of similar nature. And, due to time constraints and having to travel distances for research, many good photos went undiscovered. This book in no way reflects a complete pictorial history of the area. Other publications of this nature can, and should be done. Authors will never run out of good material. And, here in advance, I apologize for my mistakes.

In doing the second book for Arcadia Publishing I'm struck by my own personal feelings relating to these particular photos, and subjects. No photo image left me more emotional than that of the 12-15-year-old school girls, in the Altus schoolyard, in the early 1900s. They stand together, with sweet vulnerable faces, their arms about one another's shoulders. I have just now discovered their existence, only to realize they have not only grown old, but they may all now be deceased. Yet, I try not to think that they're gone. Instead, I try to think of them as preserved forever in playful innocence in an image snapped by a thoughtful photographer. I hope that you, the reader, will enjoy looking at the photos and reading about the people, as I do. And, I know you will appreciate, as I do, those who guarded, protected, and preserved the photos, and the stories. They shared their photo treasures with me, and ultimately with you.

Graveyards were part of the cultural upbringing of this region. History lessons, and morals, were taught while visiting those "who have gone on before" in the cemeteries. People of 50 to 100 years ago, in the Franklin County area, had few of the advantages that we have today, yet they enjoyed themselves to the fullest. Their hard work made this country what it is and allows us to enjoy many advantages we would not have without them. They believed in God, in themselves, and in their prospects for the future. Along with God, other main ingredients were faith and hope. Those gifts were necessary to survival.

Those days were difficult for folks who did not deal well with poverty. In the early 1900s, some coal miners struck for higher wages, which took a lot of courage. While they were idle, two brothers decided to try their hand at treasure hunting. They did not locate the "long lost treasure," but the time spent looking filled a void. In the mid-1930s, when things looked better financially, people slowed down in their quest for this particular gold mine.

The Lost Louisiana Mine served a purpose in that it took people from their despair and gave them hope for a better life. Various treasure hunters mined for the gold from 1918 all the way through the Great Depression, and on a smaller scale through the 1950s. Yet, many continue to wonder if the gold is still there, just waiting for the right person to discover it.

—Lola Shropshire

One

Altus High Point of Learning

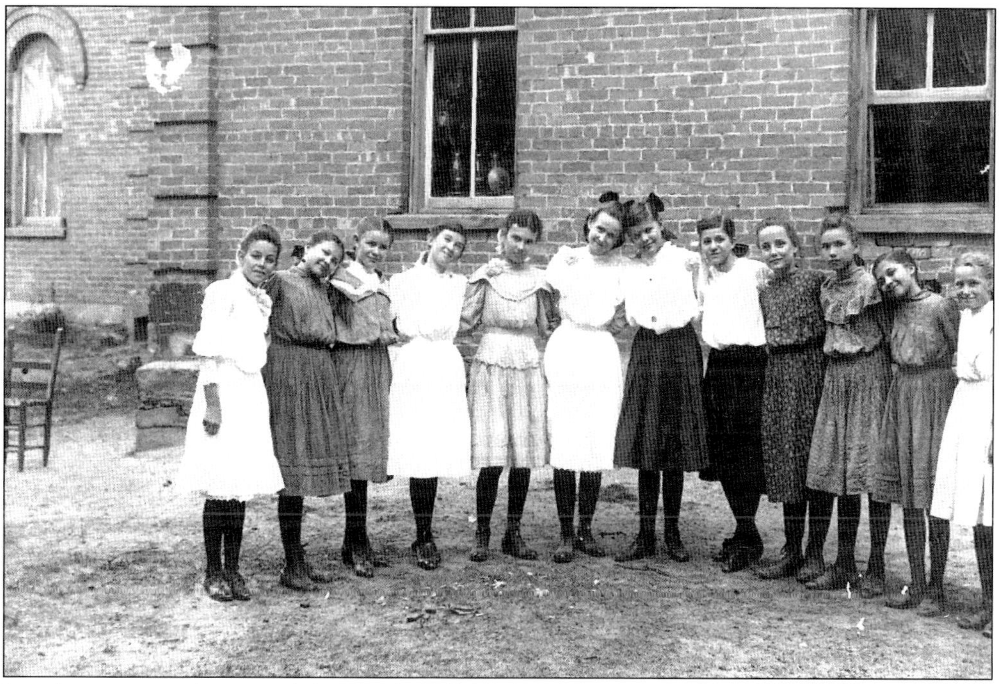

Lovely, young students, with heads playfully inclined, pose in an Altus schoolyard for a long-ago cameraman c. 1907. Their dresses are short for the era, with dark-clad knees almost to the hem. These young women, their beauty undimmed by time, are brought to life once more by the miracle of early-day photography. Students of primary and upper grades attended classes in the building shown from 1884 until 1909, when it burned. College courses were added in 1881, and were dropped in 1906. (Heritage House Museum.)

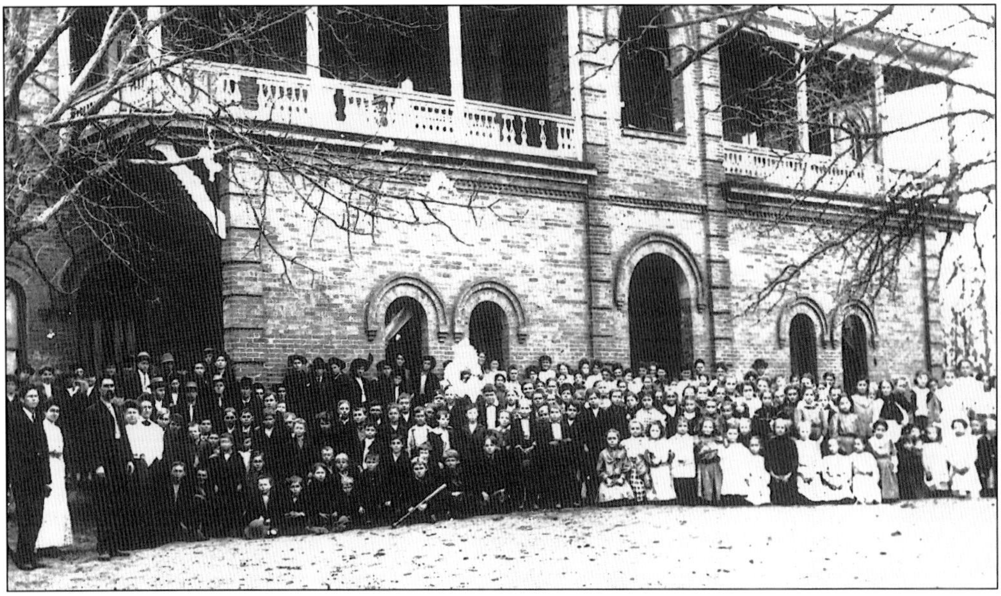

Shown *c.* 1885 is the second, and most impressive, of the two buildings of Central Collegiate Institute. Note the bearded male figure, to the left, and staff and students lined up for a school photograph. The new brick building was ready for use when the fall term opened in 1884. The massive structure enjoyed an extraordinary view of the Arkansas River Valley. This facility, and the school building before it, were used for various community functions, including church services. (Sadler H. Burrow Collection.)

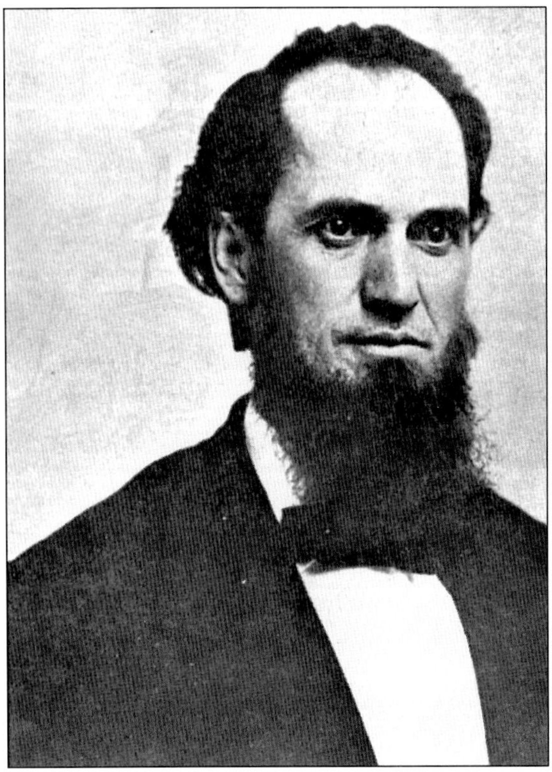

Reverend Isham Lafayette Burrow, pictured here, selected Altus in Franklin County as the site to build his school, Central Institute. A remarkable leader and teacher, it was his lifelong dream to build an institute of higher learning in an area which had great need. The name was changed to Central Collegiate Institute when college courses were added in 1881. The school, already renamed Hendrix College, was moved to Conway in 1889. The student records were transferred as well, but Burrow retained the school building in Altus and renamed it Hiram and Lydia College, in honor of his mother and father. The college flourished from 1890 to 1906, then Burrow sold the property to the Altus School District. (Submitted Photo.)

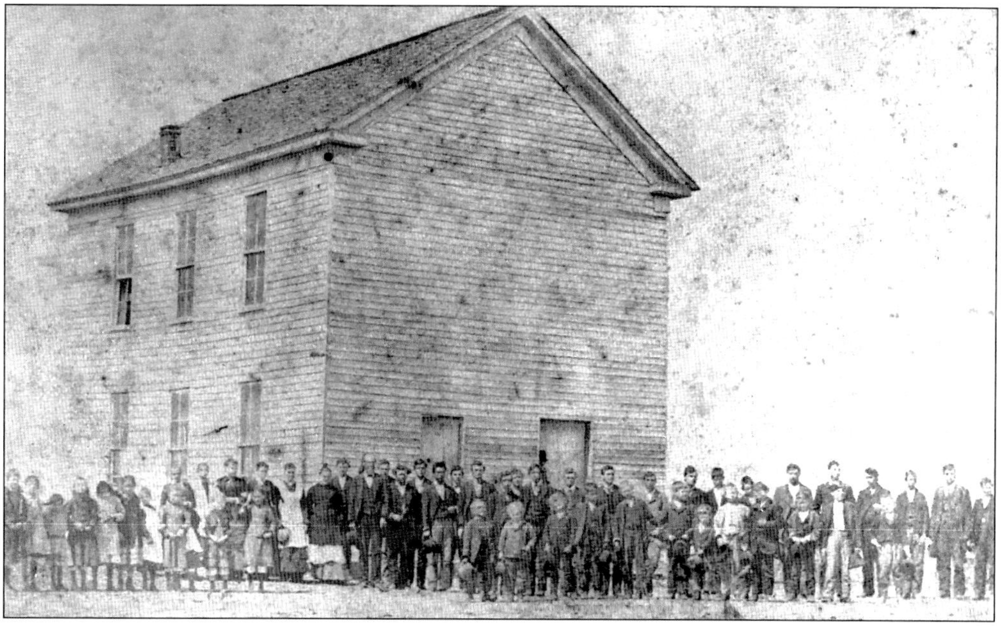

The original building of Central Institute, as shown, was constructed by Reverend Burrow in 1876, in a new-ground cornfield. The staff and student body are assembled for the official school photo. Reverend Burrow is the gentleman, left of center, with a beard. The two-story, frame building measured 24 by 32 feet in size. By October 31, 1876, regular school classes had begun in conjunction with the centennial anniversary of America's independence. (Sadler H. Burrow Collection.)

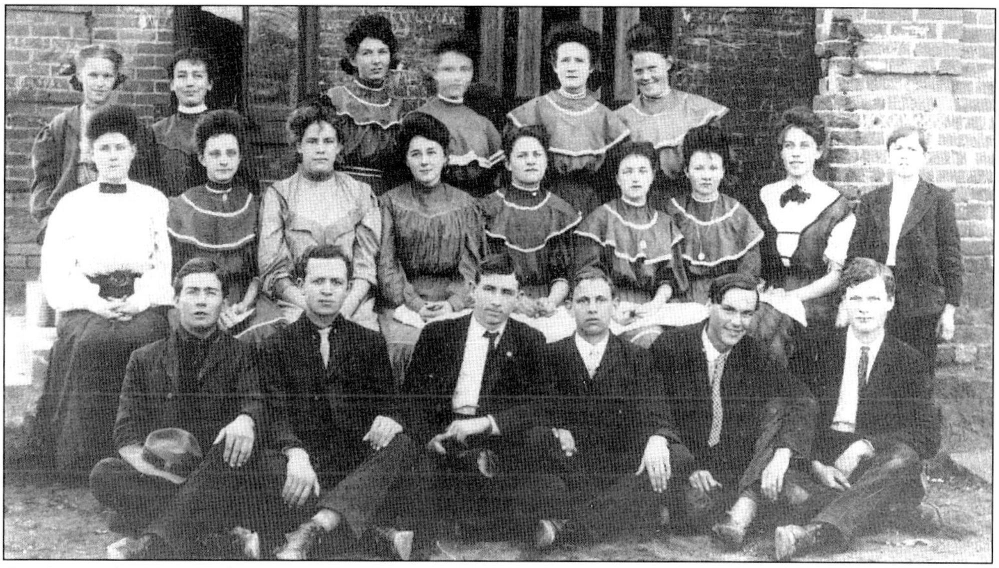

Students shown in this *c.* 1905 image at Hiram and Lydia College, are Dave Partain, Sula Kate Benson, Leona Edwards, Ida Wathern, and a Miss Watts. The young women are all wearing similar blouses with variations of the pattern. The school was noted for the number of accomplished young women enrolled. Reverend Burrow's own daughters, and son, were students and teachers here. Mathematics, English, and History were taught, as well as Latin and German. (Sadler H. Burrow Collection.)

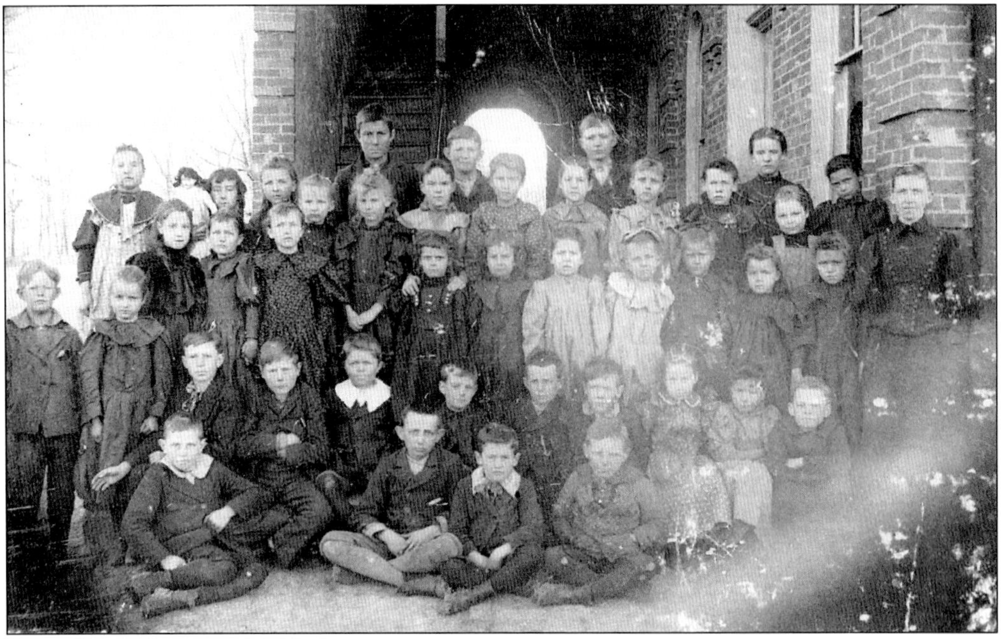

Students of primary and upper grades, shown here *c.* 1885, were also enrolled at Central Collegiate Institute. They pose at the front-entry of the school. The stairwell, behind the tall male student, led to the bell tower. The school was the focal point of the Altus community with festive dinners, dances, and annual Christmas programs. A choir and a small, but accomplished, band gave community concerts. (Sadler H. Burrow Collection.)

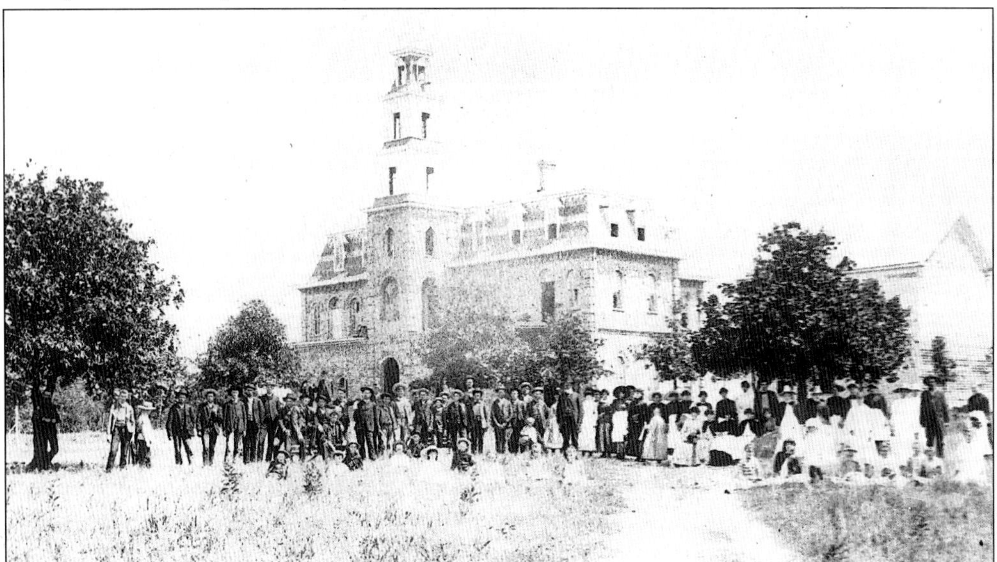

The staff and student body gather at the main building of Central Collegiate Institute in Altus. Note the dark figure of a soldier leaning against a tree to the left. Although it had been 20 years since the Civil War, he was still referred to as a Union Soldier by the community. The U.S. government continued to "inspect" large gatherings up until the1880s. Note the original frame building of Central Institute, located to the rear of the brick school. (Sadler H. Burrow Collection.)

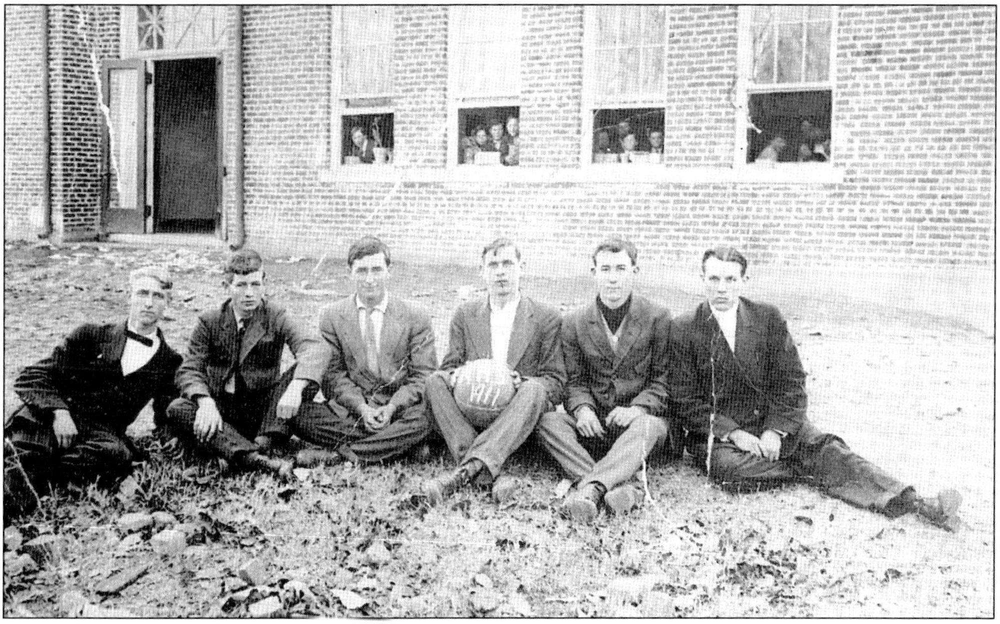

Shown is an all-male class, or basketball team, at Altus High School in 1911. The school building, in this image, was constructed after the fire of 1909. This building burned March 9, 1920. The third school, on the site of Reverend Burrow's original Central Institute, was built in 1925. Presently, Altus-Denning Schools, in yet another building, is still in service to area school children. Note the distinctive haircuts and students peering from the windows. (Heritage House Museum.)

Mary Hinton Burrow, daughter of Reverend I.L. and Rebecca Burrow, was an honor graduate of Hiram and Lydia College over a century ago. She was a musician, a writer, and an artist. In Miss Burrow's June 20, 1895 valedictory address she was hopeful for the millennium and optimistic that the world might be united in brotherly love. She lived alone in her parents home, after their deaths, and was highly revered in the Altus community. (Sadler H. Burrow Collection.)

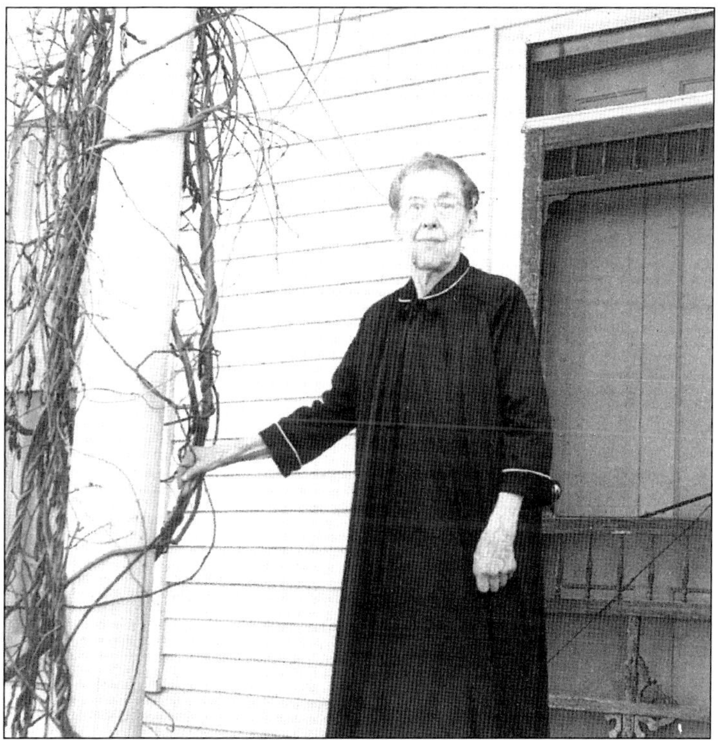

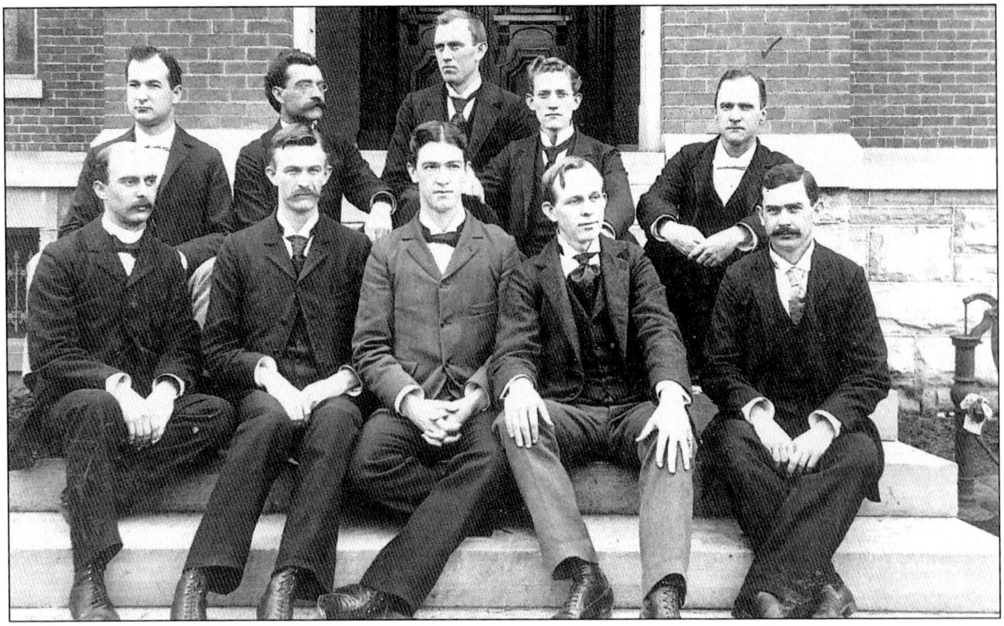

Shown is Banks Burrow, to the right rear, and fellow Methodist ministers. Banks, son to Reverend I.L. and Rebecca Burrow, was a Methodist minister and a teacher at Central Collegiate Institute and Hiram and Lydia College. Note the clean-cut good looks of these men who helped carry the Gospel to the masses in Arkansas at the turn of the century. (Sadler H. Burrow Collection.)

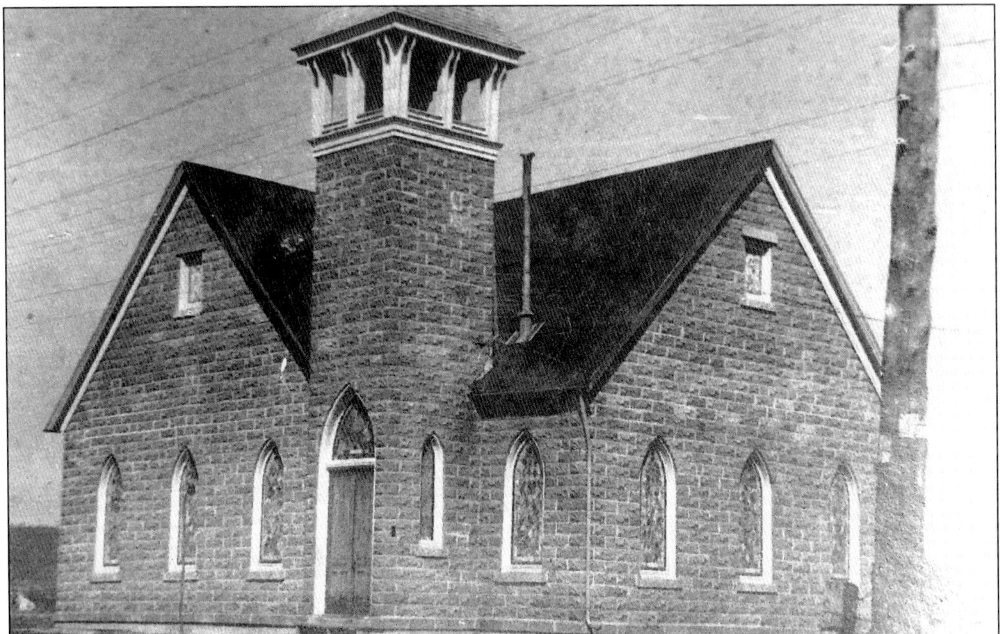

Altus Methodist Episcopal Church, South, was organized in 1875. When the Central Institute Chapel was completed, services were held there. The church building, shown here, was finished in 1905. It was constructed of concrete blocks made by members of the church. This church burned, and the present one was built in the 1950s. Note the rough, knotted utility pole in the foreground. (Heritage House Museum.)

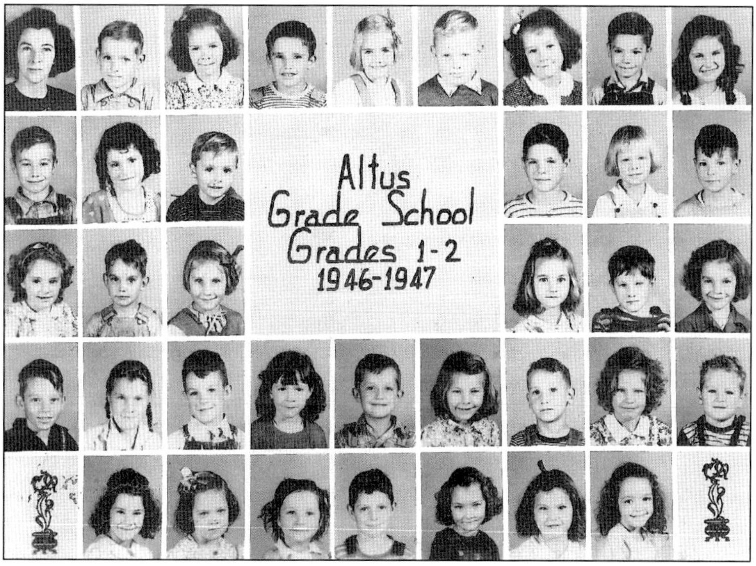

Shown is Altus' first and second grade classes, 1946–47, taught by Vesta Higdon. Still recognizable in the Altus community are many family names from this school photo. Among them are: Baker, Rickard, Edgin, Deatheridge, Ross, Hyde, Gates, Gowing, and Harbottle. (Elizabeth Muchmore Page.)

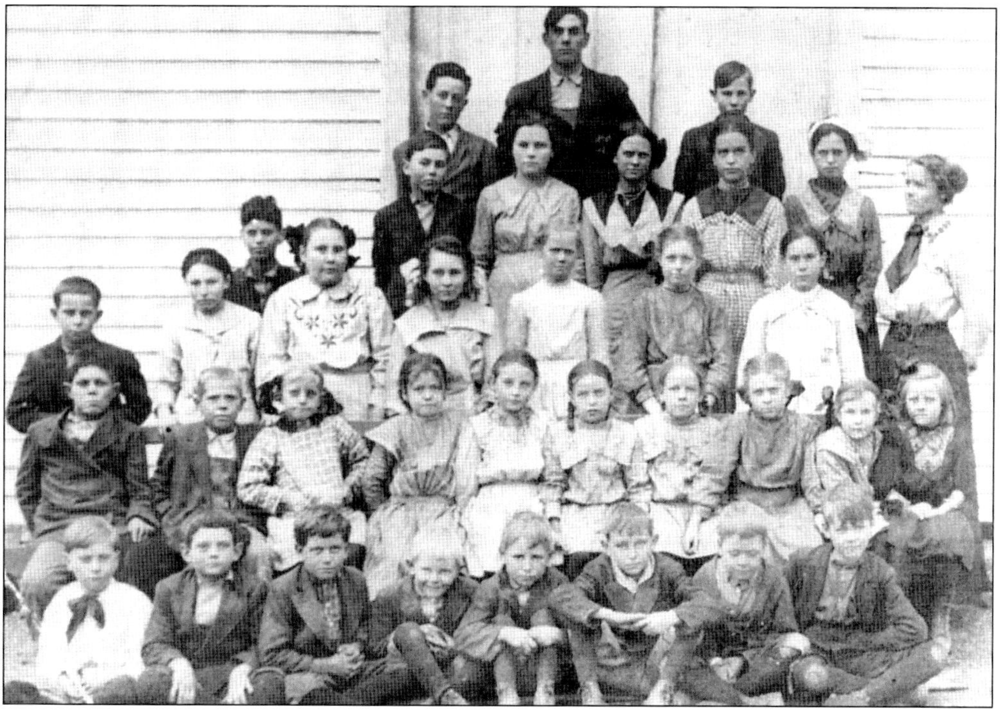

Schoolchildren are posed at Center Cross School c. 1908. Among them are Coy and Dessie Watts, George Mike, and Jim Muchmore. Coy Watts, on the front row third from left, is one of many boys who began "picking slate" at the coal mines when he was just 16. The Coy and Grace Mason Watts collection of photo images, and detailed memories of days gone by, are an invaluable historical resource. (Grace Mason Watts.)

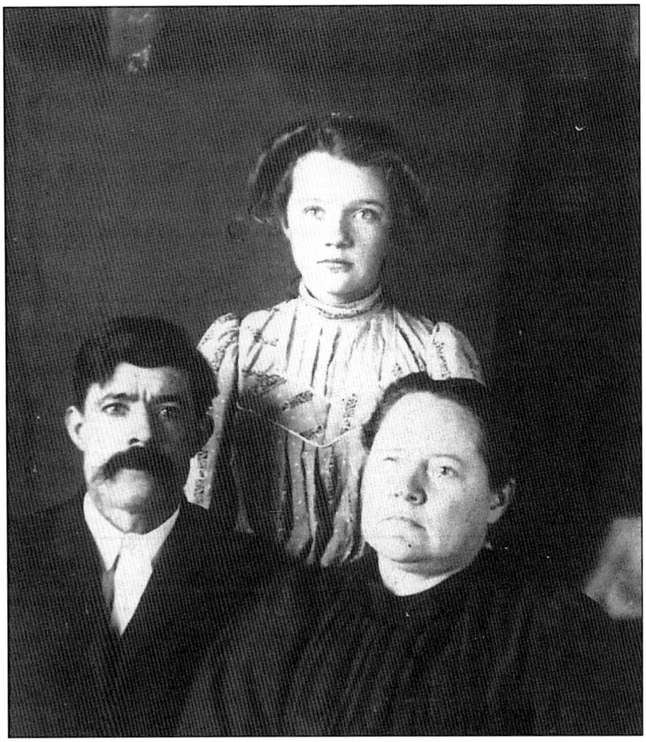

George S. and Alice Warren Muchmore, and daughter Amy, are shown *c.* 1902. George owned a grocery store and meat market in Ozark. He built fine residences in Ozark and Center Cross, which are still in use today. Alice Warren took photos and developed and printed them using her own equipment. She also wrote on how she became possessed of an evil spirit. George read his Bible, and prayed, for an hour each day before departing for work. (Virginia Muchmore Canady.)

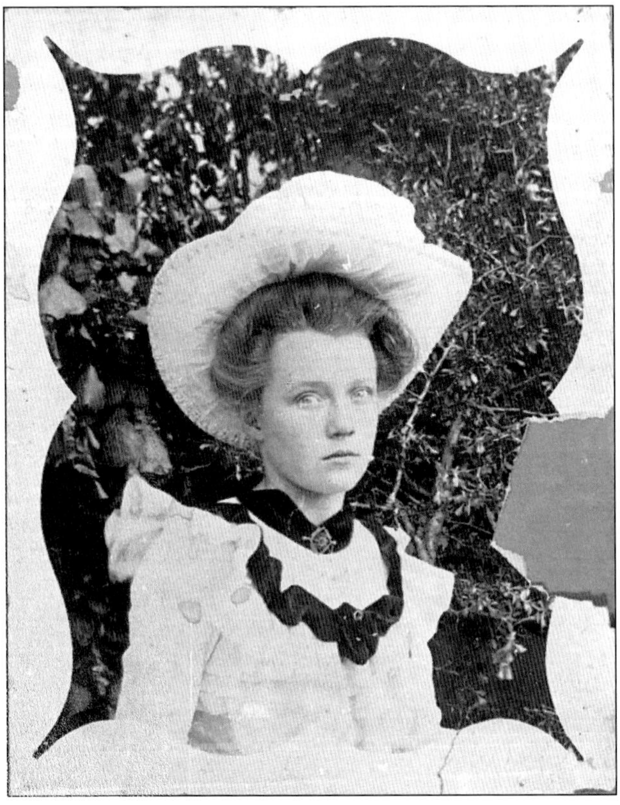

One Friday afternoon, in July 1904, Amy Muchmore, aged 14, left school after falling ill. The following day she reportedly died of a brain aneurysm. It is rumored that the attending physician practiced blood-letting. This procedure supposedly assured the remaining blood, if any, to be free of evil spirits. Although quite young, Amy had attained a degree of refinement, unusual in one so young, as evidenced by this *c.* 1901 photo. (Elizabeth Muchmore Page.)

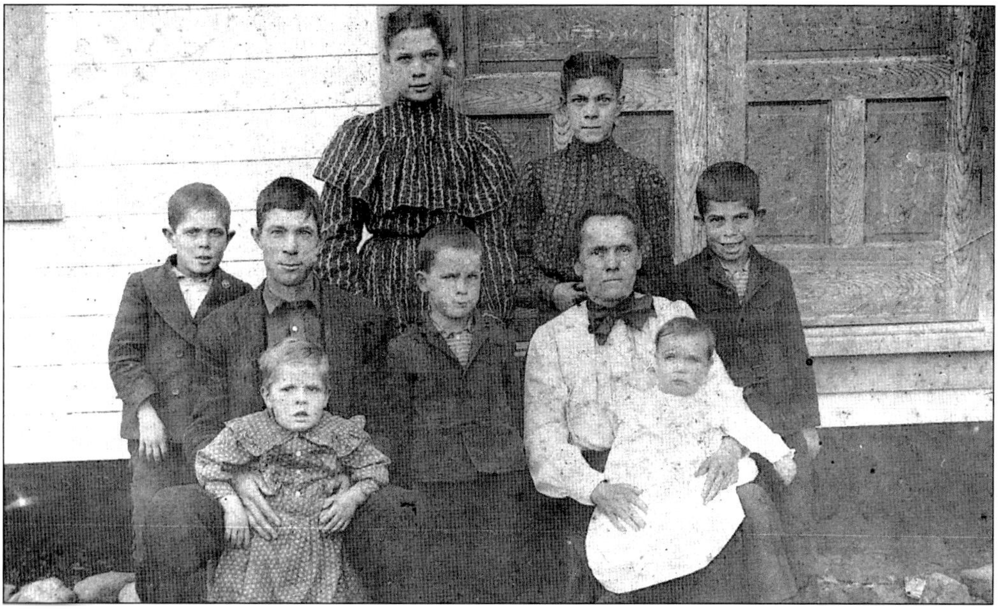

The Richard and Mary Schmitz Muchmore family is shown c. 1907 at Center Cross School. Richard Muchmore's father was from Dublin, Ireland. His mother was Amy Harsha, or Hershey, of the well-known Swiss Hershey family of Pennsylvania. Mary Schmitz, and family, sailed to America from Cologne, Germany, in 1872, to escape religious persecution. Richard and Mary's children pictured are Lena, Elizabeth, John, Mike, George, Jim, and Pearlie. (Elizabeth Muchmore Page.)

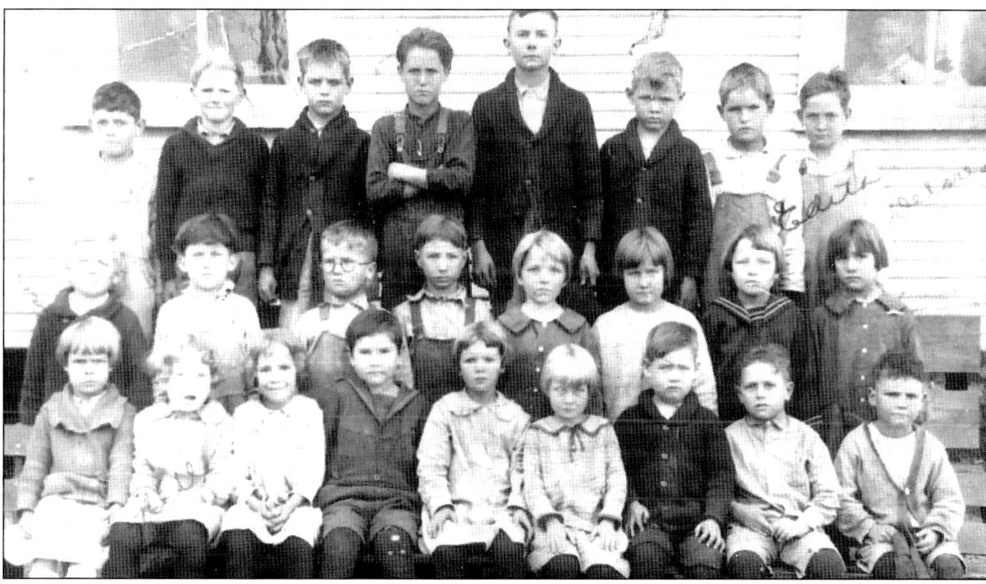

Pictured at Center Cross School c. 1924 are Vance Scribner, Benny Woods, Quincy Yother, Norman Myers, Dollis and Teela Page, Edith and Jean Page, Pauline Woods, Jack Mathis, Gussie Myrtle Gavin, and Ab Hixson. Another Hixson student is seen at the window. In 1885, Abigail Warren Hudson and J.L. Hudson deeded an acre to the school district to build a school. This is the original of two school buildings constructed at this location. (Elizabeth Muchmore Page.)

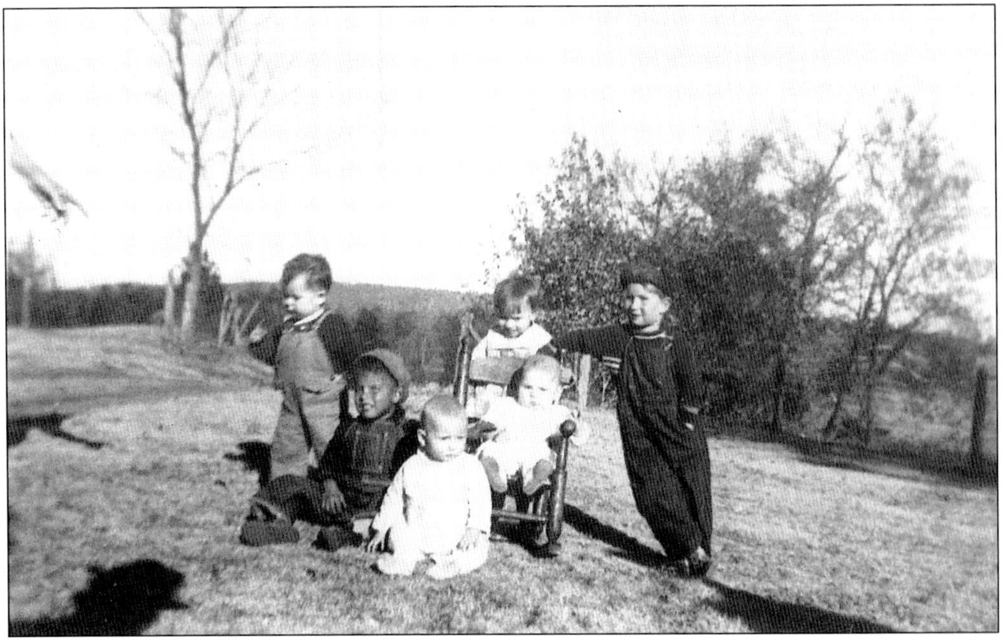

In the possession of family members for several generations, the Muchmore family homeplace is the location of this photo image *c.* 1936. Shown are George Ray and Mary Lynn Muchmore, Betty Sue Mason, Jerry Dixon, Lloyd Ray, and Bobby Page. Note Lloyd Ray's casual pose, as he leans against the rocker. (Grace Mason Watts.)

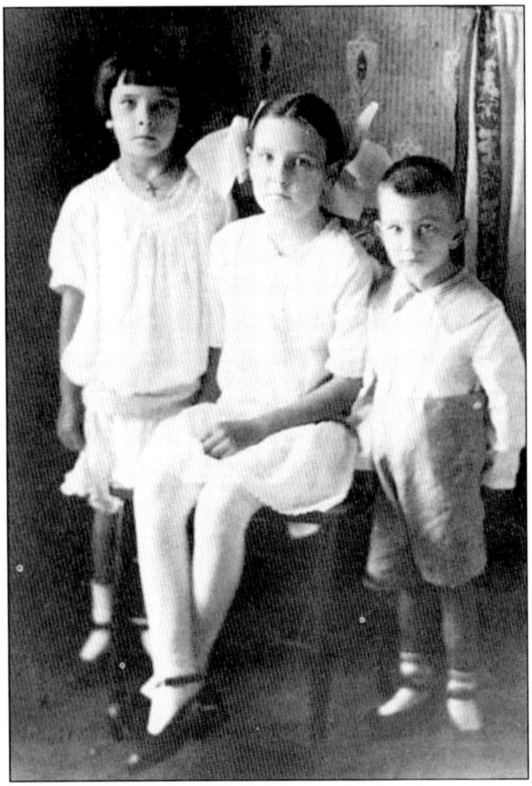

On March 28, 1905, Janice Meredith Holt was born in Altus at the home of her maternal grandparents, Dan and Catherine McGraw. In this photo image c. 1915, she is flanked by siblings Mary Catherine and John Holt Jr. Janice wrote more than 20 successful books, as well-known author Janice Holt Giles. She co-authored four books with her husband, Henry Giles. *The Kinta Years* is autobiographical and tells of her childhood in Altus. (Holt Family.)

Two

ALTUS COAL GETS UNDER YOUR SKIN

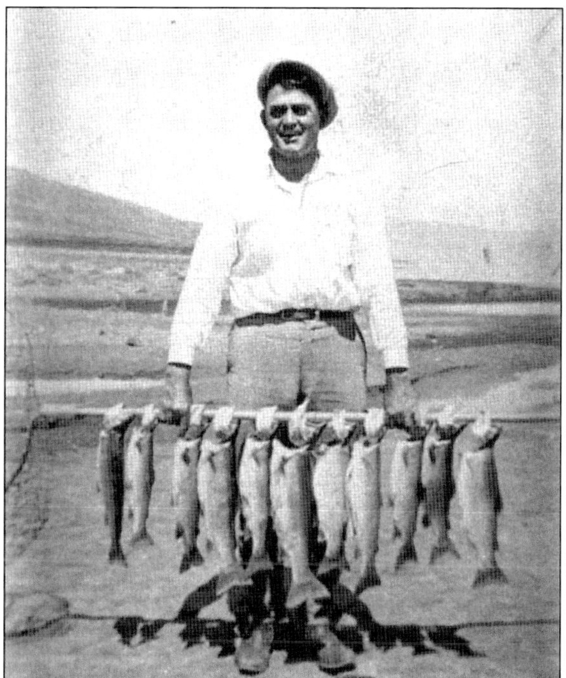

Charles "Boss" Schmidt is shown here with a string of fish. At 6 feet 4 inches tall, and 200 pounds, Boss was Arkansas' first professional athlete. He played for the Detroit Tigers as catcher from 1906 to 1911, and played in three world series. After retirement he stayed with the Phillips family, in Alix, and worked in the mines. He was only 52 when he died on November 14, 1932, at Dr. Jake Post's. The Tiger organization placed a monument on his grave at St. Mary's Catholic Church cemetery, in 1970. (Kathleen Gillespie Phillips, Heritage House Museum.)

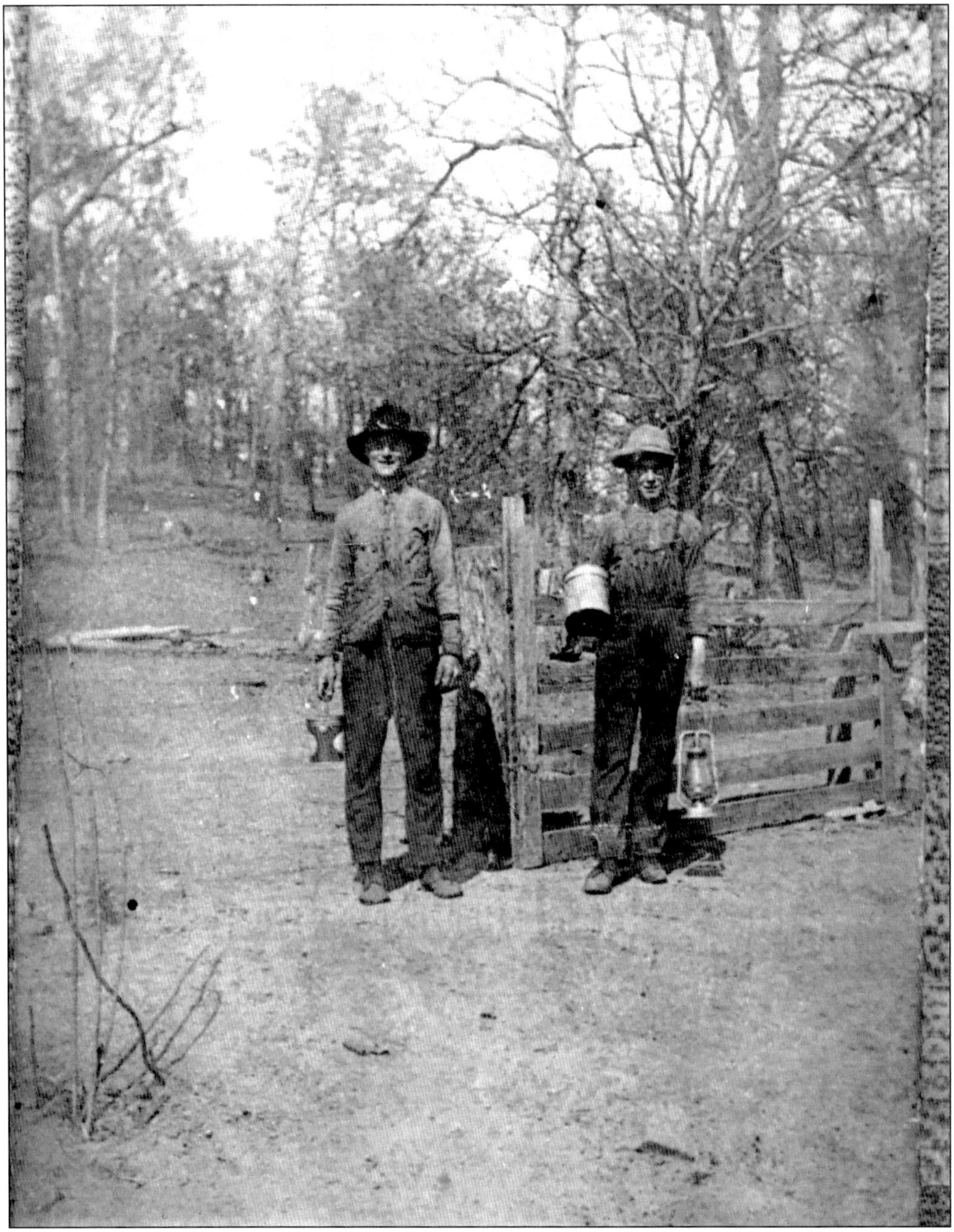

Bob Page, at right, and younger brother Wallace are shown after a day's work in an Altus area coal mine *c.* 1918. Years later Bob met with mine inspectors and took them on an unforgettable journey. They entered Number 2 Mine, toured it, and exited the entry to Number 6 Mine. It was approximately three miles topside. After detouring around rock-slides and cave-ins, it was approximately five miles underground. (Wallace Walker Page.)

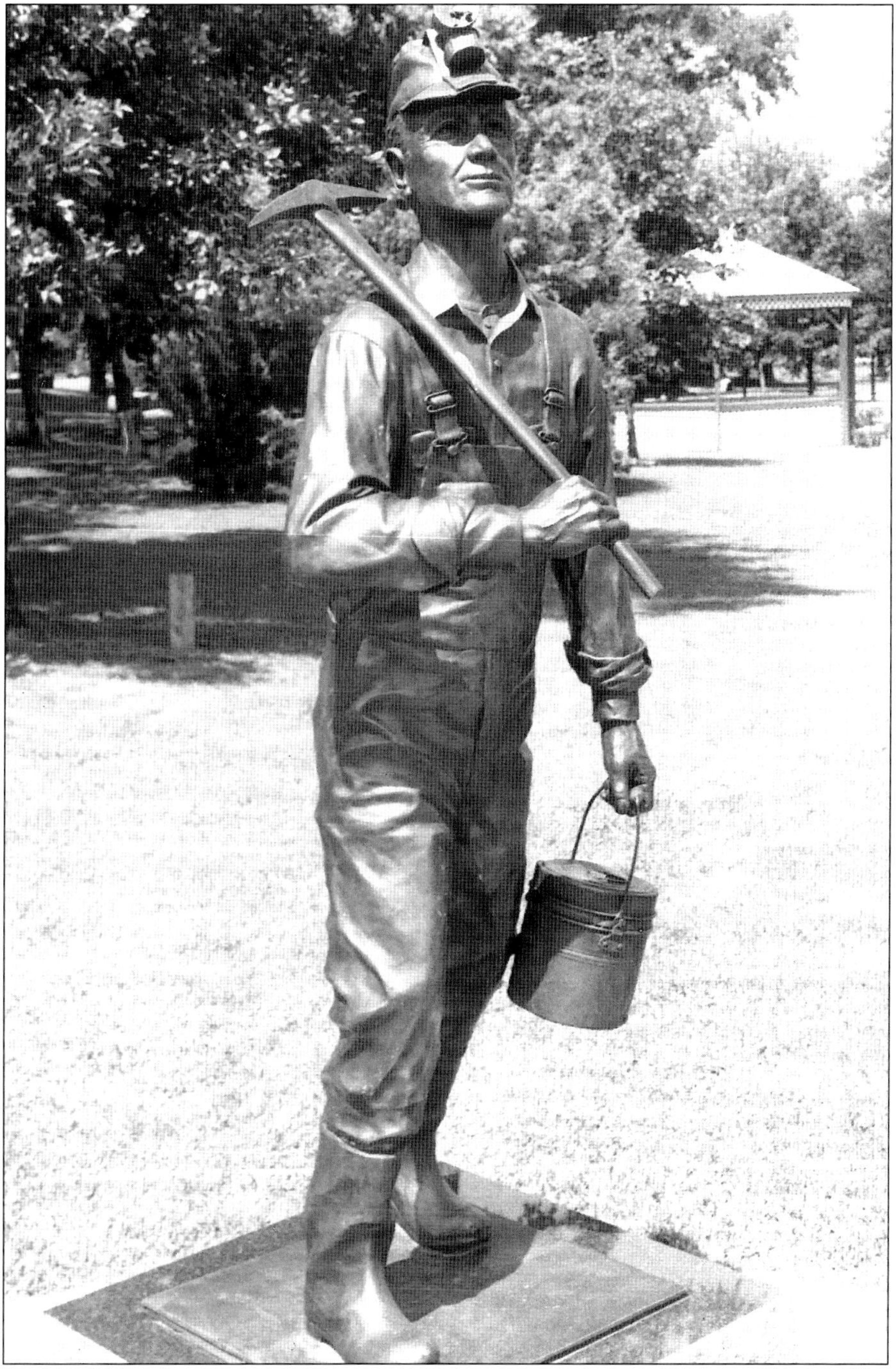

Artist Jim Westbrook's life-size bronze sculpture of an Altus area coal miner was dedicated at the Altus City Park in October 1998. The statue's rugged features reflect the culture of countless coal miners commemorated from that era. The statue is the central focus of the Coal Miner Memorial exhibit, which also features black-granite columns each bearing the names of 500 miners. The monument is dedicated to the memory of members of District 21, Western Arkansas and Eastern Oklahoma Coal Miners. (Author.)

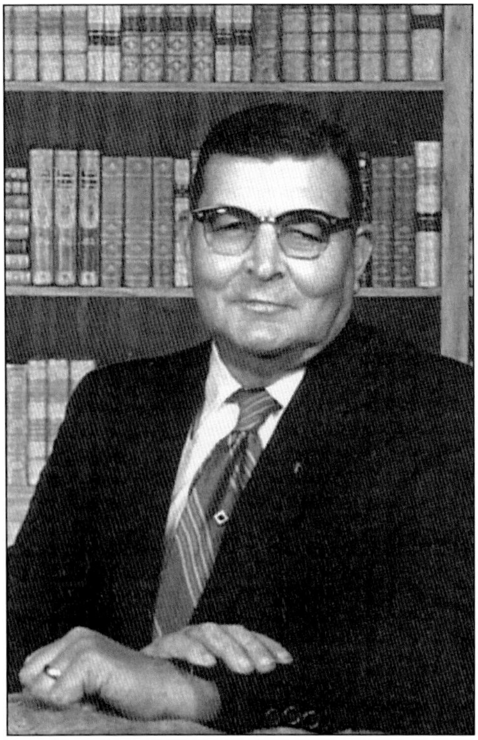

George Zolliecoffer, shown in 1981, began work in the mines with his father and brothers when he was only 16. His incomparable spirit and rugged physical stamina made him the ideal coal miner. Working until 1956, George was one of the last to labor in Altus area mines. He would frequently lie in a hole only 14 inches high, straining his back and filling his lungs with coal-dust, as he would break and load low-coal. For this he often came home with only $5 per week. Despite the hard life, George was proud of his profession. He dreamed of, one day, honoring all coal-miners with a memorial. In October 1996 George asked Louise, his wife, to approach the Altus City Council for help. The council endorsed his idea and proposed that the memorial be located in Altus City Park. The meeting took place one month before the sturdy, old miner died. Today scores of coal-mining families, friends, and admirers study the names on the black-granite columns and admire the bronze coal-miner figure. The monument has far exceeded George Zolliecoffer's dreams. (Louise Zolliecoffer.)

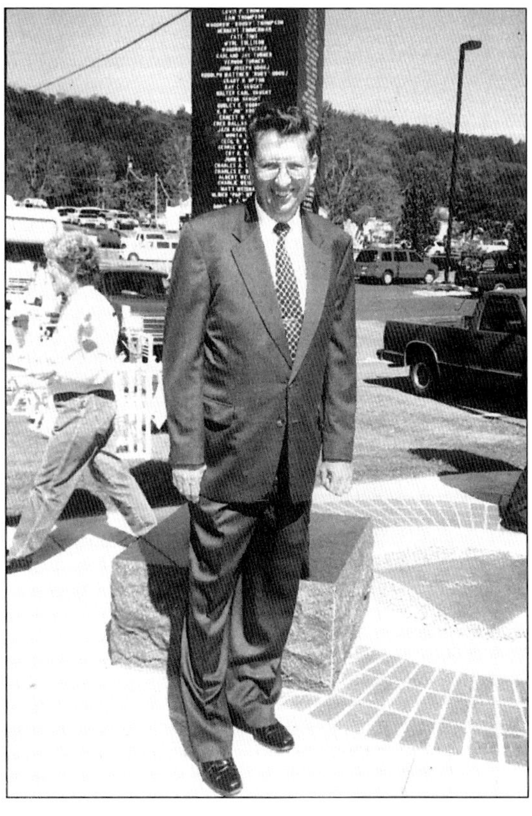

Former Mayor Jimmy Jacobs poses at the May 3, 1997 dedication of the coal-miner memorial columns. Jimmy was mayor of Altus, at each stage of the planning, installation, and dedication of the monument. Other columns have since been added along with a life-size bronze representation of a coal miner. Jimmy's father, Ferrol "Frog," and his uncle, Conley "Skeeter" Jacobs, were also miners. A youthful Conley was mayor of Altus, in 1931, when a coal-mining-related, rock-fall took his life. (Jimmy Jacobs.)

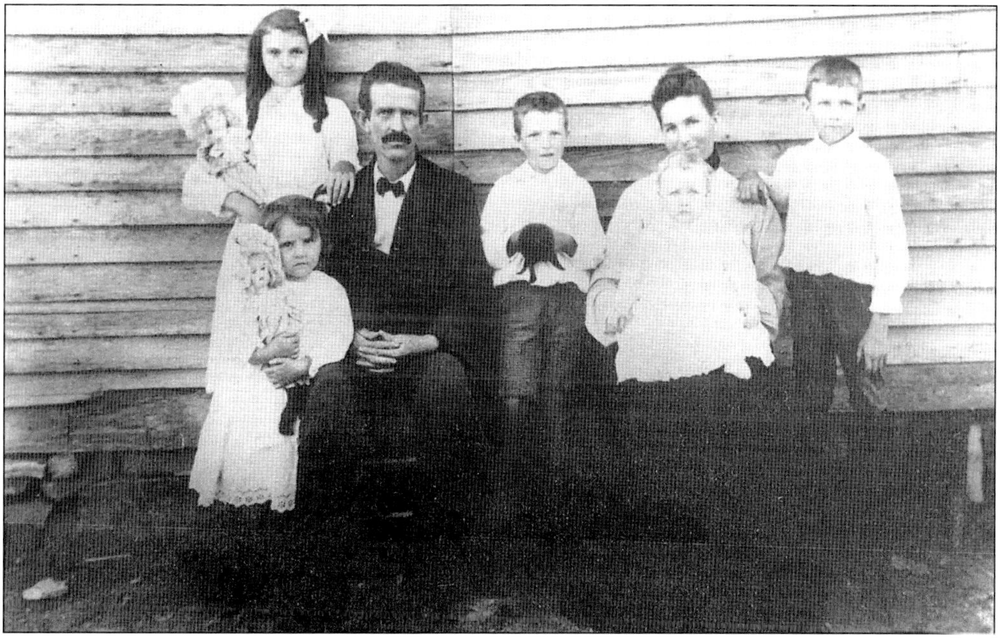

This photo image was taken c. 1905, of Dr. John and Dorthula Jacobs in Altus. Their children are Grace, Jewell, Conley, Jeff, and Ferrol, pictured c. 1905. Note the girls displaying their fancy-dressed dolls and the boy holding the little black kitten for the camera. Conley would later be elected mayor of Altus and lose his life in a coal-mining accident. (Jimmy Jacobs.)

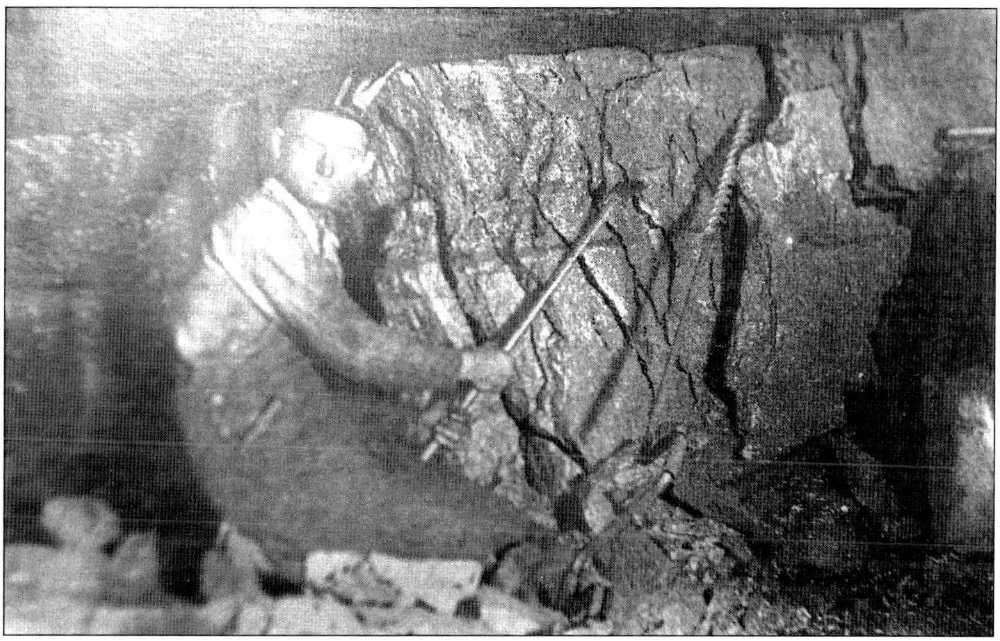

An unknown miner is shown c. 1910, in Number 2 Mine in the Denning Coal Field. In the "room," which is where the coal has been blasted, a track of steel, or wood, was laid. The coal was loaded into "pit cars" and taken by mule to the entry of the mine. If the coal-room ceiling was too low for a mule, the cars were pushed, usually by two miners, to the entry of the mine, or to where the mule awaited them in a higher ceilinged-room. (Submitted Photo.)

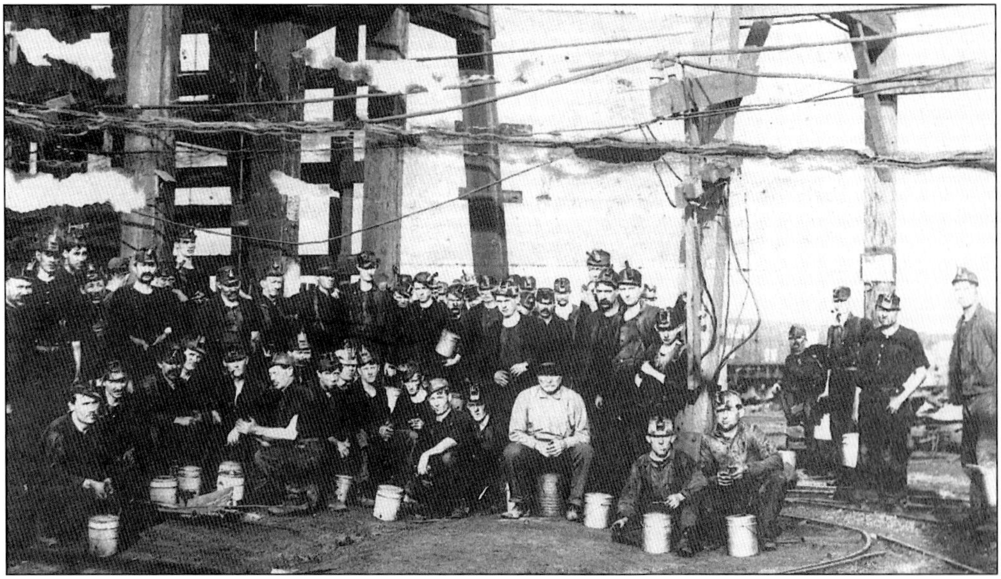

Miners are waiting to enter Number 2 Mine on December 12, 1908. The mine produced 35 tons of coal per day. Top men, who worked above ground, averaged $47 per month and worked ten-hour days. Company men who worked underground earned $53 per month. In 1899, miners struck for higher wages, shorter hours, and safer working conditions. By 1903, mine operators, faced with labor shortages, were forced to meet the United Mine Workers' demands. (Heritage House Museum.)

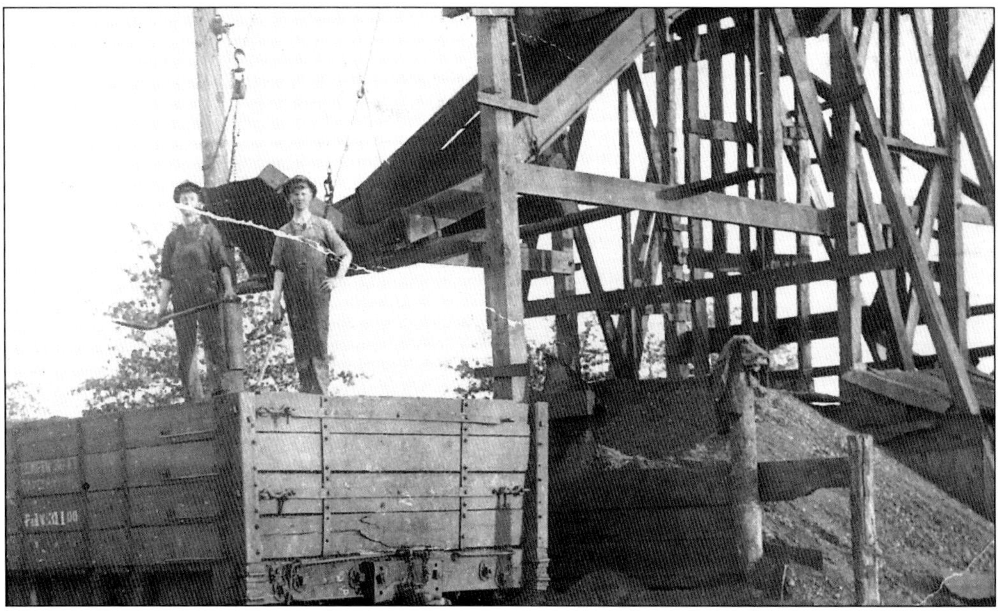

Joe Page and younger brother Wallace are shown *c.* 1908 working in a railroad coal-car at an unknown Altus-area coal mine. One Sunday morning, Wallace took his wife and daughters down the elevator into the mine where he had labored that week. The drip of the water, the falling pebbles, and the shaky elevator, plunging them into that dark, dank shaft, was never forgotten. The Denning Mine Field was developed by Sam Denning, who sunk the first shaft mine at Denning in 1892. (Wallace Walker Page.)

Shown is a miner's carbide gas lamp. The lamp's powerful flame illuminated the ceiling and was unaffected by drafts. The flame was clear, reliable, and almost maintenance free. However, its fumes caused sore throats and other ailments. When a miner walked into a methane gas pocket, found in all coal mines, the gas was ignited by the lamp. This flame enveloped the miner, burning his hair off around the perimeter of his hat. Some miners rarely needed haircuts. (Submitted Photo.)

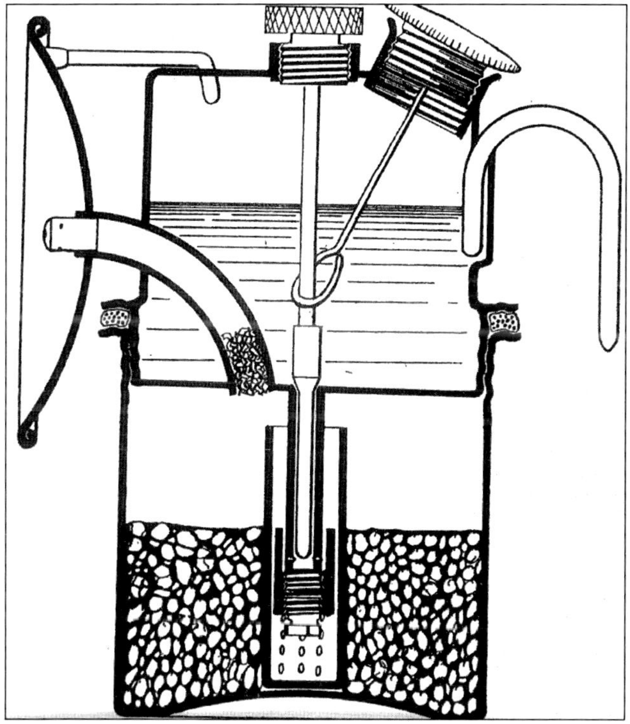

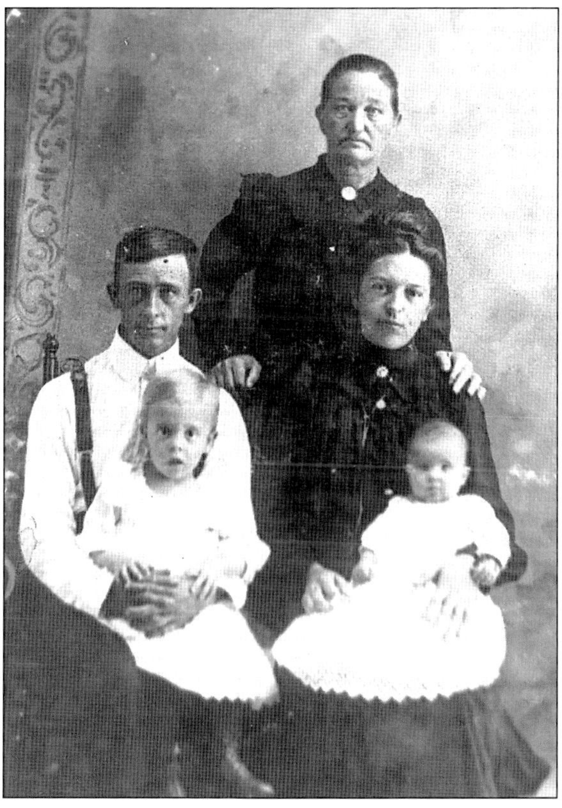

Catherine Conaster Nichols is pictured *c.* 1900. Her son-in-law, Len Berry, and daughter Elizabeth are seated with children Florence and Walter. Florence died the following year. Len began working in the coal mines at 14. The old Berry homesite is now occupied by the Chrisman Rock Chrusher. It is rumored to have sold a "million dollars worth of rock." Unaware of its value, Catherine and Elizabeth sold the property for $300. (Elizabeth Muchmore Page.)

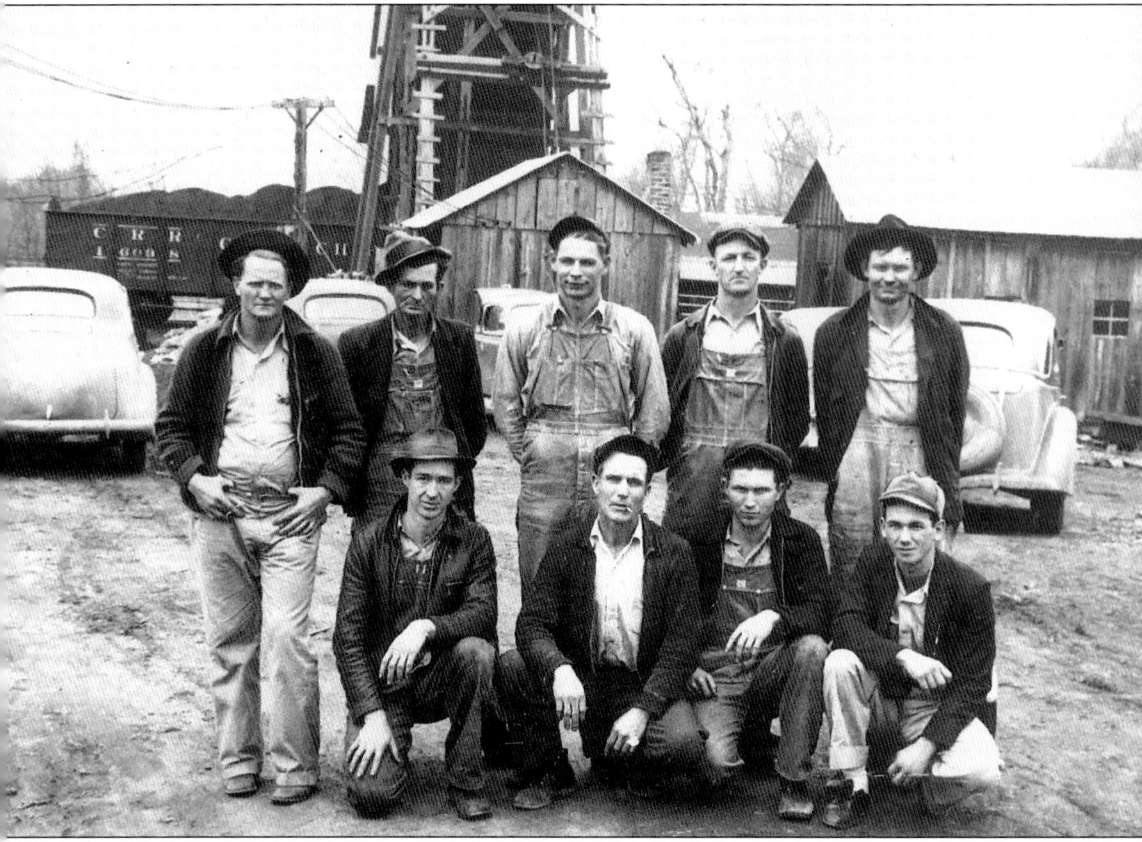

Coal miners are shown *c.* 1938 at the Bob Smith Coal Mine, near Center Cross. They are: Joe Ressie, Clarence Kelly, Basil Foster, Mike Leding, Eddie Blanscet, Ferrol Jacobs, Walter "Stormy" Mason, "Red" Horn, and Celie Foster. Note the Plymouth and Chevrolet automobiles from the 1930s in the background. Walter Mason died of the effects of cancer in one lung, and coal dust in the other. (Heritage House Museum.)

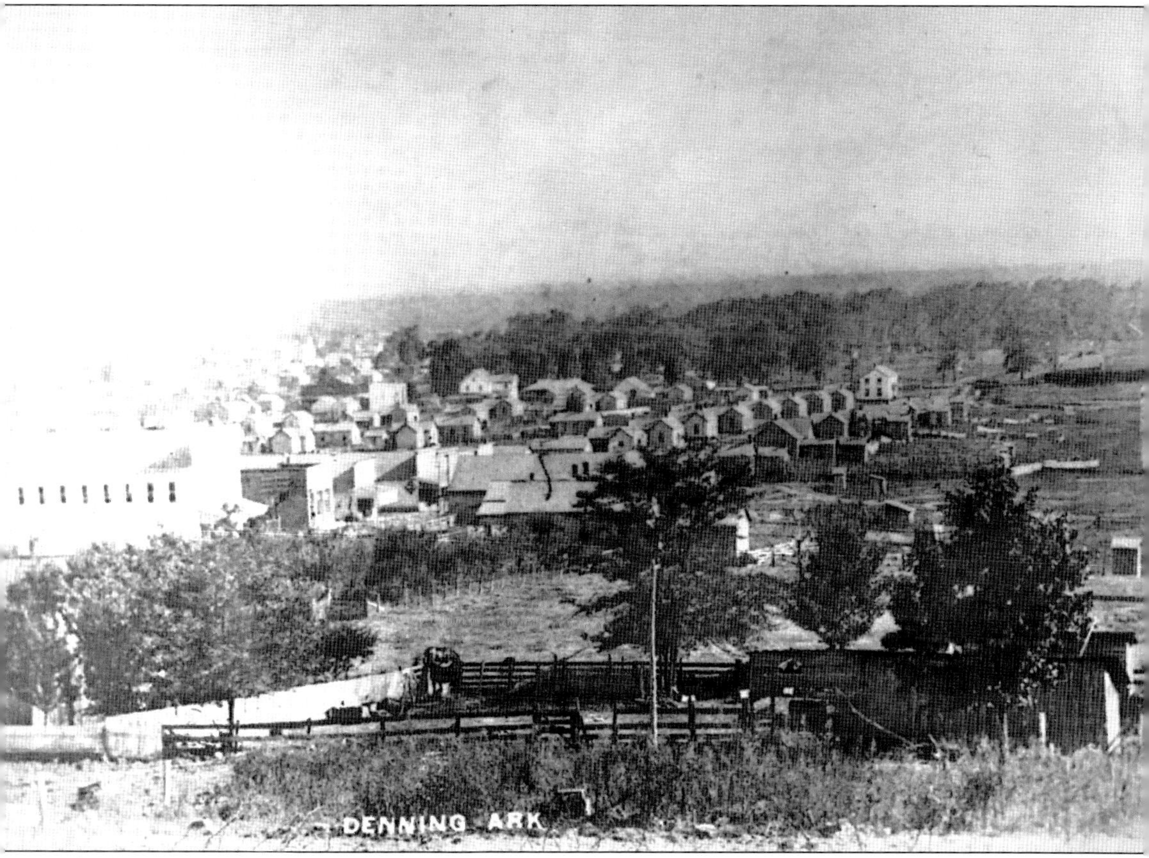

The large, white-frame building to the left, in this 1905 image, was the Denning Miner's Union Hall. It was also used for dances and community gatherings. Denning's coal-mining operations created a population of more than 1,250 citizens. It was the largest city in Franklin County. The Western Mining Company housing had from two to six rooms, and the average rent was $10 per month. There were also stores, churches, two boardinghouses, a bank, an ice house, and a school. (Dennis Baker, Sadler H. Burrow Collection.)

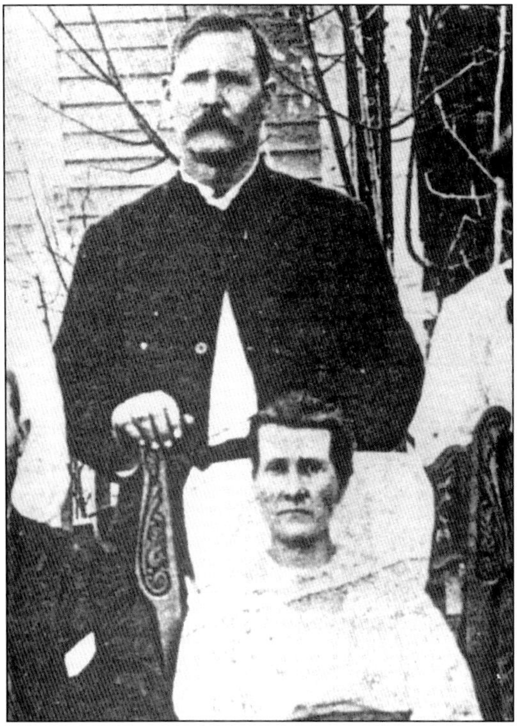

John Columbus Adams and his wife, Mary Lucinda Edgin, shown *c.* 1910, were married in 1891. They had ten children. In the early 1900s, John was the law in Denning. The jail was a 10-by-12-foot rock building in the yard of his home and was called "the calaboose." John was of such enormous size and strength that it was unnecessary for him to carry a gun. (Ronnie and Sherrill Adams Cox.)

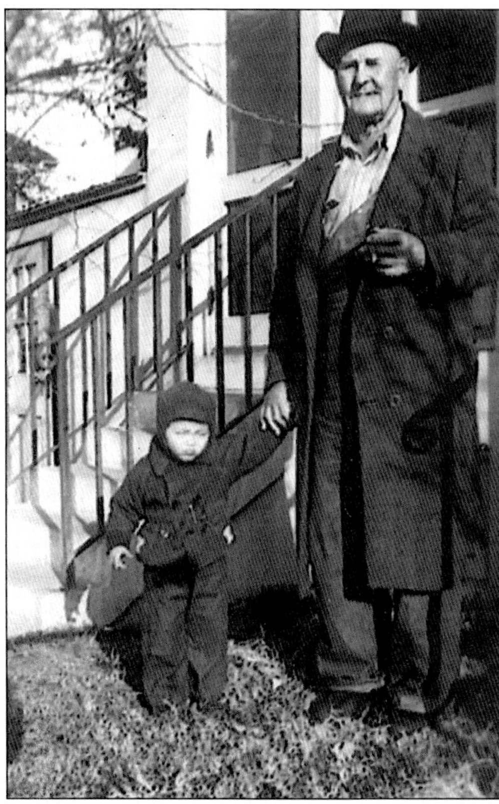

This photo image shows legendary John Columbus Adams in later years. He was marshal of the Denning community during its boom days. A large man, he was known to his many friends as "One Gallus John," a nickname he earned because of the unusual way he wore his overalls. Due to his rounded shoulders his overall gallus would slide down. To remedy this he cut off one gallus and pulled the other across and hooked it to the opposite side. (Ronnie and Sherrill Adams Cox.)

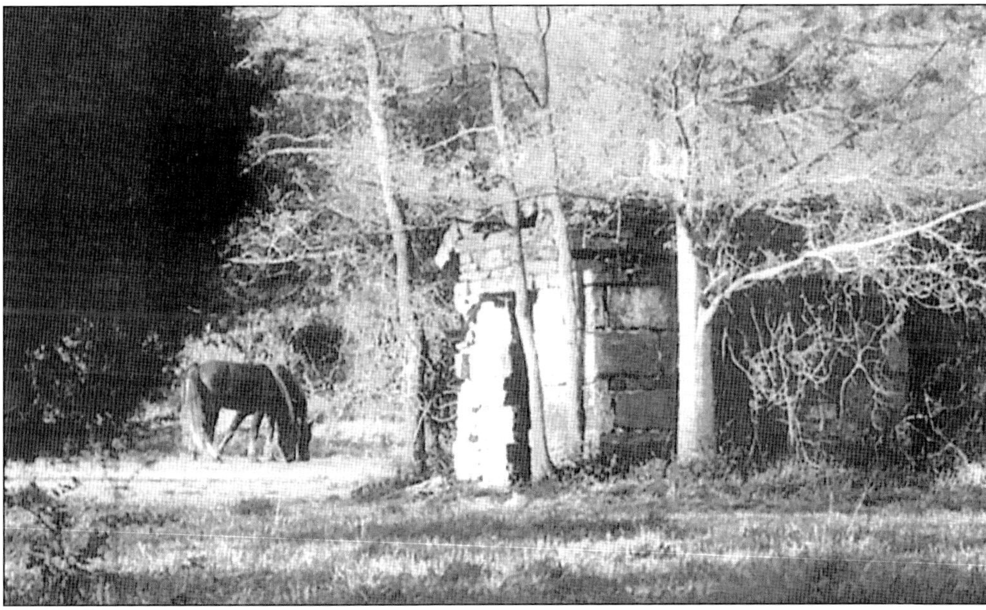

Shown is the old Denning calaboose. It is a mute reminder of the community's rambunctious past. The many active churches in Denning contended with saloons, gambling joints, and pleasure houses for the souls of the miners. On weekends the jail would be full of drunk miners, and others, whooping and yelling through the night. At least one prisoner died in the calaboose of unknown causes. Note the fine horses grazing in this peaceful scene. (Ronnie and Sherrill Adams Cox.)

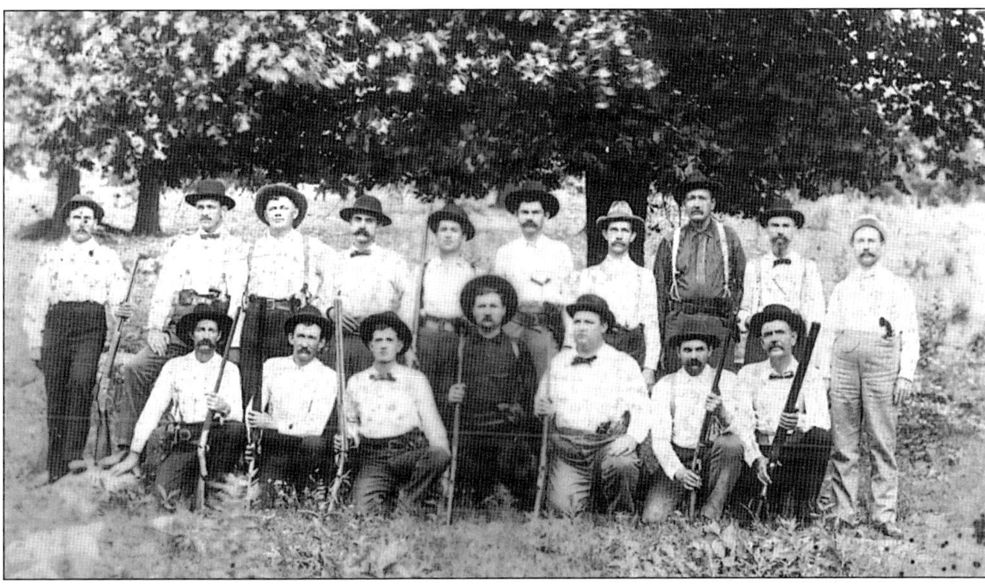

Coal Mine Guards, in this image c. 1900, were called in to quell disturbances caused by strikes and other disruptions. The man shown to the far right, with a pistol in his trouser-band, was hired by the mining companies and was organizer of the group. He was an employee of the Pinkerton Agency. Their local leader, kneeling in front, was E.B. Milton, sheriff of Franklin County. Among others they are Dow Huggins, John Stanley, Taylor Jackman, Dan McGraw, and Demus Huggins. (Sadler H. Burrow Collection.)

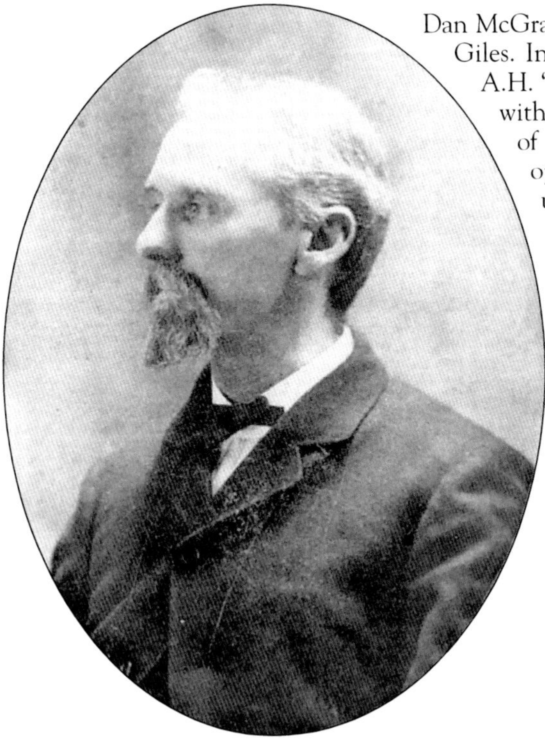

Dan McGraw was grandfather to novelist Janice Holt Giles. In 1882, he became a deputy under Sheriff A.H. "Hub" Sadler and was wounded in the face with buckshot. Later he became superintendent of Western Arkansas Mining Company's operations. He was ambushed, and beaten up, by disgruntled miners, and another time beaten and robbed of the gold payroll. It was necessary for doctors to implant a silver-plate over one eye. (Holt Family.)

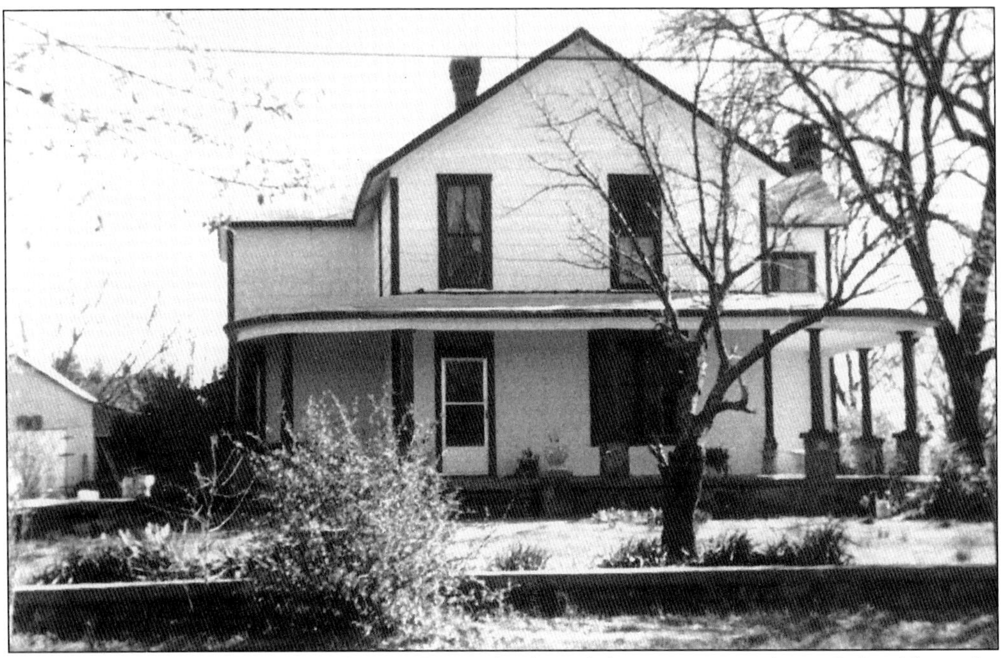

The McGraw Family Home, as shown, boasted a formal dining room with an Oak table, eight chairs with red plush seats, and a sideboard. A snow white tablecloth contrasted with the fine Haviland China. The white porch, sporting fancy scrollwork and a banister, was surrounded by pots of red geraniums. Originally, an iron picket fence enclosed the lawn, and an iron gate gave entry to the slatestone walk. Ash saplings were planted by Dan McGraw. (Jimmy Jacobs.)

Three

Altus Fruit of the Vine

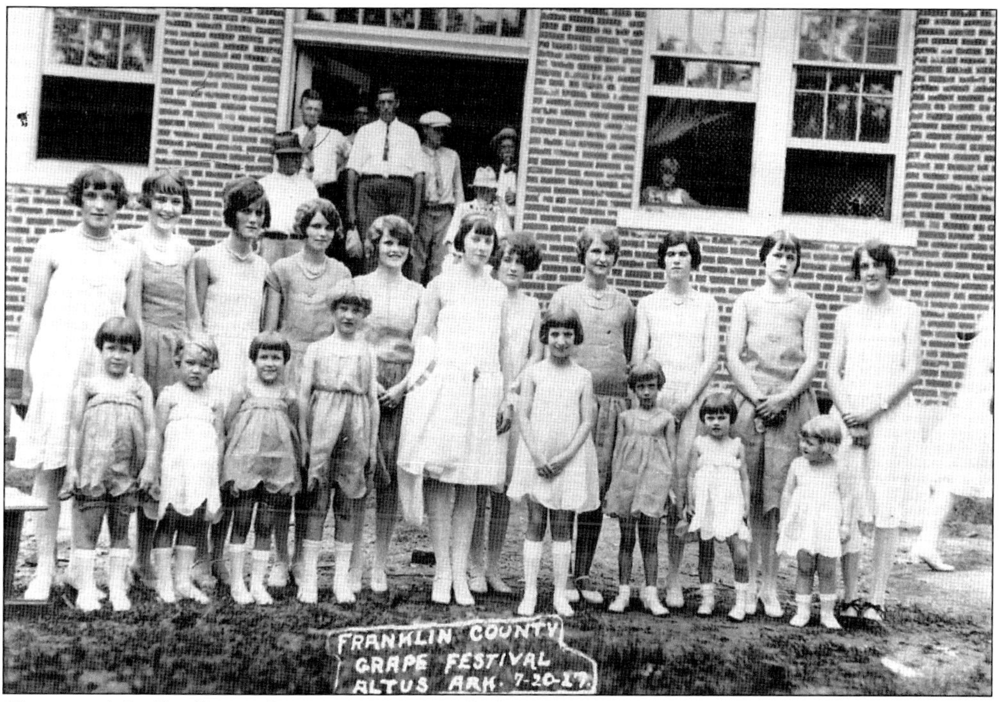

Shown is Ada Shaffer, in the crown, Queen of Altus' second annual Grape Festival, July 20, 1927. Her maids were: Mary Ford, Eula Sublett, Reba Brison, Neva Hogan, Maxine Musgrave, Eunice Hollowell, Vera Clay, Allene Greene, Minnie Leding, and Anna Dot Eveld. Entertainment, food, and tours of the vineyards were available to thousands of visitors and dignitaries at the festival. (Dollis Page Rickard.)

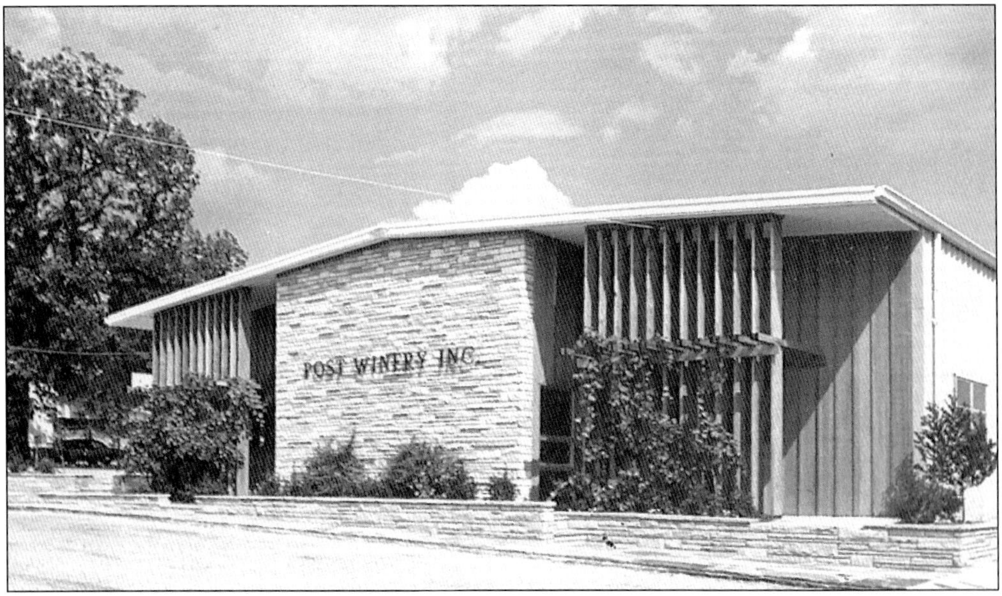

This 1964 postcard features the Post Familie Vineyards and Winery one block north of Highway 64, in Altus. It is a modern steel and native-stone building which houses a gift shop, offices, sales, and tasting room. The original winery, east of this location, was built in 1905. Since 1872, six generations of the Post Family, originally from Bavaria, have been American vintners of fine wines. They have grown grapes in Altus since 1880. Sax and Wiederkehr Wineries, located atop beautiful St. Mary's Mountain, dates from the same year. (Paul Post.)

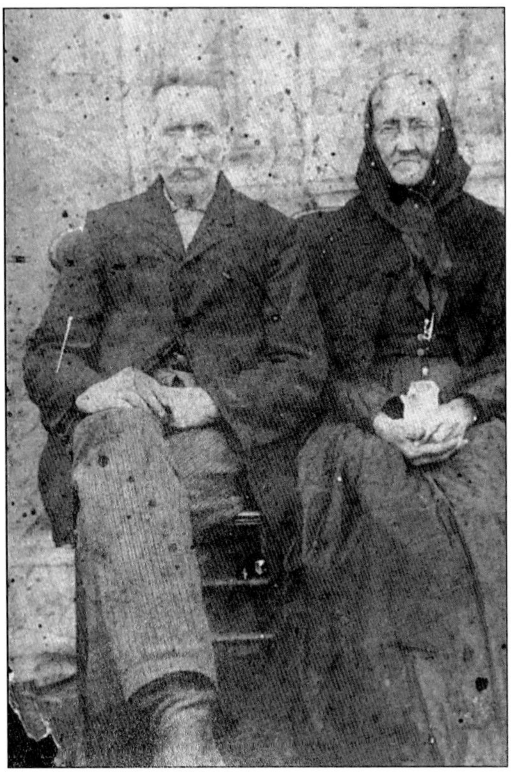

Paul Post, vice president of Post Familie Vineyards and Winery, is shown at Altus' Heritage House Museum. The grape crusher wine press, on display, belonged to his grandfather, James "Jake" Post. Paul restored the Mulberry wood, bottom tray, and sanded and cleaned the remaining wood. The family made a gift of the press to the museum. Paul's wife Veronica was elected mayor of Altus in 1998. Paul works with his father, five brothers and a sister, continuing the tradition of an Arkansas Winegrowing family. (Author.)

This photo image was made during WW I of James "Jake" Post and a friend, with grapes loaded into a boxcar ready for shipment to market. The Post family also sold grapes to Iron Mountain train passengers. Railroad personnel disapproved of hulls and seeds because they made a mess on the floor. Mount Bethel Winery, owned and operated by Eugene and Peggy Post and their son Michael, is the second-generation site of the Post Winery. Their grapes are handpicked, fermented, and aged in redwood barrels. (Paul Post.)

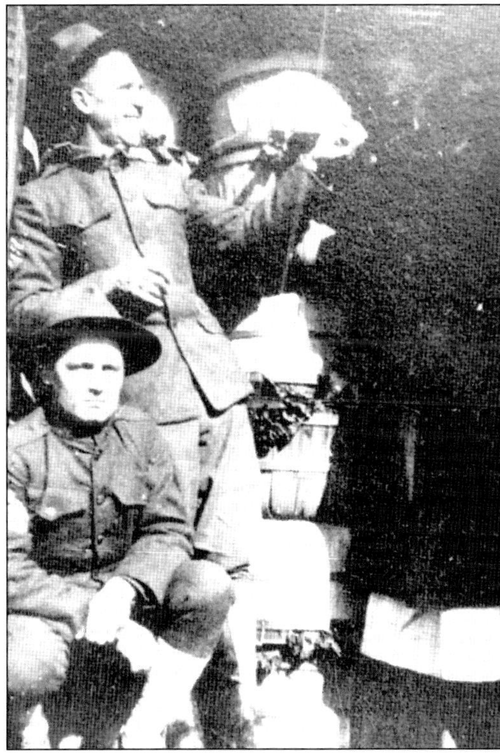

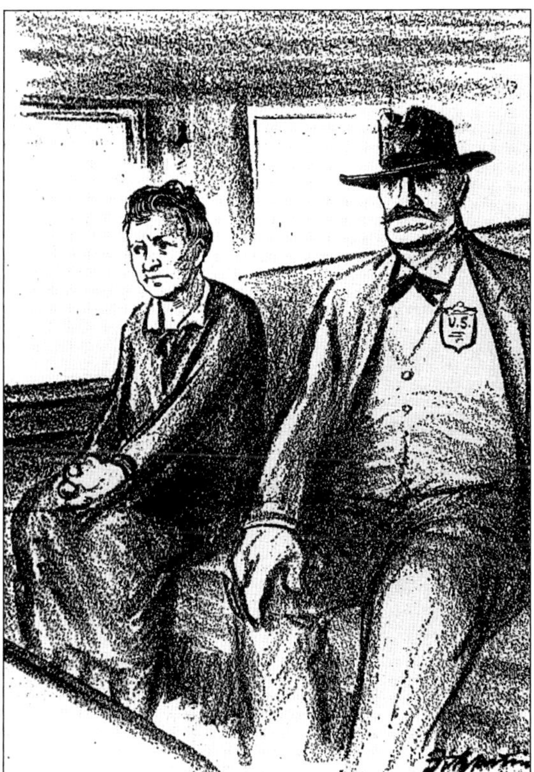

Katherine Post, aged 56 years, was sketched in June 1929, while being transported to prison. The wife of fruit farmer Joseph Post, she pled guilty to selling wine and whiskey during prohibition, a violation of the Volstead Act. She was sentenced to serve 18 months. Katherine admitted that repeated crop failures, and a need to pay for her children's education, tempted her to break the law. At the time, she was mother to 16 children, five still living at home, under the age of 18. (Paul Post.)

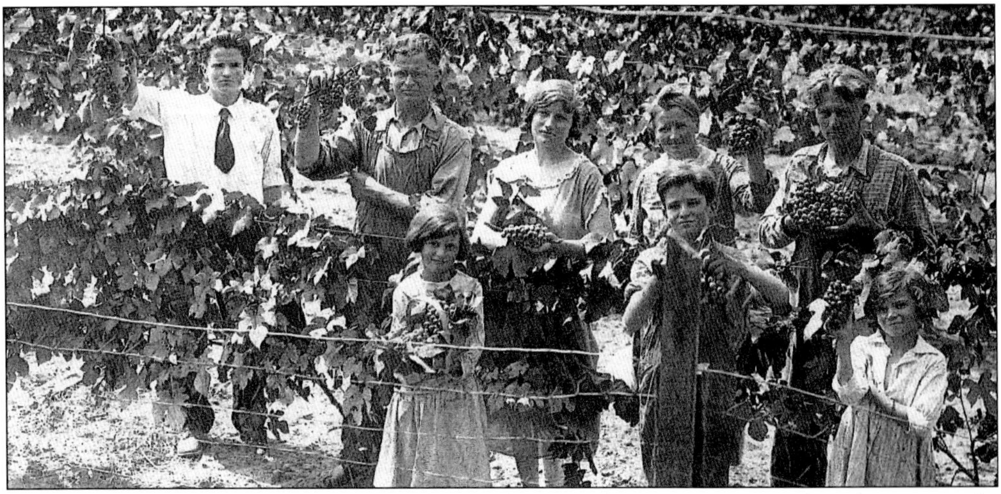

Second and third generation Post family members, as shown in 1926, gather the vineyards, plentiful harvest. Katherine Post, right of center on the back row, poses with her large family among the grapes. After prohibition, the Arkansas State Legislature requested that James "Jake" Post, Joseph and Katherine's son, help them rewrite the law to allow wine growing, again. Jake, and son Mathew, founded the Post Winery at its present location. It is now known as the Post Familie Vineyards and Winery. (Paul Post.)

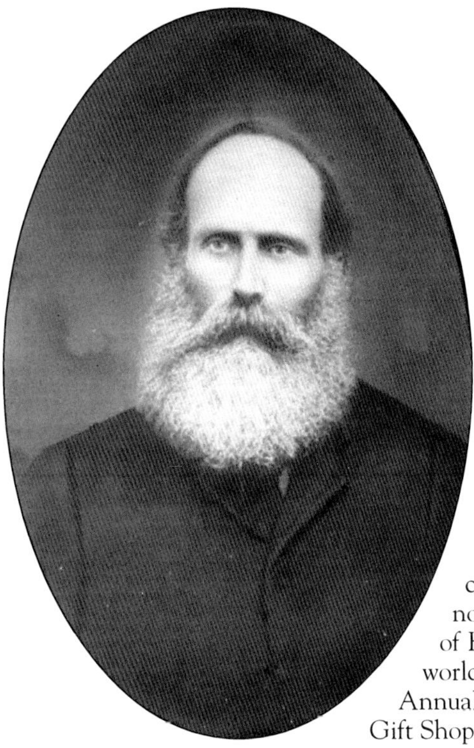

Shown is Johann Andreas Wiederkehr of Switzerland, who arrived in Altus c. 1880, with wife Katharina. They boarded with Father Ziswyler of St. Mary's Catholic Church for six weeks until their log cabin was finished. That cabin and the original hand-dug wine cellar are now preserved and listed on the National Register of Historic Places. Today the wine cellar serves old-world cuisine as Wiederkehr's Weinkeller Restaurant. Annually, thousands of tourists visit the Swiss Chalet Gift Shoppe and wine-tasting room. (Gary Udouj.)

Katharina Guller Wiederkehr, shown here, and Johann Wiederkehr eventually had nine children. When Katharina was 49 years old in 1903, she gave birth to their youngest child, Mary, who became Sister Mary John. In 1927, the same year Johann and Katharina were to celebrate their Golden Wedding anniversary, Johann died at age 72. Plans were made to use the famous Edelweiss, from the windswept byways of the Swiss Alps, to decorate for the anniversary occasion. The rare and beautiful flower was used, instead, at Johann's funeral. (Gary Udouj.)

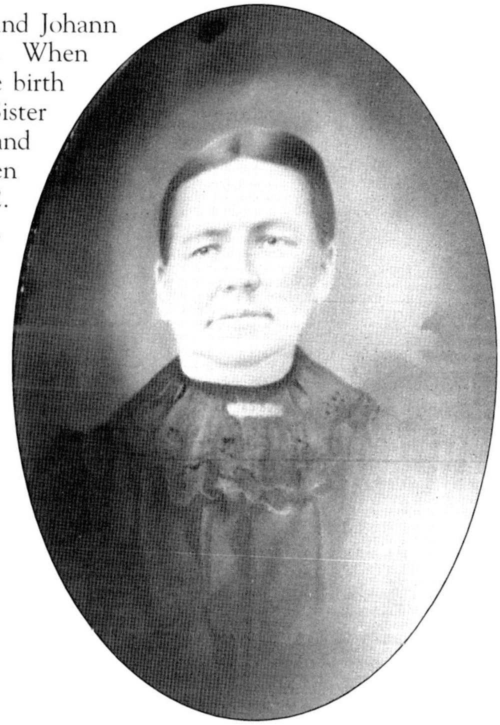

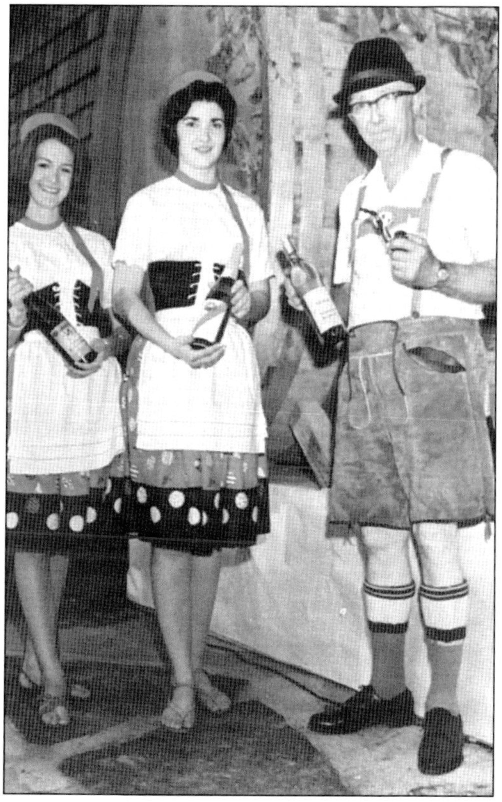

Herman Wiederkehr in this picture postcard remembers his father shipping barrels and kegs of wine all over the United States and delivering wine locally in a hack. Even during prohibition, the Wiederkehrs produced sacramental wine. Shown with Herman are Gayle Gibbons and Mary Long. As a student, at Arkansas Tech under the GI Bill, Herman was asked to teach plant-propagation, grafting, and other horticultural techniques to students. (Gary Udouj.)

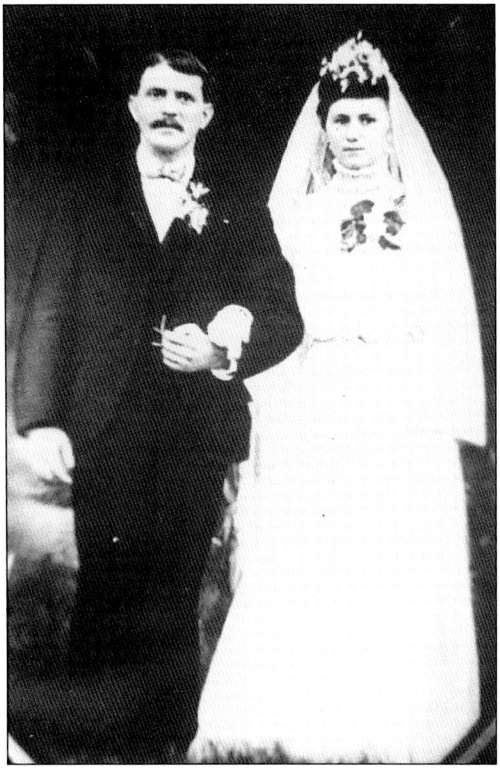

Joannes and Katherine Wiederkehr Udouj are shown in their wedding photo c. 1905. They were married at St. Mary's Catholic Church in Altus. Joannes and Katherine eventually had eight children. All of the children graduated from St. Mary's Catholic Church School. Joannes supported his large family as a coal miner working in Coal Hill. Two of his sons also worked the mines. (Gary Udouj.)

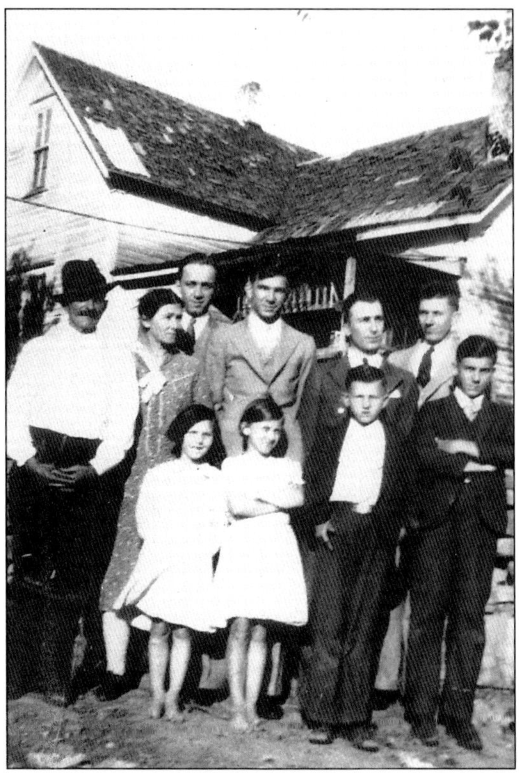

Joannes and Katherine Wiederkehr Udouj pose in front of the old homeplace in Altus in November 1934, with their children. They are John, Rudolph, Alphonse, Herman, Henry, Carl, Theresa Marie, and Catherine. Joannes Udouj was born January 1876, in Dolenjas Austria-Hungary (Yugoslavia), and died in 1941. Katherine Julianna Wiederkehr was born January 1886, in Altus, and died in 1977. (Gary Udouj.)

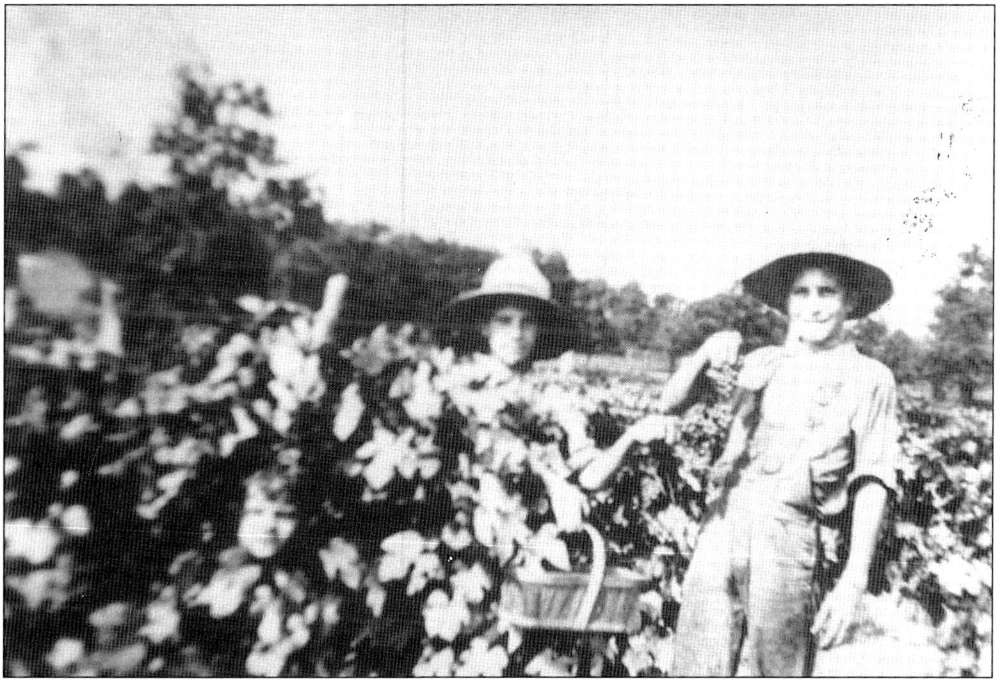

Henry Udouj, whose face can be seen down on the left in the grapevines, and his older brothers are shown in the Altus vineyards c. 1928. The Udouj family became involved in area coal mining and later moved to Fort Smith and began other professions. Herman founded Fort Smith's Riverside Furniture. Other Udouj family members have gone into medicine, law, engineering, real estate, and other well-respected and prosperous occupations. (Gary Udouj.)

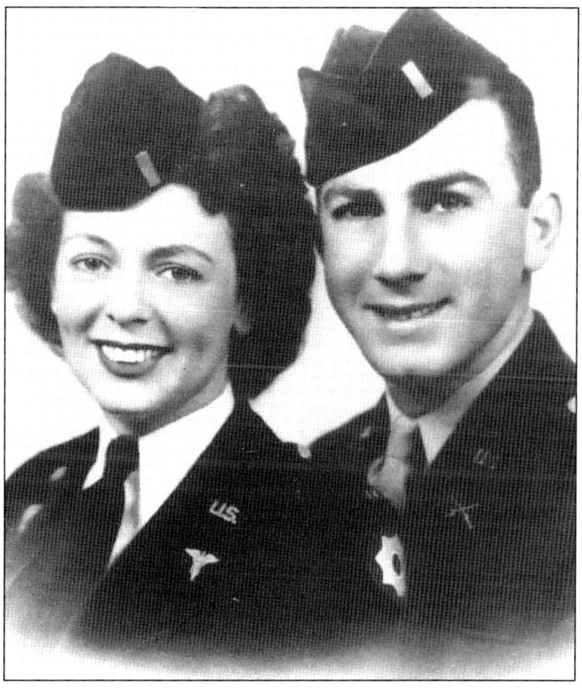

Shown are Lieutenant Henry "Hank" J. Udouj and Lieutenant Ida "Ken" Kinzle. The photo image was made in France in 1944. After serving their country during WW II, the two lieutenants became husband and wife. They met at Camp Fannin, Texas, where Ken was serving as a registered nurse in the Women's Army Corps. Hank grew up in the Altus community. (Gary Udouj.)

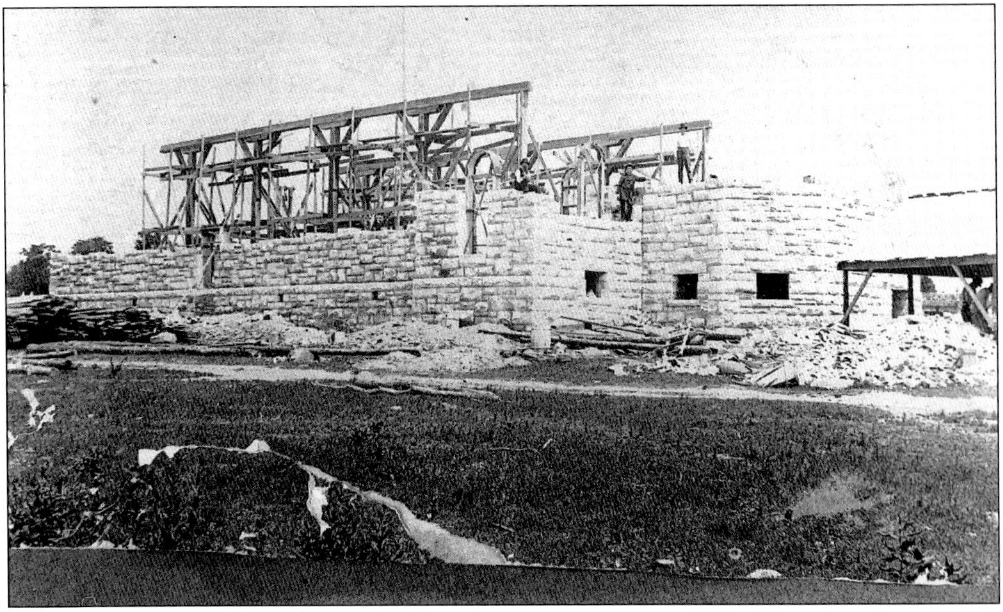

St. Mary's Catholic Church is shown under construction c. 1901. The church organized on November 21, 1879, originally served the German-speaking Catholics in Johnson and Franklin Counties. The increase of coal-mining operations in Denning enlarged the church's membership. As a result, on November 28, 1900, the congregation voted to build a new church. The beautiful, coarse-grain, granite-like, sandstone, found on the bluff at the edge of St. Mary's Mountain, was used in the church's construction. (Heritage House Museum.)

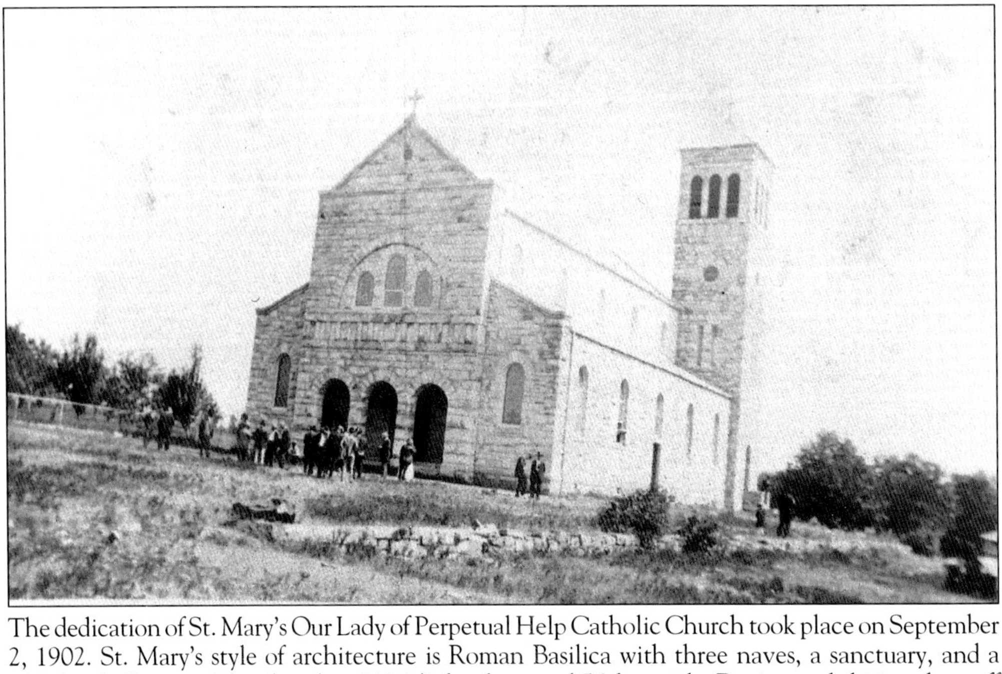

The dedication of St. Mary's Our Lady of Perpetual Help Catholic Church took place on September 2, 1902. St. Mary's style of architecture is Roman Basilica with three naves, a sanctuary, and a 100-foot bell tower. The church is 117 1/2 feet long and 56 feet wide. During prohibition the staff hid sacramental wine under the floorboards to prevent its destruction by authorities. The original St. Mary's was wood frame with an onion-shaped belfry. (Gary Udouj.)

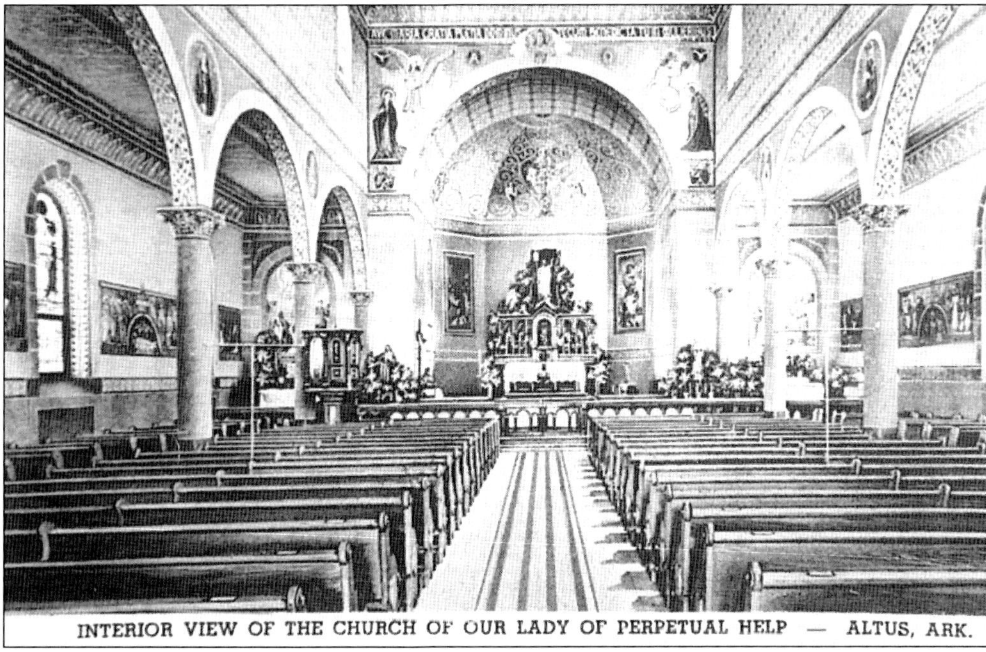

The interior of St. Mary's Catholic Church is shown on this postcard. Members experienced years of self-imposed sacrifice as the magnificence of the church's interior unfolded. In 1915, Artist Fridolin Fuchs, of Berlin, Germany, painted the interior walls with religious scenes. Early residents of Altus, including Fuchs, modeled for many of the saintly figures. On October 31, 1999, Bishop Andrew J. McDonald presided at the dedication of the church's $500,000 renovations. (Heritage House Museum.)

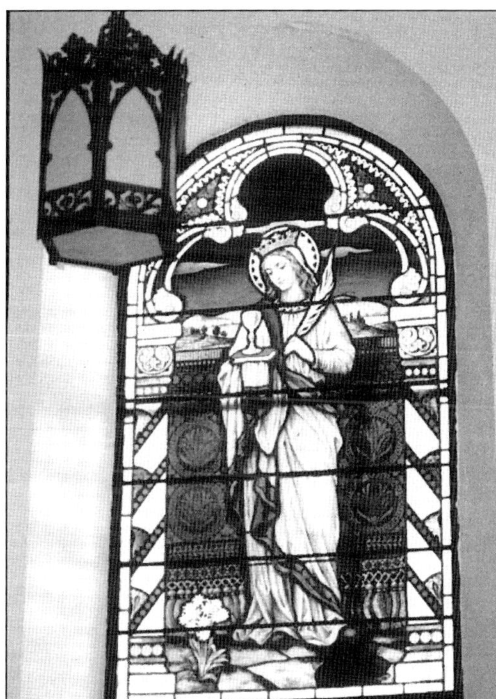

One of the many stained-glass windows of St. Mary's Catholic Church is that of St. Barbara, Patron Saint of Miners. St. Barbara was a virgin and martyr. The window was a gift of the Santa Barbara Society of coal miners, with emphasis on the Slavic community. Immigrants of European descent added greatly to Altus' Catholic population. Most of the Slavic miners lived in mining company houses in Denning. (St. Mary's Catholic Church Photo Collection.)

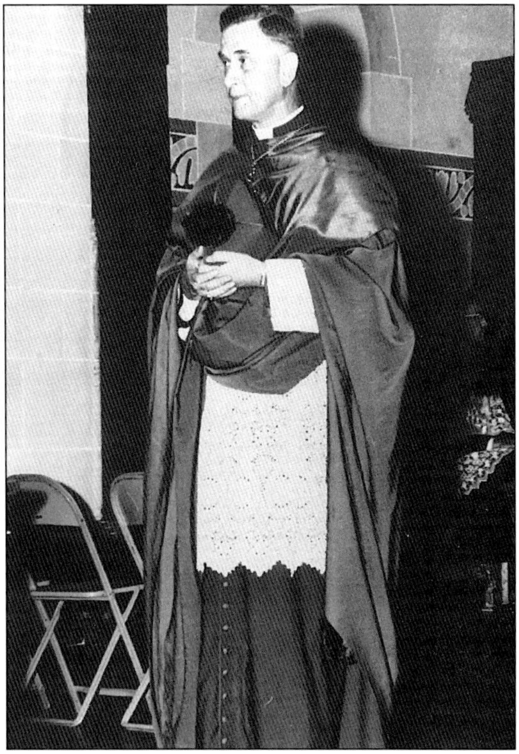

Shown is Bishop Albert L. Fletcher, D.D., confirmed as the fourth bishop of the diocese of Little Rock. The Most Reverend Fletcher was the first native of Arkansas to be so honored. The announcement of his appointment on December 11, 1946, was made from Rome in the name of Pope Pius XII. Bishop Fletcher was confirmed on March 16, 1947, at St. Mary's. (St. Mary's Catholic Church Photo Collection.)

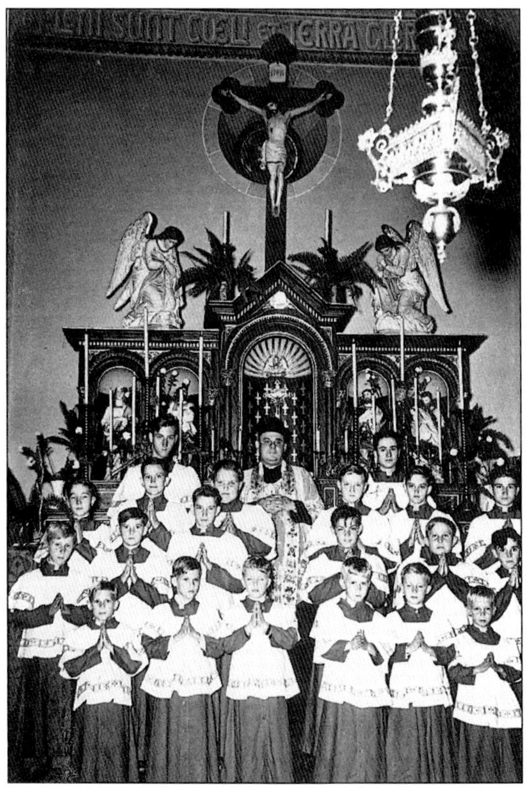

St. Mary's Catholic Church Choir is shown with angelic, young men dressed for their performance in beautiful robes. The St. Mary's choir has been outstanding over the years. Young men and women of St. Mary's, members of choirs, and others, have gone on to outstanding vocations. From St. Mary's has come priests, an abbot, a mother superior, and numerous nuns. Some lost their lives in defense of their country. The young man on the top row right, whose hands can be seen folded, is Alquin Wiederkehr, of the Quorum Court. (Gary Udouj.)

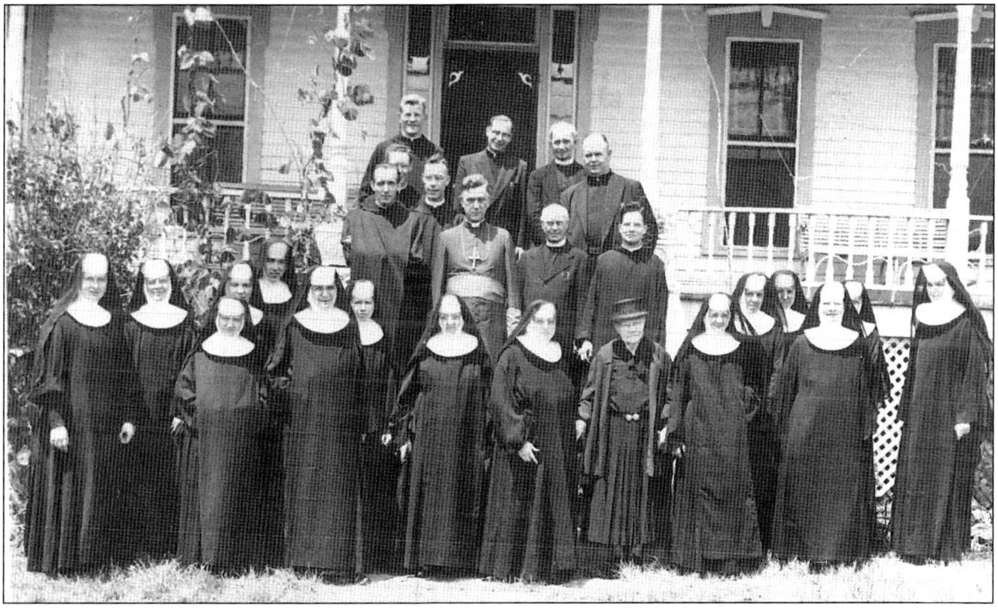

Priests and Nuns pose outside the Priest's rectory during St. Mary's Diamond Jubilee Celebration in 1954. Also called the parsonage house it was dedicated on March 21, 1896. It had a mansard roof and porches along three sides, with 232 running feet in upstairs and downstairs total length. Later the home became dilapidated and leaked throughout. It was torn down c. 1965. The original estimated cost to build it was $4,500. (St. Mary's Catholic Church Photo Collection.)

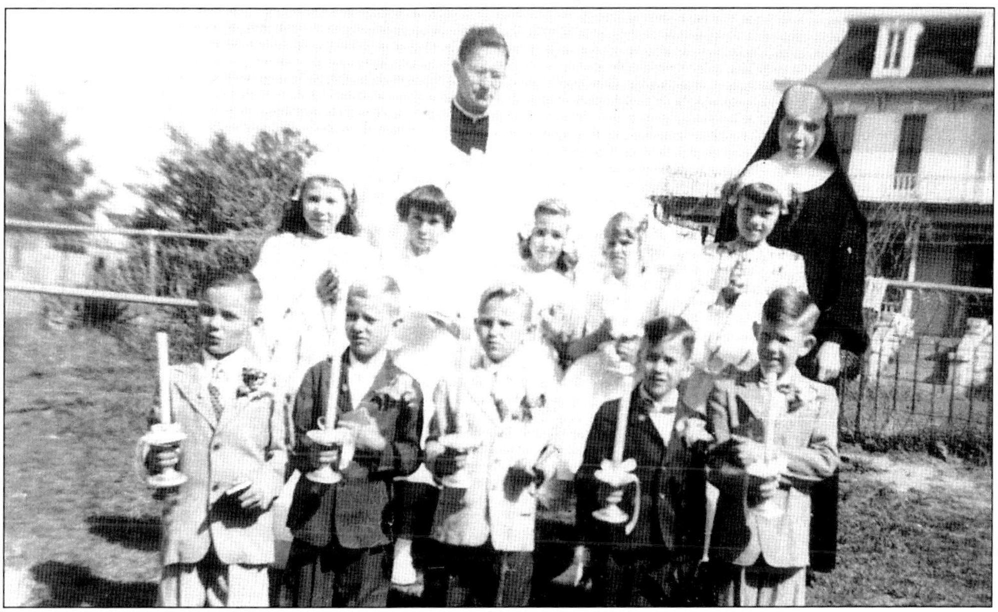

Children of St. Mary's Parish who received their first Holy Communion on March 27, 1960, pose with Sister Madeline Clifton. They are Zeta Myers, Matt Post, Paul Vaught, Steve Timmerman, Bill Mark Schaffer, Virginia Thomas, and Stan Eveld. Sister Madeline taught at the church school from April 1956 through 1960. At that time she was known as Sister Monica. Later the sisters began using their given names. (Bill Mark Schaffer, Sister Madeline Clifton.)

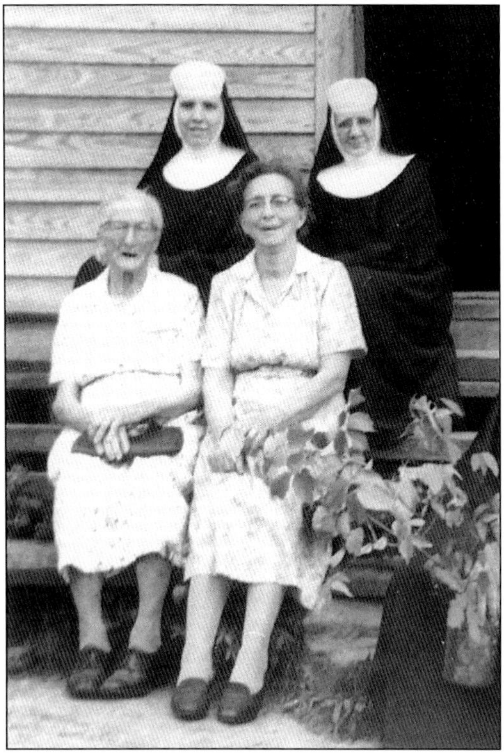

These venerable ladies, Mary Elser Sax to the left and her daughter Agnes Sax Post, pause for a photo with Sister Ottilia and Sister Madeline Clifton at St. Mary's Catholic Church, in the Altus community, c. 1959. Sister Madeline, who is now a chaplain at St. Edwards Mercy Medical Center, taught grades one through four at St. Mary's Parish, in Altus, in the 1950s. (Sister Madeline Clifton.)

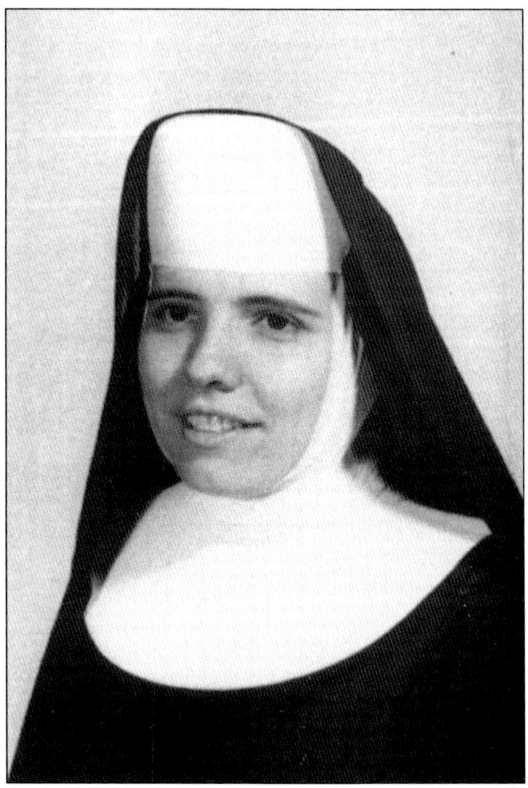

Some folks still believe that a "real" Nun must wear a habit. Sister Madeline Clifton no longer donned hers by c. 1960. The fabric worn on Sunday, and big feast days, was a heavy serge material, and was hot. Fabric, referred to as coolcloth, was not cool. Old habits had to literally wear out before replacement. After washing, the white-coif's pleats were shaped, and the coif set out to dry. Then the pleats were pulled around the neck and the rest of the material pinned on top, under the veil. Often there were four layers of starched cloth on top of the head. In the summertime "you sweated out your coif." (Sister Madeline Clifton.)

Four

Altus Is Its People

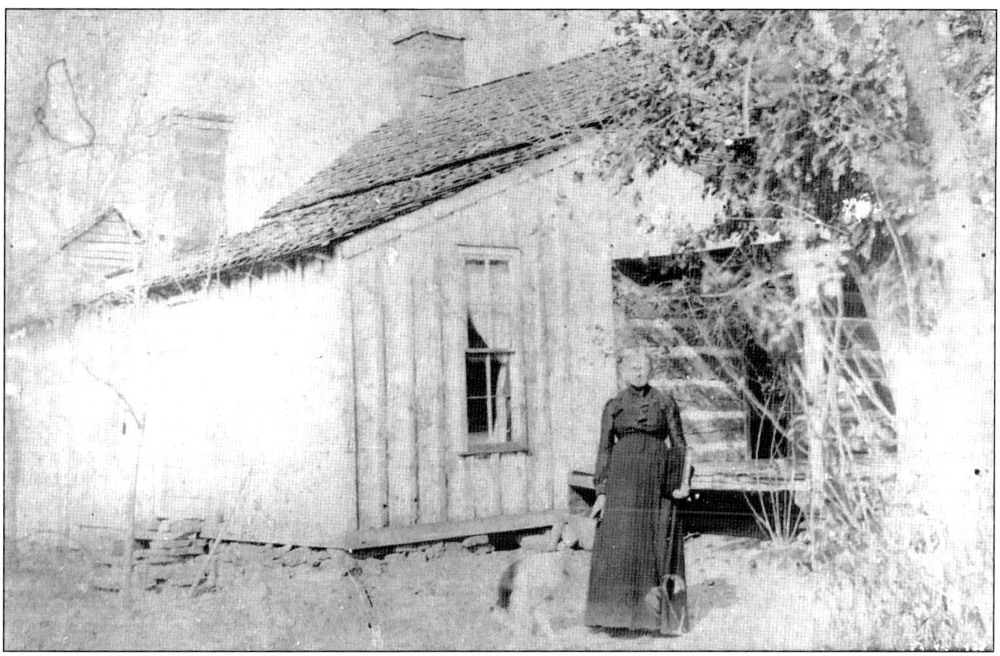

Abigail Parker Warren Hudson, with Bible in hand and faithful dog at her side, stands in front of her log home built *c.* 1861. She and Ambers Warren, her first husband, were married the same year he built the home for her. He was 24 and she was 21. He was murdered in the front yard by Civil War bushwhackers and is buried near where she is standing. For years after his death, people spoke of his blood-stained clothing still in an attic trunk. This was considered a rather fine home for the 1860s era, in this part of Arkansas. (Elizabeth Muchmore Page.)

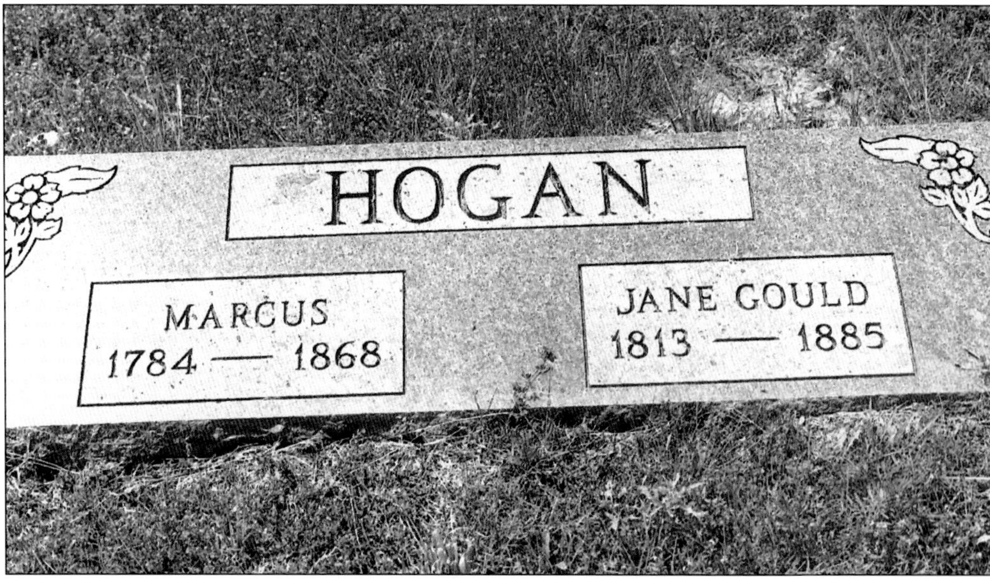

Pioneer Marcus Hogan's tombstone inscription bears the name of his last wife, Jane Gould. Marcus was among the first to settle the area. In 1849, as Justice of the Peace, he performed the first marriage in Franklin County. In 1875, Hogan Township was named for him. During the Civil War he refused to reveal the hiding place of his gold and food staples, even after bushwhackers burned his feet and hung him. His slaves and Jane, his 16-year-old daughter, cut the rope and saved his life. Marcus was almost 80 at the time. (Author.)

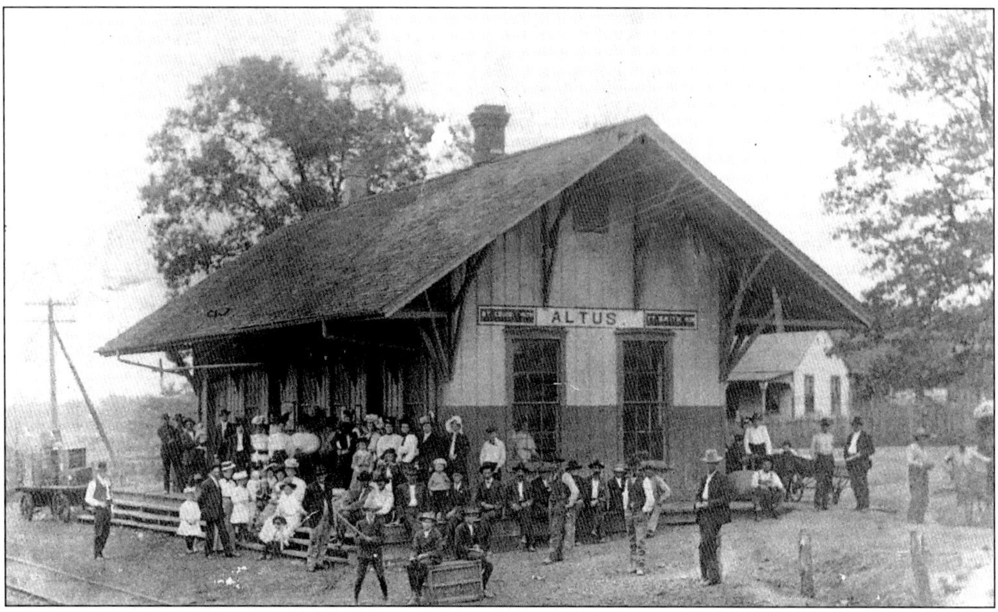

Altus Depot is shown before its expansion. Originally another depot was located one-half mile east. Many German, Swiss, Slavic, and Irish immigrants came to America by way of Ellis Island through New York Harbor, in the 1870s. They were informed of Altus' large Catholic community and that work was available at the Fort Smith and Little Rock Railroad. Another bonus, when they arrived in Altus, was similar geography to their own homelands. (Katherine Cherry Parmalee, Heritage House Museum.)

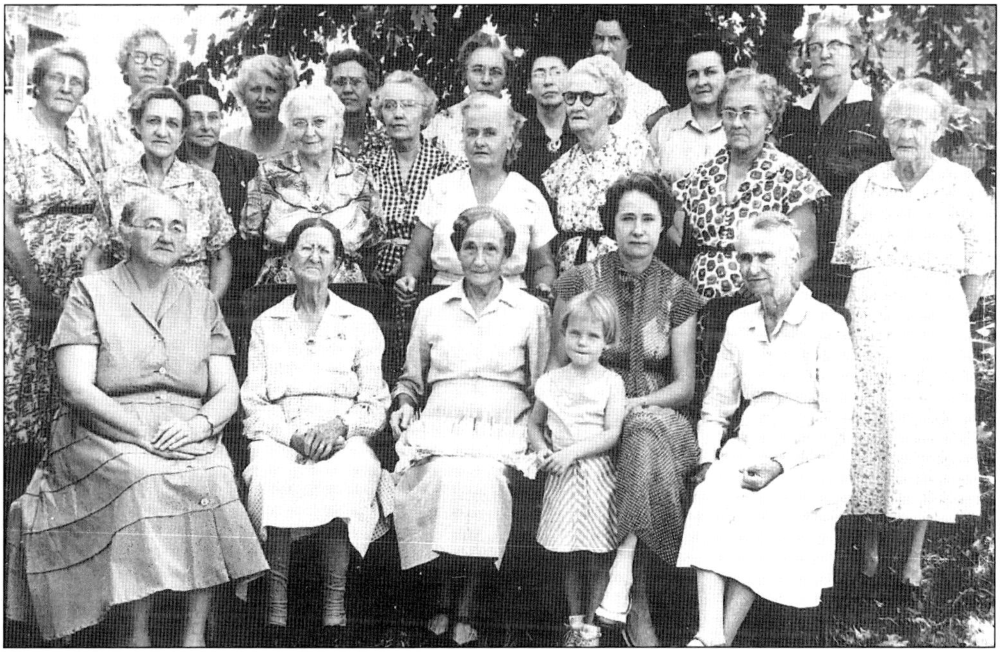

This is a photo of Ida Hale's 81st birthday party, September 12, 1957. Others are: Rose Hopper, Gertie McNabb, Cumi Edgin Jacobs, Vannie Lee Jacobs, Maud Baker, Rena Pyron, Anna Lee Zolliecoffer, Agnes Hampton, Guss Harbottle, Maggie Baker, Vera Jennings, Maggie Cherry, Maud Denton, Ethel Stutchman, Med Muldoon, Addie Dunahoo, Mrs. Edgin, Mary Adams, Pearl Mathis, Mrs. Hale (with cake), Viola Quaile, Martha Quaile, and Sally Jackman. (Jimmy Jacobs.)

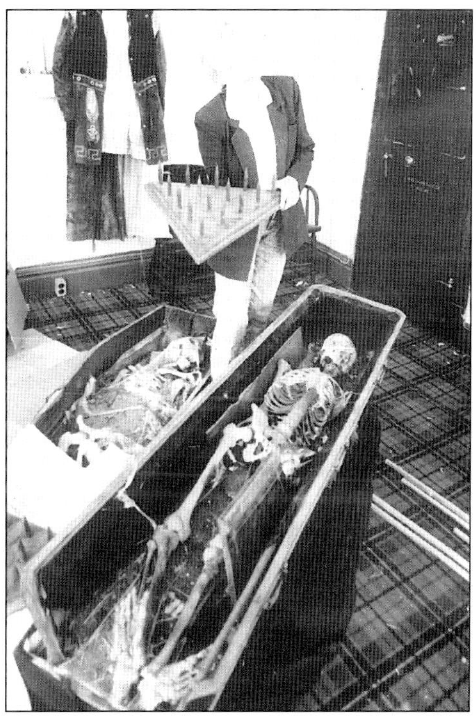

Joy Wilcox, former Altus mayor, c. 1994, displays a skeleton in its ornate, velvet-lined coffin, used in Knights of Pythias ceremonies. Note the ceremonial robes hanging on the wall. The Knights assisted the sick and widowed. When the Altus Chapter of the Knights disbanded, on March 18, 1991, they left their money to Children's Hospital in Little Rock, and they left their meeting place, the old German-American Bank, to the city of Altus. (Spectator, Heritage House Museum.)

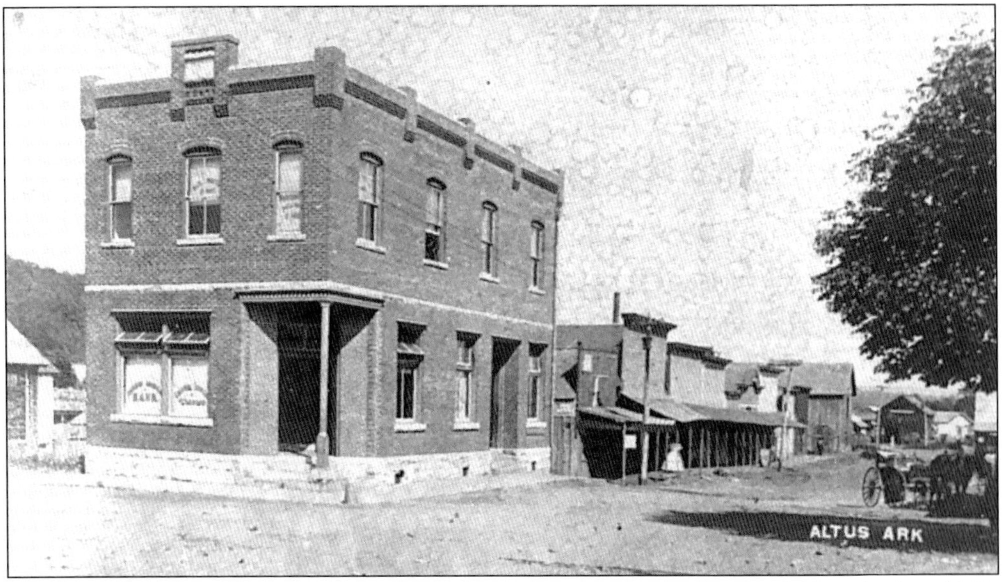

Shown to the left, in this c. 1909 image, is the German-American Bank of Altus, built c. 1900. The German portion of the name was dropped during WW I. This part of town, looking east, was called "Smoky Row," due to questionable activities which took place there after dark. Most of the buildings you see in this image, with the exception of the bank, no longer exist. The Heritage House Museum, which opened in 1994, is now located in the bank building. (Sadler H. Burrow Collection.)

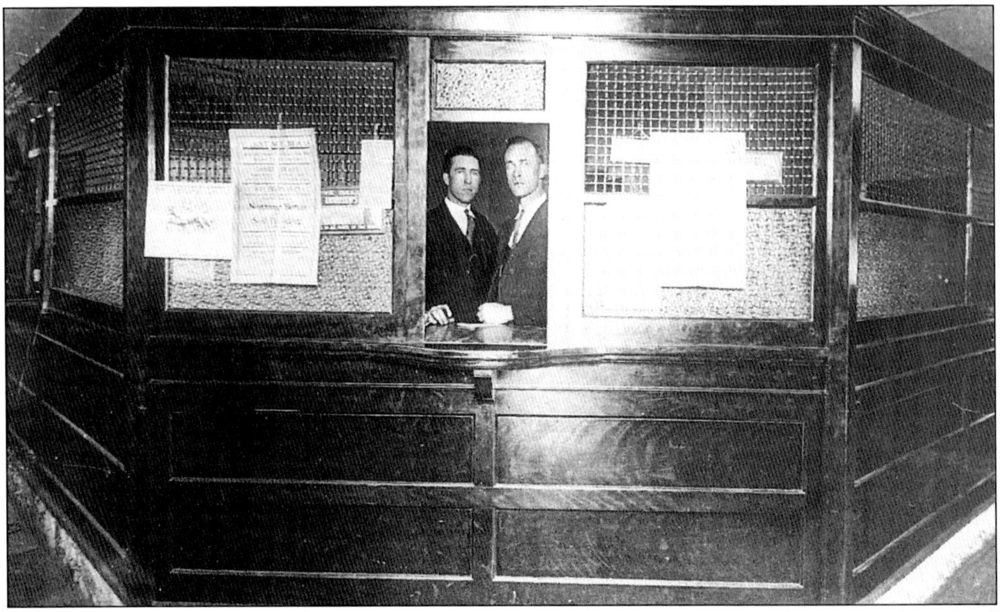

The men posed in the bank window in this c. 1928 photo image are Edgar E. and Garland Nichols. The German-American Bank, organized in 1904, closed in June 1938. The Altus chapter of the Fraternal Order of the Knights of Pythias owned the building and held their meetings upstairs. They rented the downstairs to the U.S. Postal Service. Note the Wanted Poster listing a $500 Reward and an admonishment to "please count your change." (Norval A. Nichols, Heritage House Museum.)

Lewis and Virginia Muchmore Canady were visiting Grace and Coy Watts in Altus when this photo was snapped, c. 1954. For many years, Lewis worked on B-52 airplanes at Boeing Aircraft in California. After retiring in 1969, he and Virginia returned to Altus. In January 1970, they opened a grocery and dry goods business, which they operated for a number of years. Virginia is president of the Altus Historical Society and is largely responsible for the development of the Heritage House Museum and for efforts to preserve Altus area history. She authored an account called *Altus History 1888 to 1988*. (Virginia Muchmore Canady.)

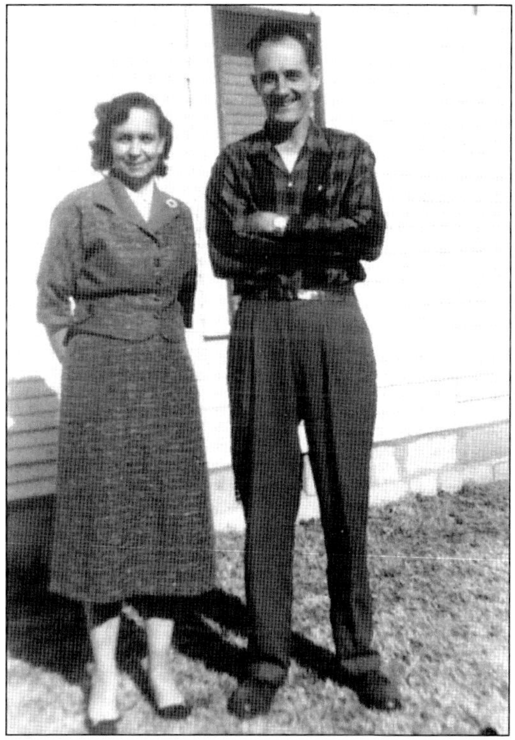

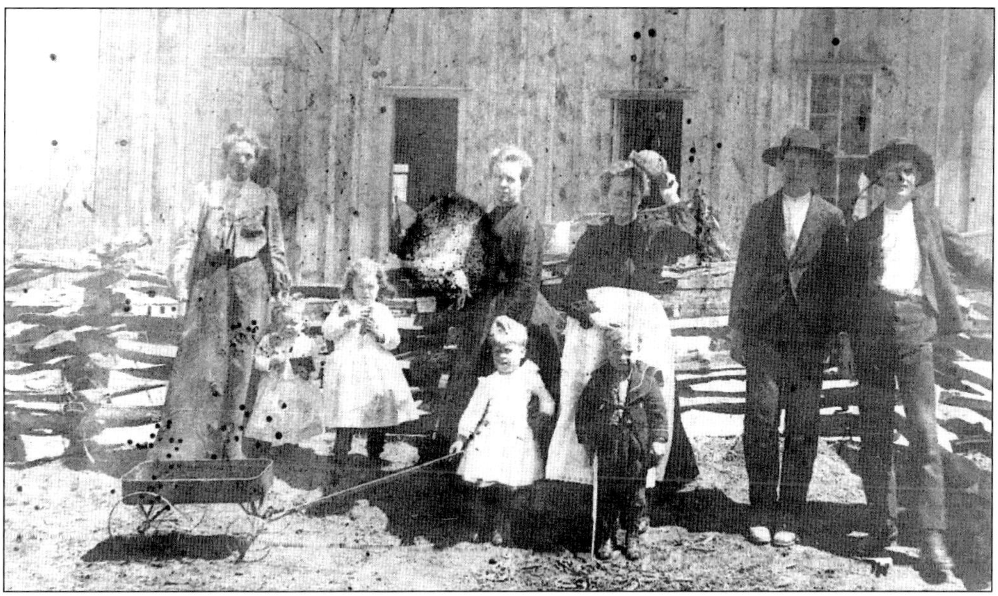

Shown among others are Lynn Snider Page and her daughters Jewel and Dessie c. 1910. Also pictured are Laura Page Sublett and possibly two Page boys. The location was near Center Cross. When the literary society was not meeting at Center Cross School, they met at the Snider home. People shared music, books they read, and poems they wrote themselves. It involved things of a creative nature. Despite the bare look, the yard was continually filled with flowers and attractive bushes. Note the split rail fence which kept grazing livestock out of the yard. (Virginia Muchmore Canady.)

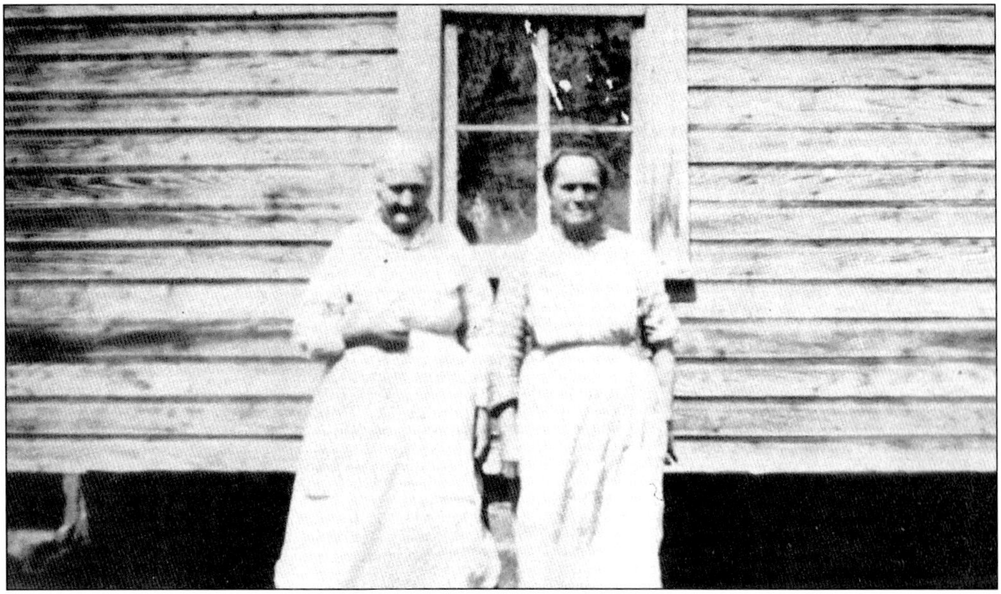

Mary Schmitz Muchmore, on the right, is pictured c. 1948, with Martha English Brown near Center Cross. Mary's grandchildren recall that people would often come and get her to take care of ill family members. She acted as midwife delivering a number of babies in the Altus community. She doctored with herbs and medicinal trees and plants. Herbalists like Mary were important to the physical well-being of early-day citizens. Mary's gift was learned from her mother Carolina Schmitz. Mary and her family immigrated to America from Germany in 1872. (Edith Page Wright.)

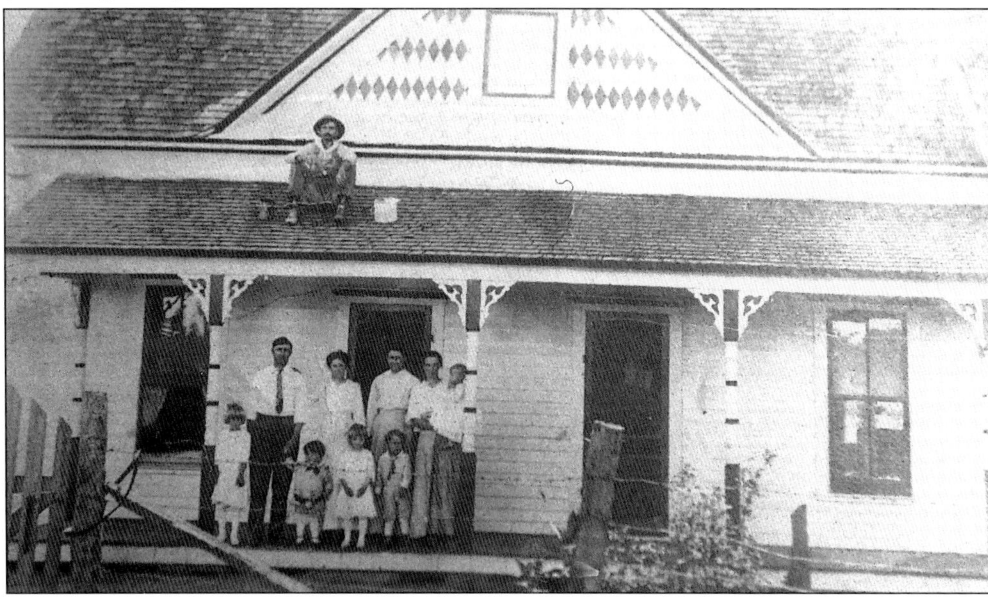

Pictured are Scott and Rose Bailey and children Essie Faye and Lola Mae c. 1917. Also pictured are George Muchmore, Joanna Lowe, Lena Mason, and children Grace and Walter. On the roof is Mr. Scribner, the house painter. Electric lights and radios did away with the comforting, family custom of sitting on the farm porch after dark. Families might discuss the day's work and make plans for the next, or just sit quietly without speaking. (Grace Mason Watts.)

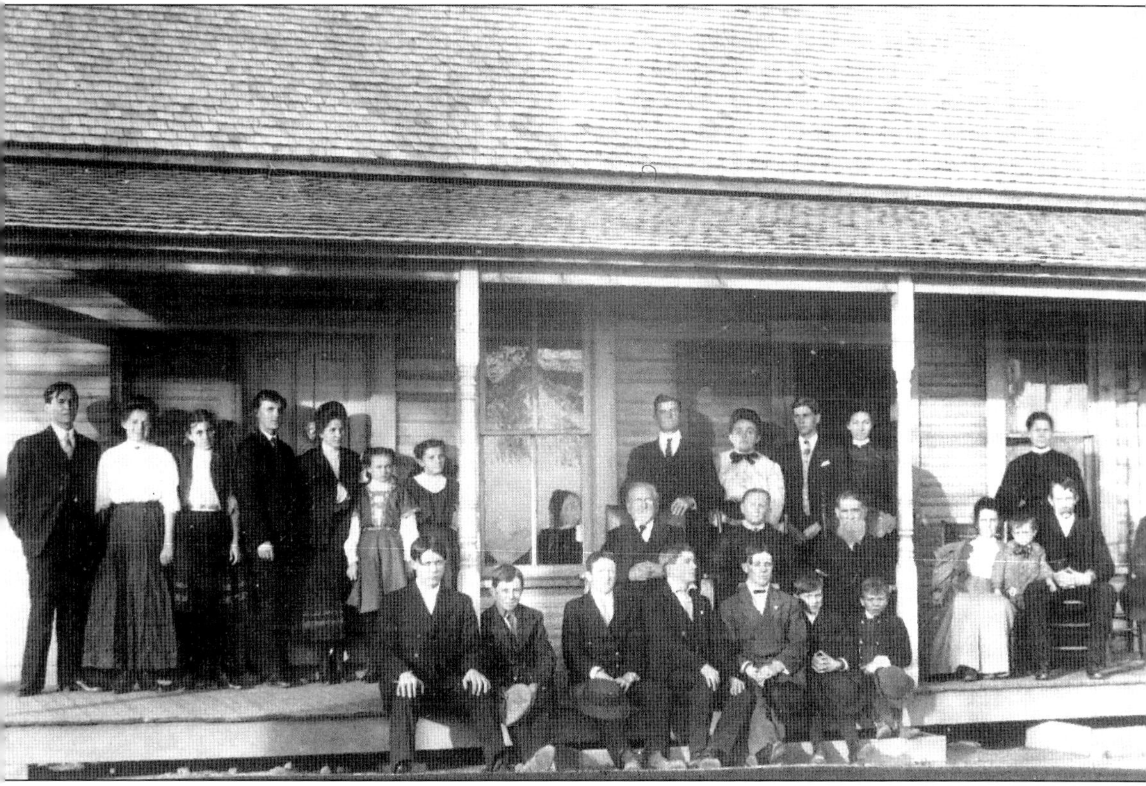

Sharing Christmas in 1907 are Lester Hardgrave, Clemmie Hunt, Annie Nichols, Jack Cleeton, Bonnie Hunt, Floy "Gyp" Hunt, Charles McDonald Hunt, Lucy Jackson Hunt, Walter Jackson Hunt, Sallie Nichols, Cynthia Ogden Hardgrave, Martha Kirley, Frank Kirley, Gabe Kirley Raefel, Earl Crutchfield, Jack Cheek, Horton, Harlan, Cleave Morris, Jim Kirley, and Jake Kirley. (Heritage House Museum.)

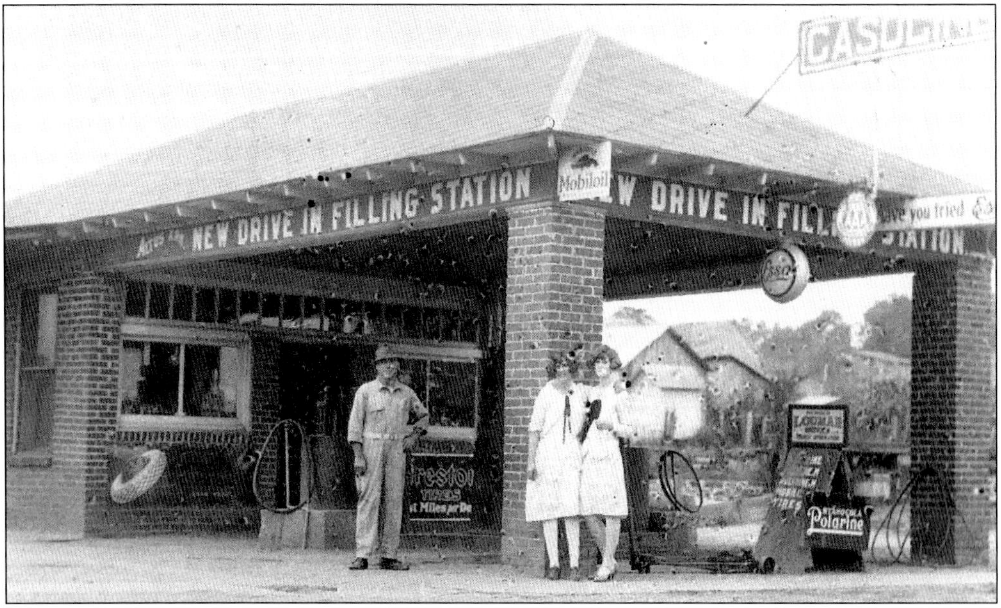

This Triple A Service Station, owned by Joe and Bonnie Forneris, was located on the corner of Ozark and Main Streets, west of today's city hall in Altus. Joe is the station attendant, and Bonnie, in white, is shown with an unknown lady. The station was built in1923. This station was torn down and a similar station built here in 1931. Note the residences to the south and west. (Grace Mason Watts.)

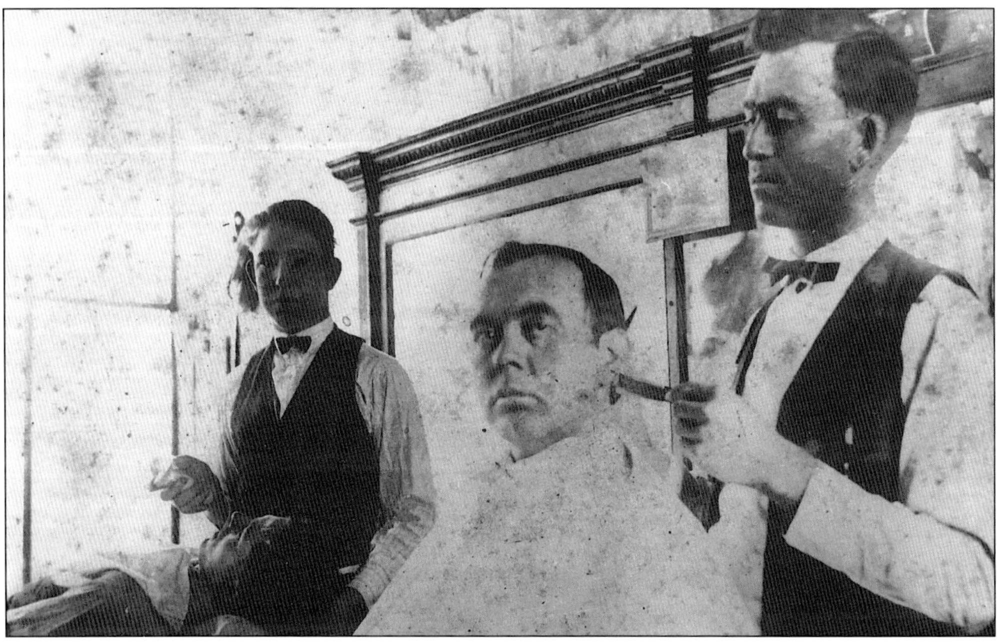

Molard Jacobs is shown to the left in this photo along with a fellow barber in Altus. Later Molard moved to Ozark. He cut the hair of men, their sons, and finally their grandsons. One fateful day Molard tried to intervene as two men began an argument in his barber shop. He knew it was serious since they were both armed. When they told him to leave he did as they asked. Tragically, both of those men died that day. (Sadler H. Burrow Collection.)

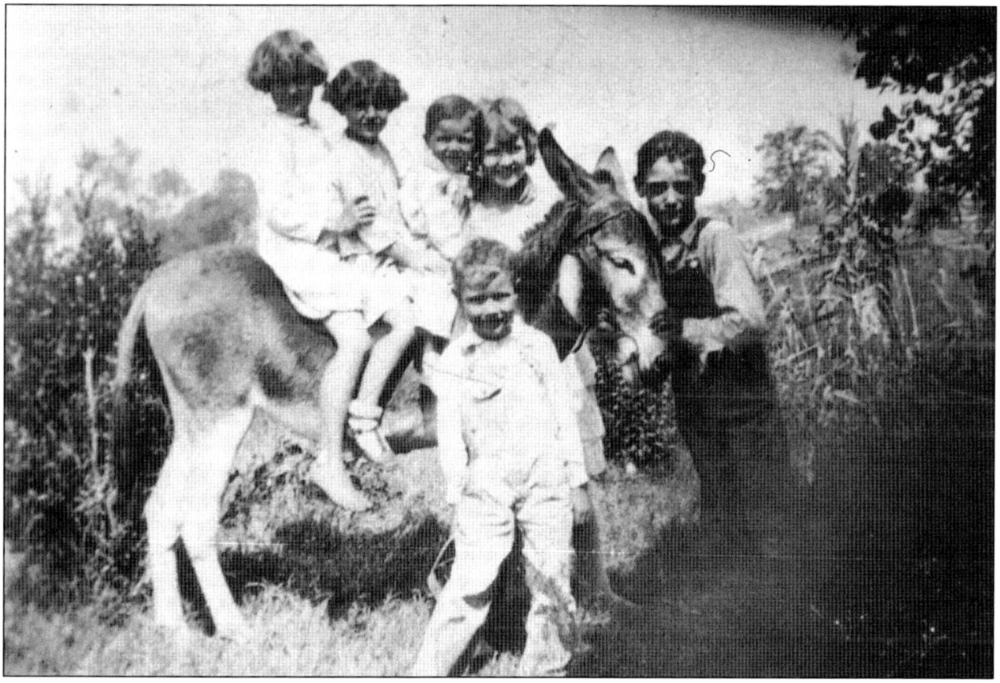

The Blythe children and friends are playing on a donkey, in 1928, in the little Greenwood Community. They are Dennis and Arvil Blythe, Mary Bell McDonald, James Pruitt, and Rosa Beth and Eunice Blythe. With no television, or shopping malls to amuse them, kids learned to entertain themselves. (Blythe Collection, Heritage House Museum.)

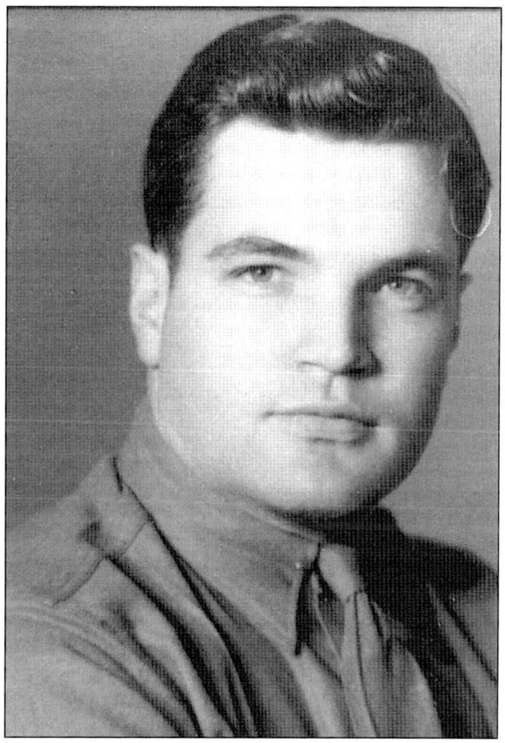

Harold Gene Blanscet joined the Marines on August 14, 1941. He was awarded the *Purple Heart medal* for injuries sustained in battle at Tinian on August 1, 1944. Other medals were the Honorable Service Lapel button, WW II Victory Medal, Good Conduct Medal, and the American Theater SV Ribbon. He married Margaret "Marie" Hardwick on October 21, 1944, in Ozark. Corporal Blanscet was discharged at Camp Lejeune, North Carolina, October 1, 1945. (Marie Hardwick Blanscet.)

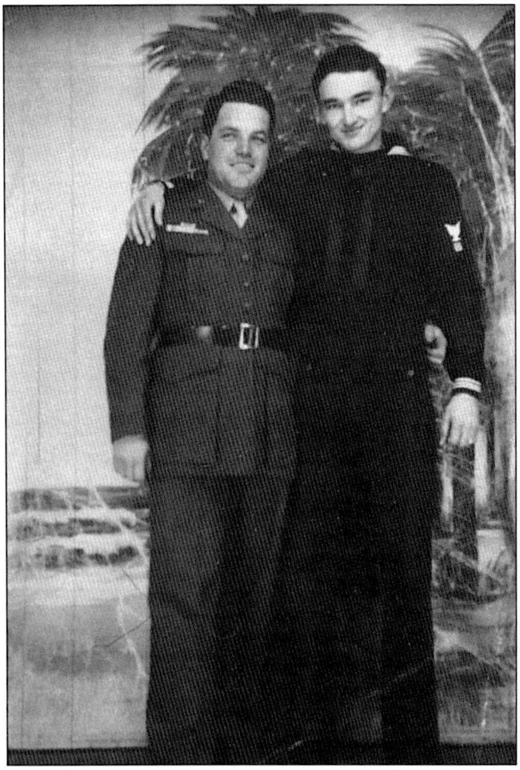

Marine Corporal Harold Gene Blanscet and his buddy, Raymond Burns, of the U.S. Navy, another Altus boy, posed for this photo taken in 1944, in Charleston, South Carolina. Corporal Blanscet was a member of the Marine Corps military police. He was transferred to Camp Chaffee where he continued to serve in a military police capacity. Harold Gene also participated in action against the enemy at Tarawa, Atoll; Gilbert Islands; Saipan; Marianas Islands; Tinian; and Guadalcanal. (Marie Hardwick Blanscet.)

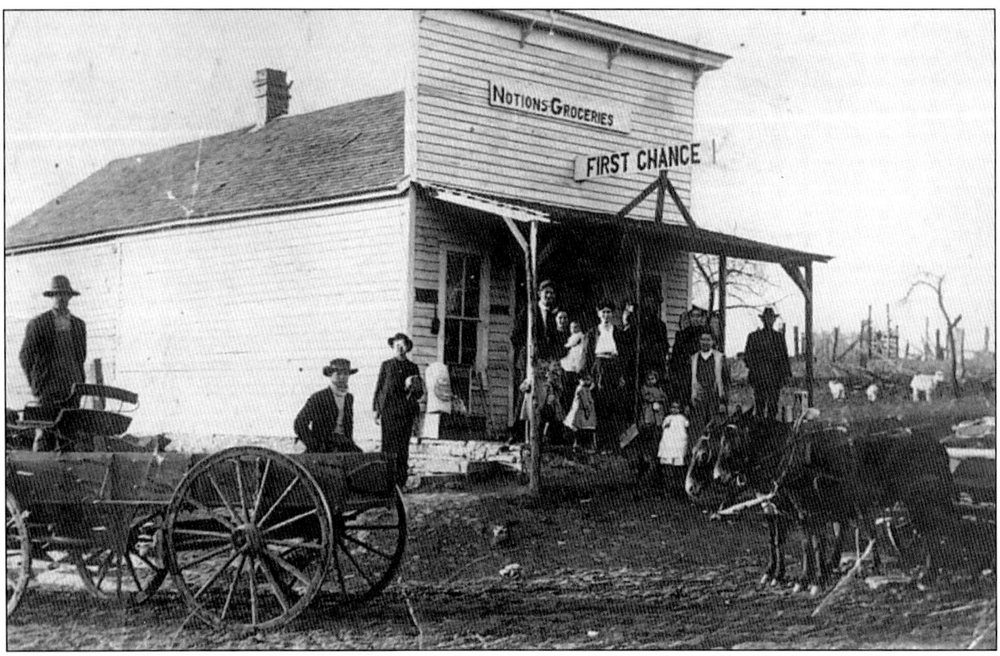

The *First and Last Chance Grocery Store* was owned by J.P. Higdon. The sign said First Chance when going to town and Last Chance, on the other side, when leaving town. The store was located at the cross-roads near Altus Schools. Note the number of small children and the nanny goat with her babies. (Grace Mason Watts.)

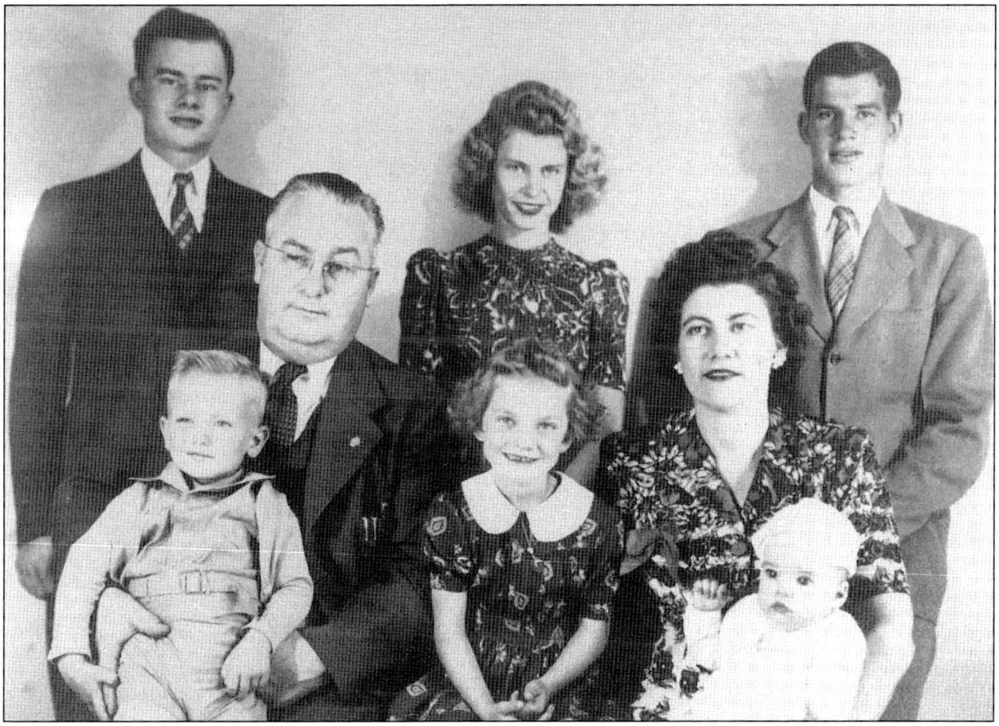

Dr. E.W. Pillstrom, shown here with his family, practiced medicine in Altus until his death in 1957. He was Franklin County coroner for many years. Mary Adeline Newton Pillstrom, Dr. Pillstrom's wife, was the first licensed midwife in the state of Arkansas. She also set broken limbs and treated other complicated cases in Dr. Pillstrom's absence. Children of the Pillstrom's are DeEsta Rose, Mary Ann, Sally Jane, Edward William, and Lawrence G. (Dr. Lawrence G. Pillstrom, M.D.)

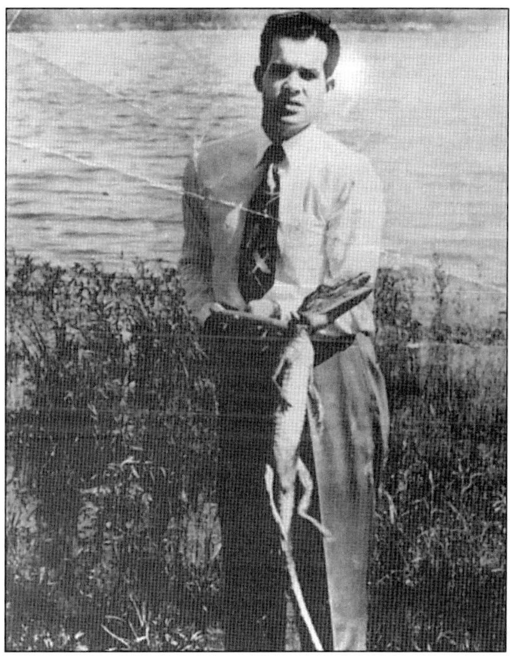

Larry Pillstrom, as a University of Arkansas pre-med student in 1953, began the study of snake venom and poisonous bites. With no safe way to capture and control the reptiles, he invented, and perfected, the Pillstrom Snake Tongs. He is shown here holding an Alligator with the tongs. The tongs are now used by Disney world, recreational areas in Africa, zoos, animal control agencies, and special animal handlers and collectors. (Dr. Lawrence G. Pillstrom, M.D.)

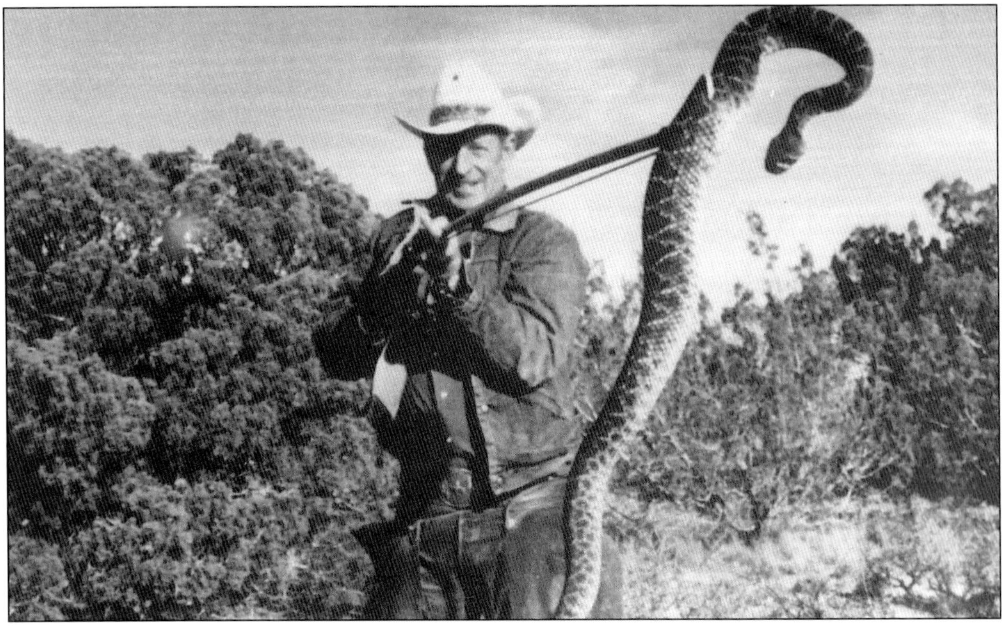

Don Bennett in a picture postcard is holding a 6-foot-4-inch, 10-1/2-pound Diamondback Rattlesnake with the Pillstrom Snake Tongs. The tongs were invented by Dr. Larry Pillstrom. Other uses of the tongs are: controlling small pets safely, barbequing, and picking up trash. They are also used by wheelchair-bound people to secure out-of-reach items. Dr. Pillstrom has several lengths depending upon the need. (Dr. Lawrence G. Pillstrom, M.D.)

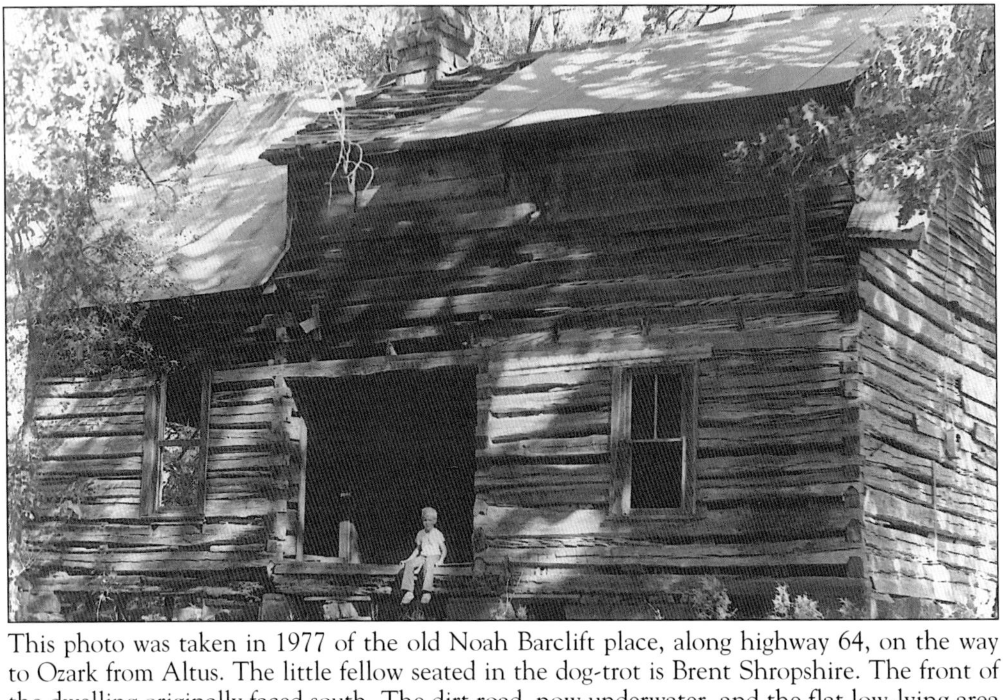

This photo was taken in 1977 of the old Noah Barclift place, along highway 64, on the way to Ozark from Altus. The little fellow seated in the dog-trot is Brent Shropshire. The front of the dwelling originally faced south. The dirt road, now underwater, and the flat low-lying area nearby were called Barclift Bottoms. According to local legend, when the last owner of the old loghouse died, his mattress was found to be stuffed with $100 bills. (Author.)

Five

Ozark
The Bend of the River

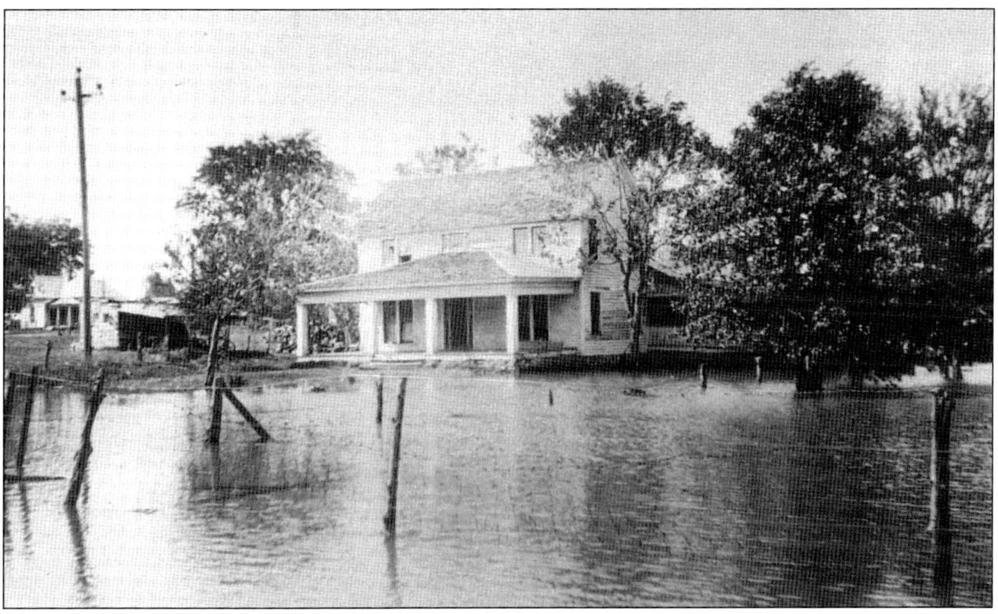

This photo, taken one block northeast of the courthouse *c.* 1943, reveals Gar Creek floodwaters ready to overflow the porch of an Ozark residence. To combat this periodic flooding, millions of manhours and tons of dirt and concrete were used in the construction of the Ozark-Jeta Taylor Lock and Dam. The work was done under the supervision of the United States Army Corps of Engineers, Little Rock District. (Sadler H. Burrow Collection.)

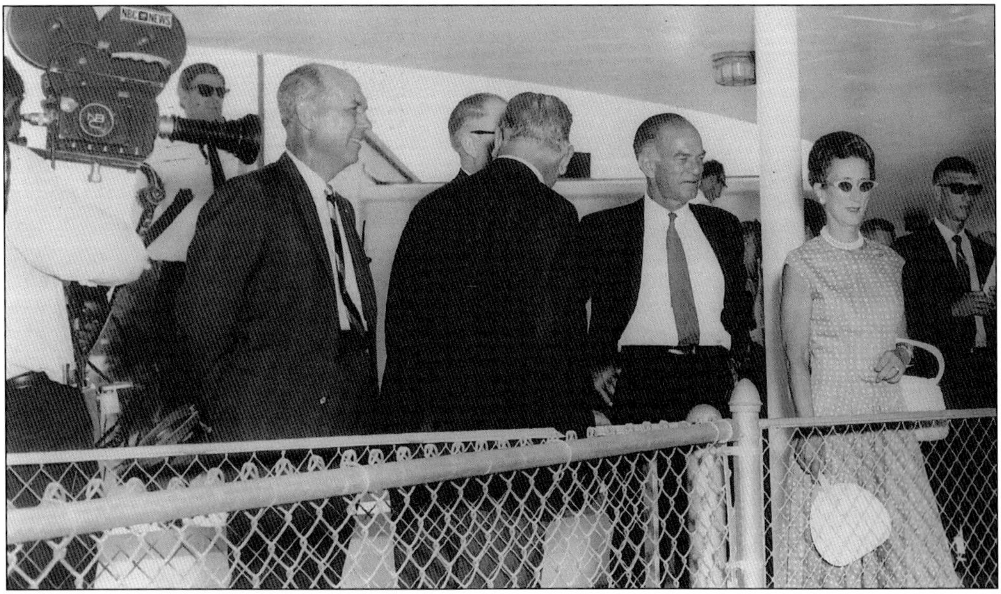

The dedication of the Ozark Jeta-Taylor Lock and Dam featured Senator J. William Fullbright, on the right, at Reed Mountain overlook. This monumental project was initiated in 1965, and completed in November 1969. The dam, a vital component of the McClellan-Kerr Arkansas River Navigation System, the most expensive waterway ever constructed at that time, assures the citizens of this region that they will never again experience widespread flooding. (Greg Miller, Ozark Field Office and US Army Corps of Engineers, Little Rock.)

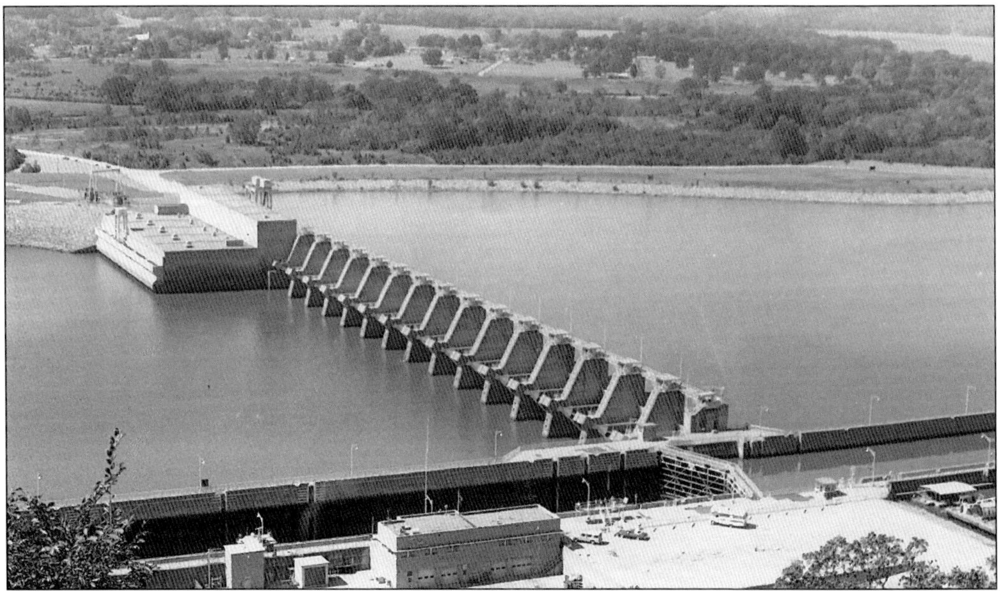

The Ozark-Jeta Taylor Lock and Dam between Altus and Ozark is shown in this 1977 image, taken from Reed Mountain. The estimated cost of the lock and dam alone was $83 million. There are 17 locks and dams in the project, with 12 of them in Arkansas. In 1837, from this vantage point, near the bend of the river, folks likely witnessed steamboats, keelboats, and canoes plying Arkansas River waters. The goods brought to Ozark by steamboat were distributed inland by horse-drawn wagons. (Author.)

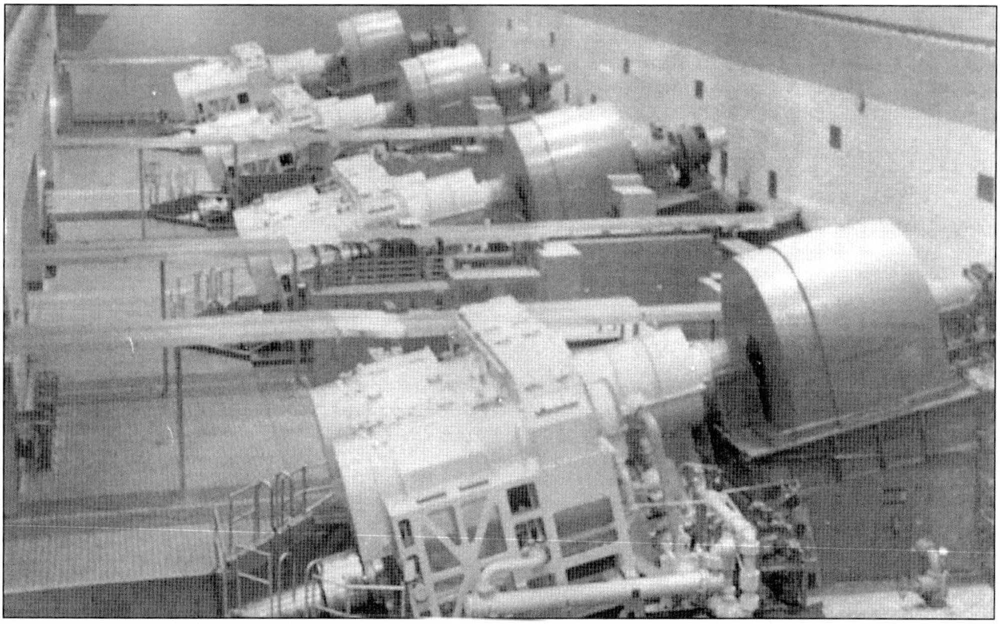

The powerful turbines of the Ozark-Jeta Taylor Lock and Dam, shown here, generate hydroelectric power which is sold to public and private utilities. Marketed by the Southwestern Power Administration, the power is delivered over a network of high-voltage, transmission lines. The powerplant contains five inclined axes and hydraulic, turbine-driven 20,000 kilowatt generators. The Ozark Powerplant is maintained, and operated, by the US Army Corps of Engineers. (US Army Corps of Engineers.)

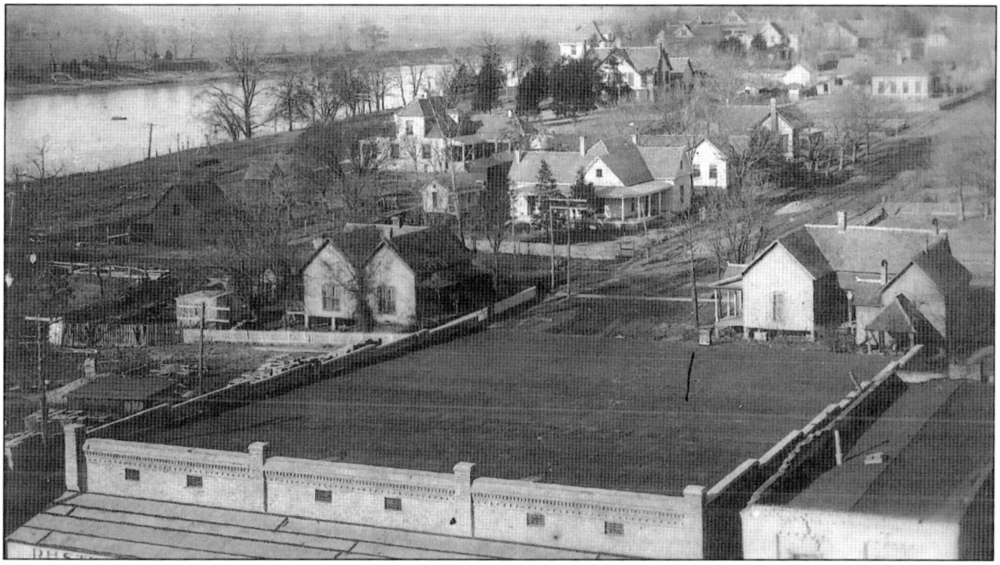

The Arkansas River is shown looking southwest from the courthouse clock tower *c.* 1909. Some pioneer settlers to the Ozark area were Cureton, Walker, Yell, and Hail. They surveyed the town and held the first public auction of lots at a July 4, 1836 barbecue. Settlers Alston, Barclift, Booth, Eichenberger, and Littleton were also in the area. William Cureton was owner, in part, of the area where Ozark is located today. He operated a ferry, from the boat landing, which he established prior to 1836. (Sadler H. Burrow Collection.)

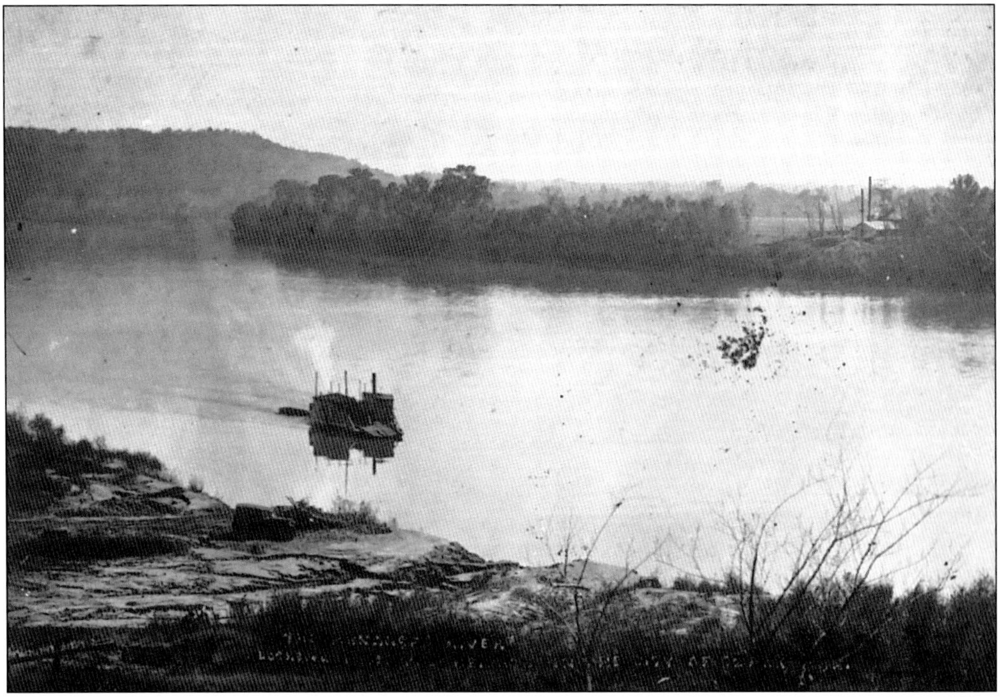

The ferry in this *c.* 1920 image was used prior to the construction of the Ozark-Webb City Bridge. Beneath its deck was an engine-powered paddle wheel. The ferry was not always available. Mrs. T. Moore said that during the Civil War a messenger told of letters from loved ones (soldiers) written to families living in Ozark. The letters were delivered to Webb City, which was across the Arkansas River from Ozark. Although the river was high and had drifts, Mrs. T. Moore and Serena Webb Turner crossed over in a canoe to retrieve these letters. They had only a wash pan to use as a paddle. (Sadler H. Burrow Collection.)

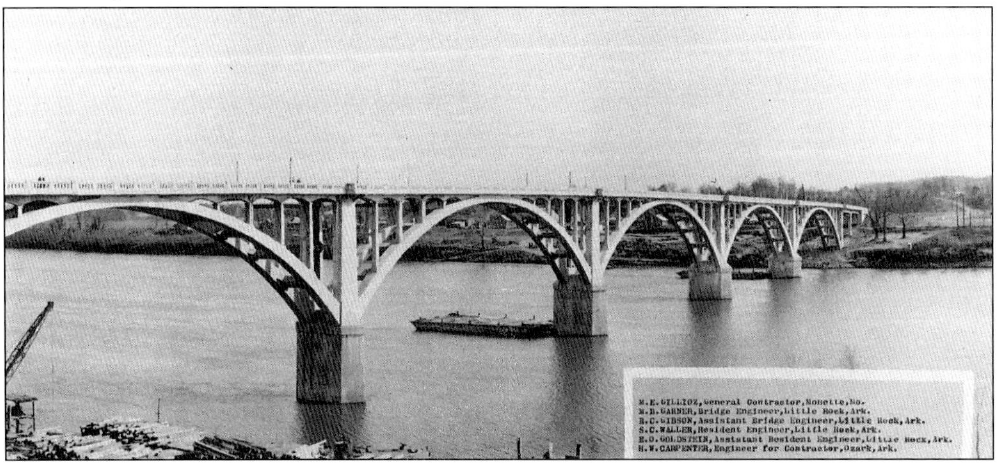

Shown is the Ozark-Webb City Bridge, referred to as the concrete bridge. The bridge had six arches, with five visible here. It was built in 1931 by contractor M.E. Millioz of Monette, Missouri, on the Toll Pool Plan. Many such bridges were built using the same funds. Taylor Pierceson and J.W. Harmon were the first toll collectors. By 1938, the debt had been paid and there was no longer a toll. Initially the bridge was recognized as one of the 11 most beautiful bridges in the world. (K.C. Studio, Wallace Walker Page, Mike Guittare.)

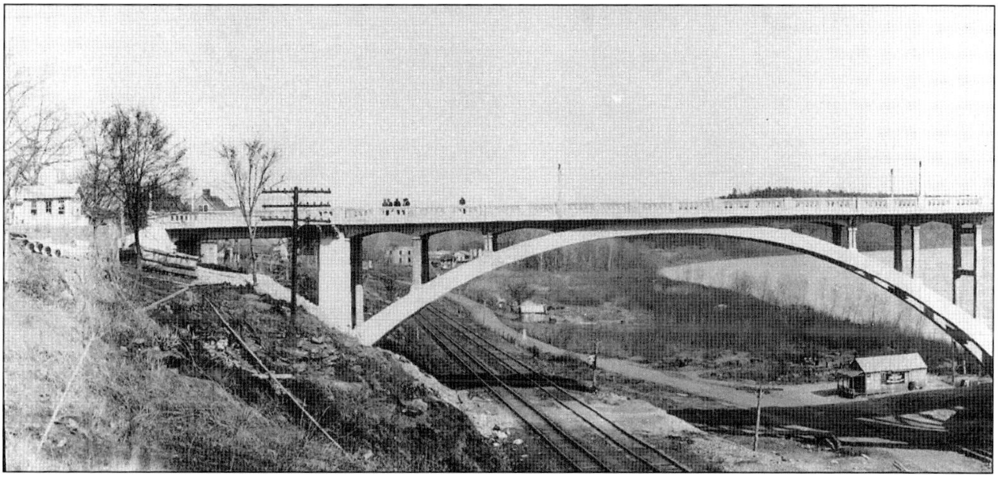

Looking from the north river bank, on March 19, 1931, one can see the first of six arches of the Ozark-Webb City bridge. On that date three cars belonging to bridge builders and Ozark officials were the first to cross the bridge: contractor M.E. Millioz, S.C. Waller Project Engineer; Judge T.A. Watson; Guy Duvall; Claude Wakefield Jr.; Mr. and Mrs. J.R. Davidson; Mrs. J.B. Carter; Claude Carter; and Mrs. S.C. Waller. Note officials posed at various locations along the bridge. (K.C. Studio, Wallace Walker Page, Mike Guittare.)

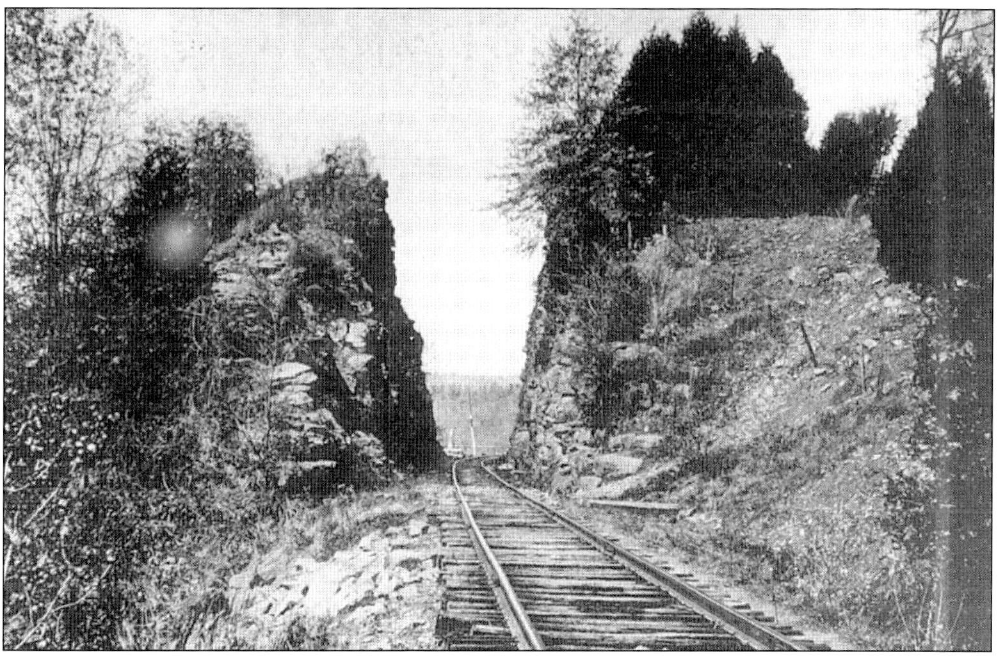

The "railroad cut," also known as the "slate cut," is shown in this picture postcard. Many lives were lost, near the cut, on the bluff west of Ozark both during and after the railroad's construction. In 1883, a large boulder slid down the hill, above the cut, and a freight plowed into it. William Voss, the engineer, died when he was pinned beneath the engine. In 1911, the fill and trestle east of the cut washed out and wrecked five railroad cars of corn and flour. Residents carried it off by the wagonload. (Harry Blackman.)

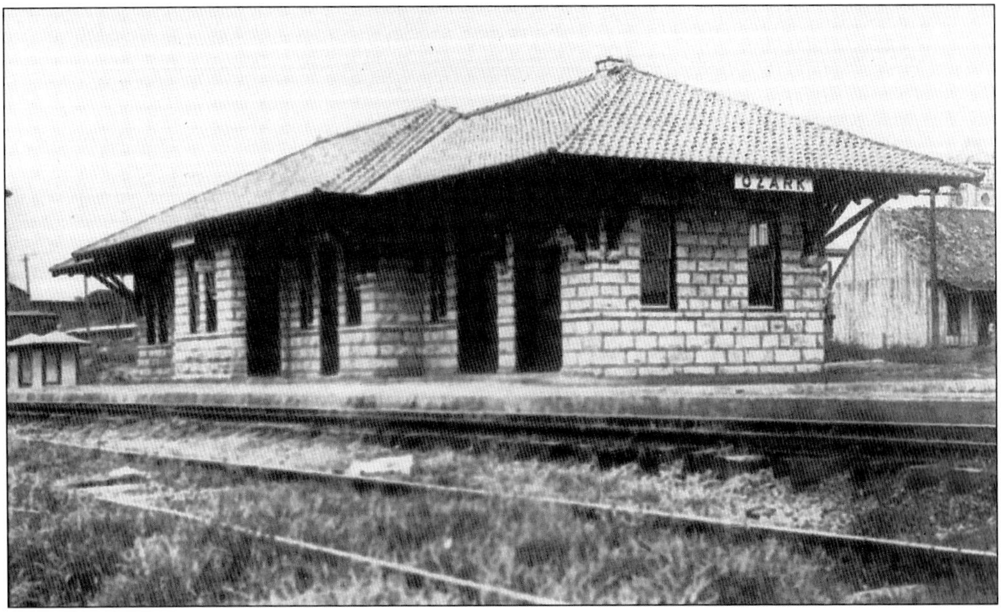

The Iron Mountain Train Depot, shown in this picture postcard, was constructed in 1911. The 200 people who attended the dedication listened to a day-long band concert. The first depot was located east of the present building and was wood frame. The first train to enter Ozark was a freight which came from the east in January 1876, at 8 p.m. A great crowd gathered to greet it. (Sadler H. Burrow Collection.)

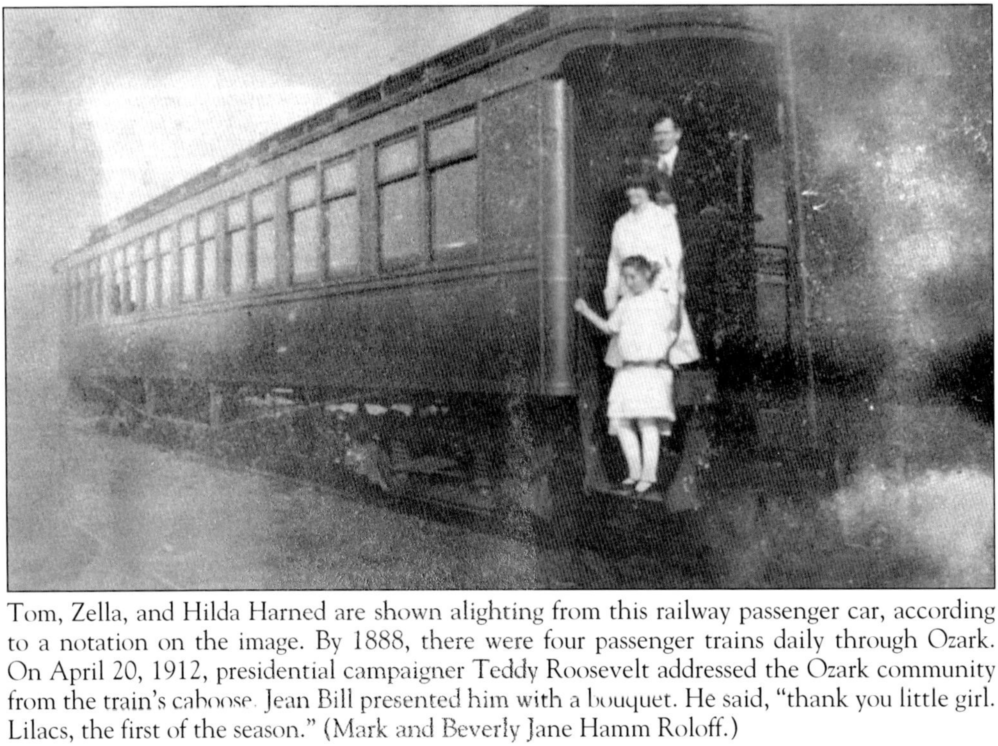

Tom, Zella, and Hilda Harned are shown alighting from this railway passenger car, according to a notation on the image. By 1888, there were four passenger trains daily through Ozark. On April 20, 1912, presidential campaigner Teddy Roosevelt addressed the Ozark community from the train's caboose. Jean Bill presented him with a bouquet. He said, "thank you little girl. Lilacs, the first of the season." (Mark and Beverly Jane Hamm Roloff.)

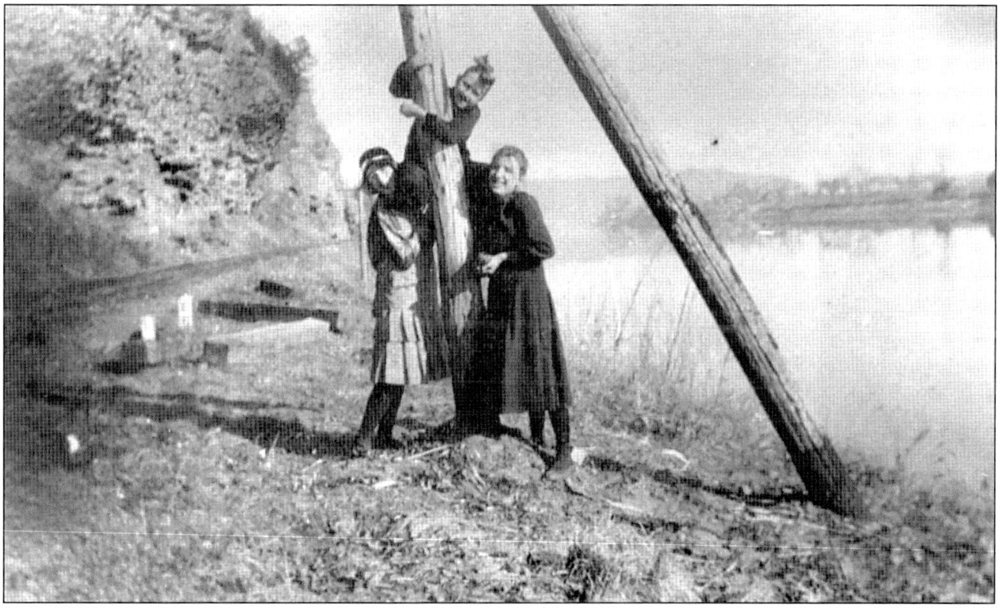

Three girls are shown at play by the bluff near the railroad cut. Farther west, in February 1876, a so-called treasure chest was unearthed by a Little Rock and Fort Smith Railroad construction crew. The chest, which was buried three feet deep, contained tools and materials for making counterfeit money. (Mark and Beverly Jane Hamm Roloff.)

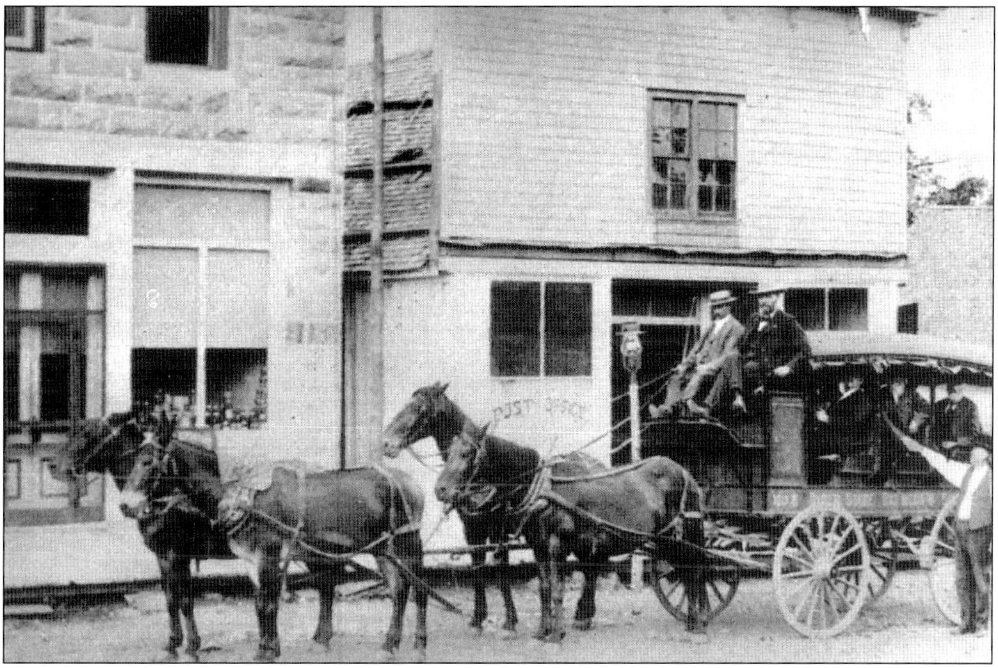

A stagecoach line was launched between Dwight Mission and Fort Smith in the summer of 1838. The coach in the image, c. 1905, in front of the post office, was pulled by a mixed team of mules and horses. Ozark was a stagecoach terminus for supplies and passengers during the Civil War. After leaving Ozark, the coach rumbled down the Altus to Clarksville Road, which turned left at the foot of the big hill east of Ozark. (US Forest Service.)

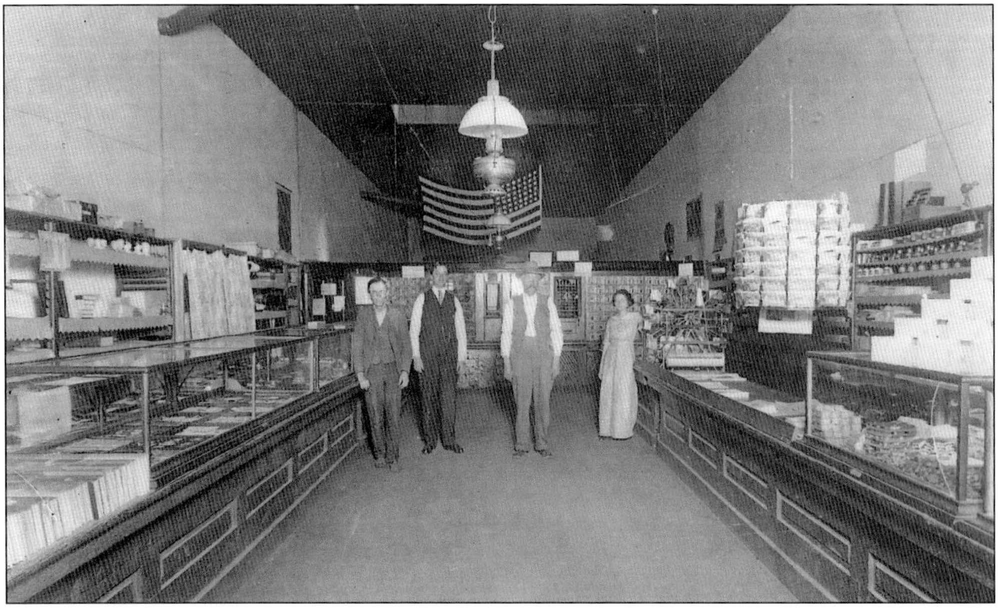

The transport of the U.S. Mail to Ozark has been varied and unique. One unusual method was by canoe on the Arkansas River and another by stagecoach, twice per week before the Civil War. The driver sounded a bugle, long and loud, as he pulled into town with the mail. In 1926, the post office, in one of its many moves, was transferred from the Masonic building to the new brick building constructed by John Davidson. It is shown here at the rear of this dry goods or drug store. (Sadler H. Burrow Collection.)

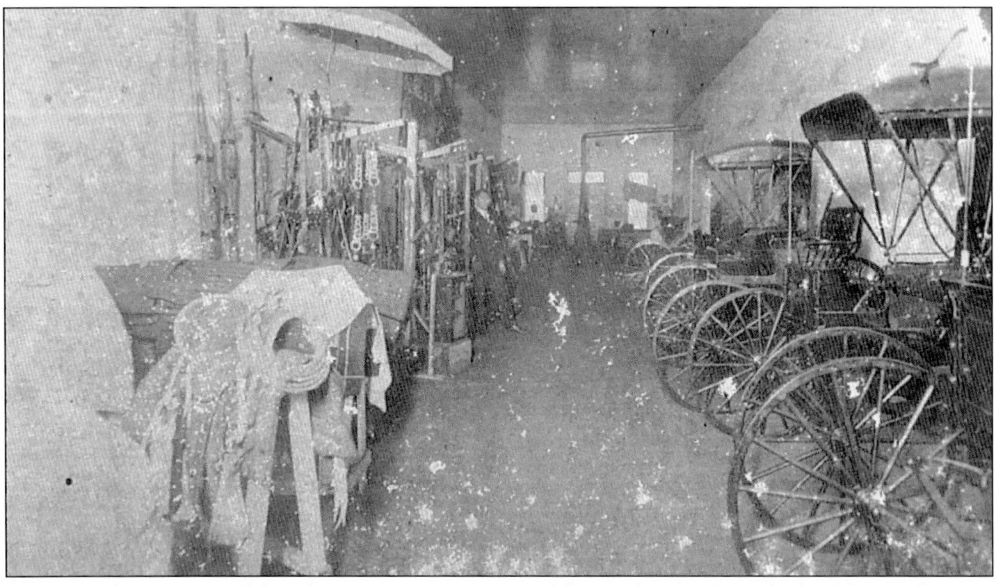

Shown is the interior of the Elsey Harris Harness, Saddles and Vehicles. The building still exists today on Commercial Street, West. A young girl who eventually became Mrs. Harris walked by the shop one day. Mr. Harris saw her, and the next time she walked by, he walked along with her. She was born in the year 1900. Mrs. Harris, at 99 years old, still lives in her own residence in Ozark. Note the umbrella to the left in the image; it would have been used to shade riders in the carriages. (Norman Powell.)

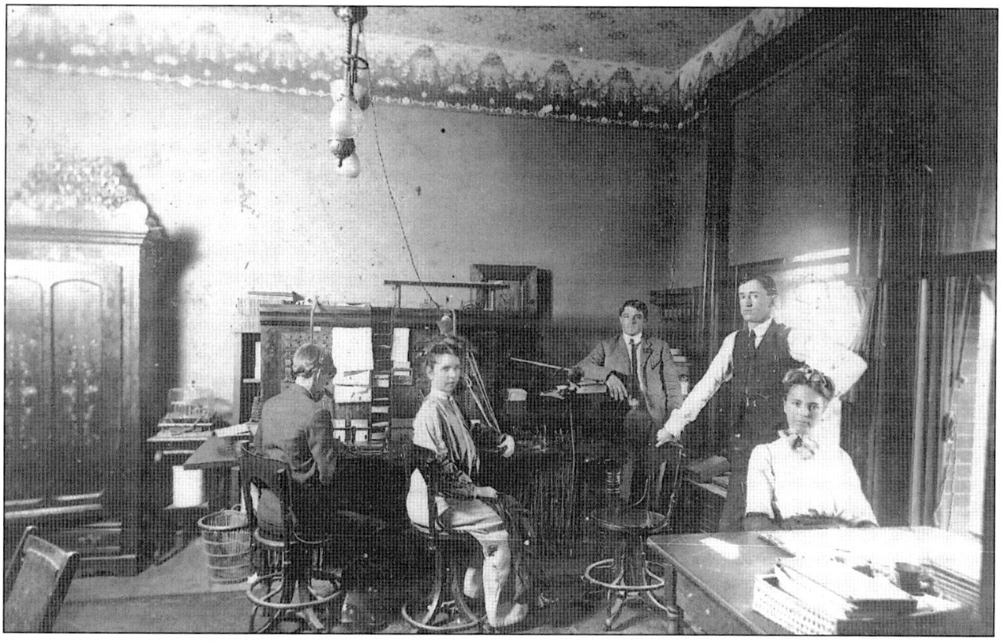

At one time, the telephone company, as shown, was located inside the Arkansas Valley Bank building. The telephone system in Franklin County was established in 1895. The first Ozark telephone network, in 1891, consisted of a line from Eugene Hail's home to the post office and another line to Mrs. T. Moore's. On September 8, 1926, Arthur Dupreast replaced D.B. Anderson as manager of the Home Telephone Co. (Sadler H. Burrow Collection.)

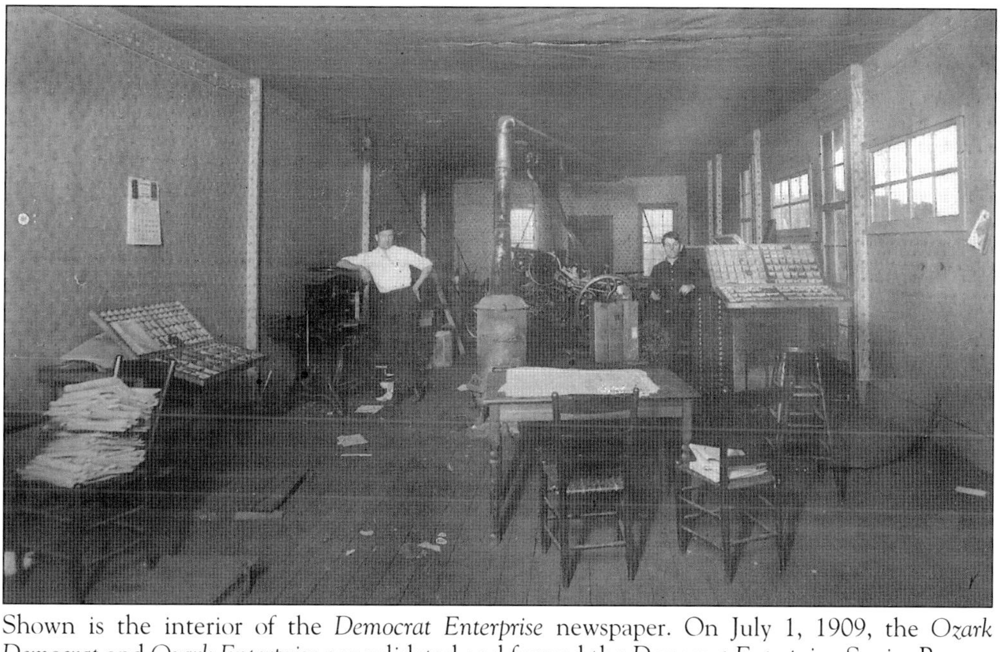

Shown is the interior of the *Democrat Enterprise* newspaper. On July 1, 1909, the *Ozark Democrat* and *Ozark Enterprise* consolidated and formed the *Democrat Enterprise*. Squire Boone, an attorney and descendant of the noted Daniel Boone family, was editor of the first newspaper published in Ozark. Established in 1858, it was called the *Southwestern*. It survived only one year. (Sadler H. Burrow Collection.)

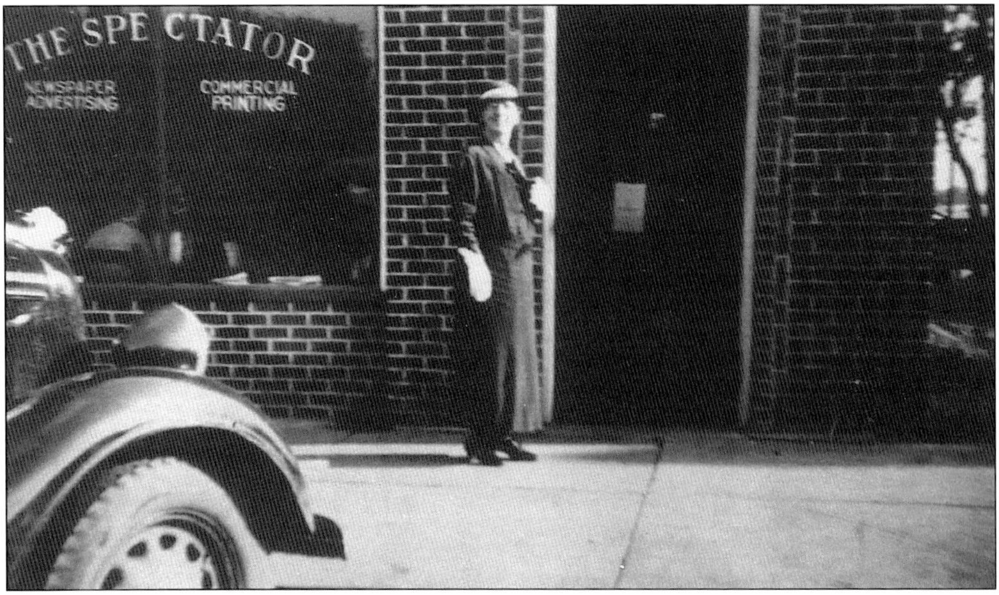

Daisy Sadler Burrow is shown c. 1920 posed in front of the *The Spectator* newspaper office. Her husband was newspaper founder Reuben H. Burrow and her father was A.H. "Hub" Sadler, once sheriff of Franklin County. As a Cass school teacher, Daisy rode a horse to school each day, fording overflowing creeks in wet weather. In Ozark she ran a small dairy business and made sure fresh milk was available to all new babies. (Sadler H. Burrow Collection.)

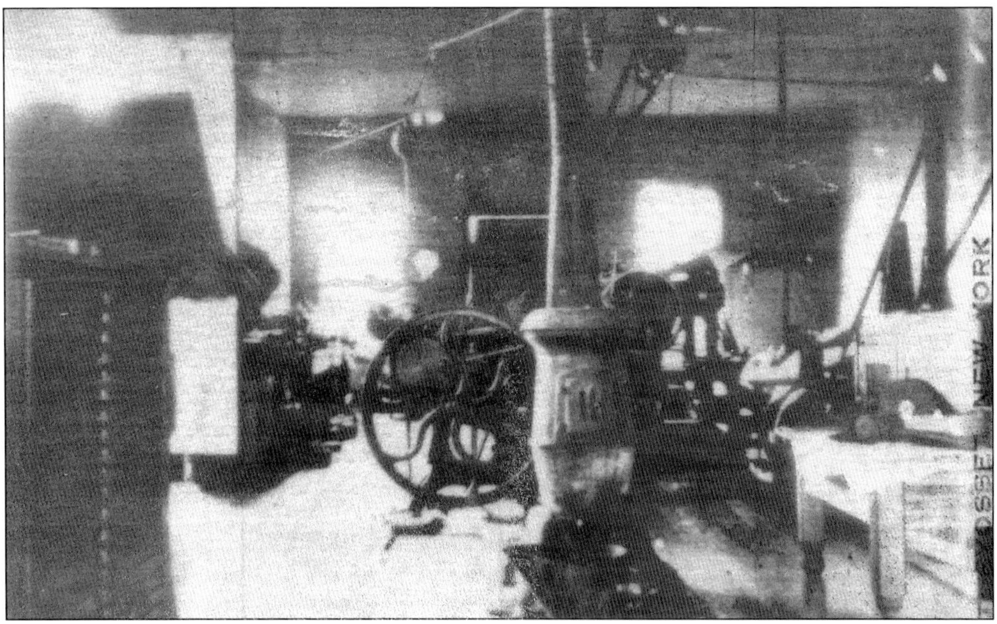

This image of the interior of *The Spectator* newspaper office, shown c. 1920, was taken from a photo positive. The newspaper job press, powered by a Fairbanks Morse, one-cylinder, gasoline engine was located at the rear of the office. At night the office was lit by a gravity-fed, gasoline, mantle light. The Reuben H. Burrow family operated *The Spectator* until 1967, when it was purchased by Orval Faubus and Francis Murray. Jo Eveld is now editor of *The Spectator, Inc.* (Sadler H. Burrow Collection.)

Six

OZARK FROM DEATH TO LIFE

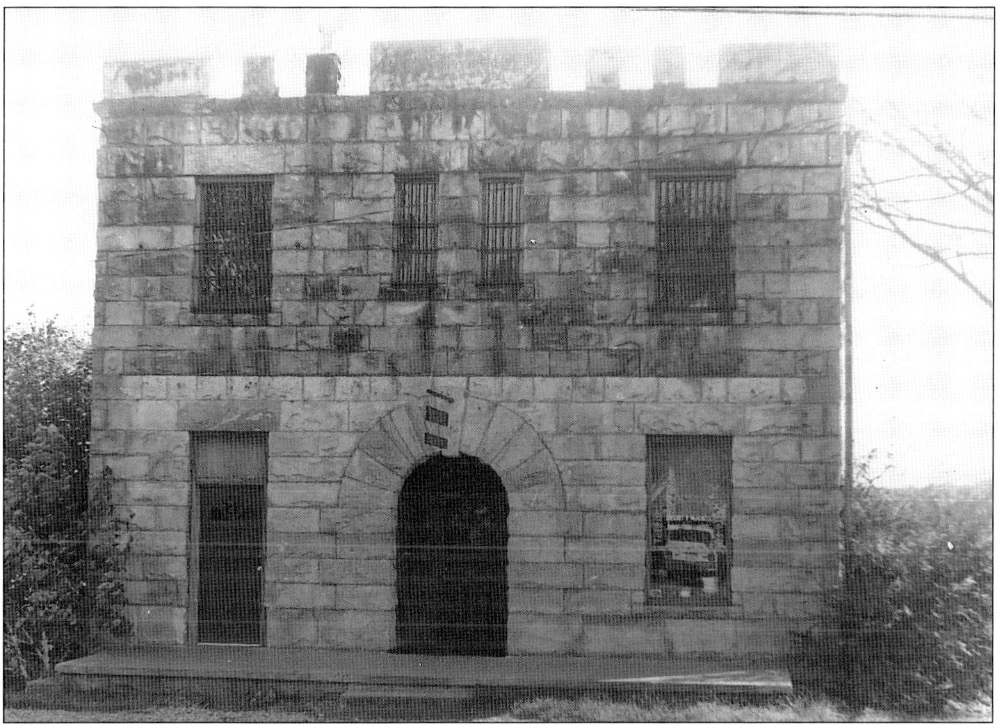

The Ozark Jail, as shown c. 1977, was constructed in 1914, utilizing an earlier iron cell block. Its architecture is an example of vernacular native-stone construction. Another of Ozark's first jails was built of heavy logs, with a high log fence around it. One-armed Sheriff A.H. "Hub" Sadler and his family lived across the street from the jail and were the jailers, responsible for guarding and feeding the prisoners. (Author.)

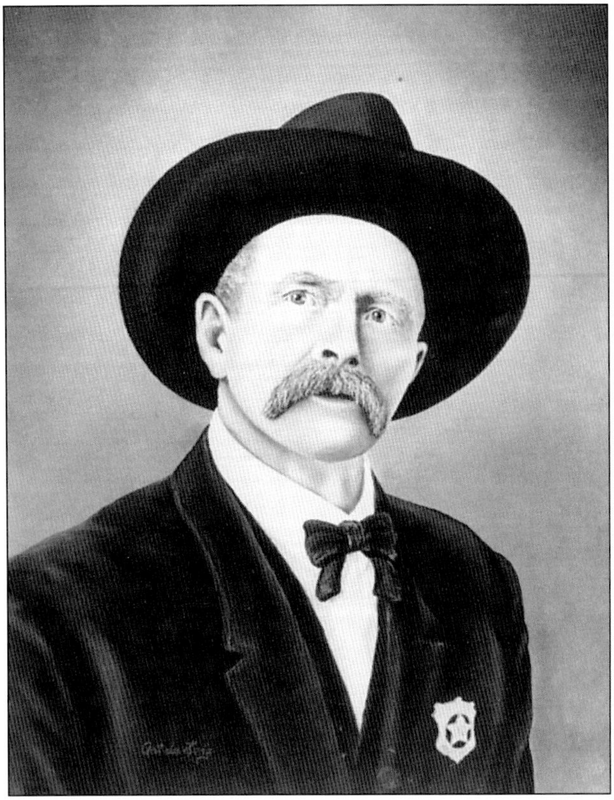

This photo image of James Franklin "Bud" Ledbetter was taken from a painting by Art daLong. In March 1883, Deputy Ledbetter, Johnson County Sheriff Bud McConnell, Deputy Paden Tolbert, and Franklin County Sheriff Hub Sadler arrested the gang that killed Conductor John Cain in a train robbery attempt. Ledbetter was known for standing in plain sight when having a shoot out. This strategy proved psychologically devastating to outlaws. Instead of having to worry about cover, Bud could concentrate on where to put his next bullet. (Photo by William Beebe, Fort Smith National Historic Site.)

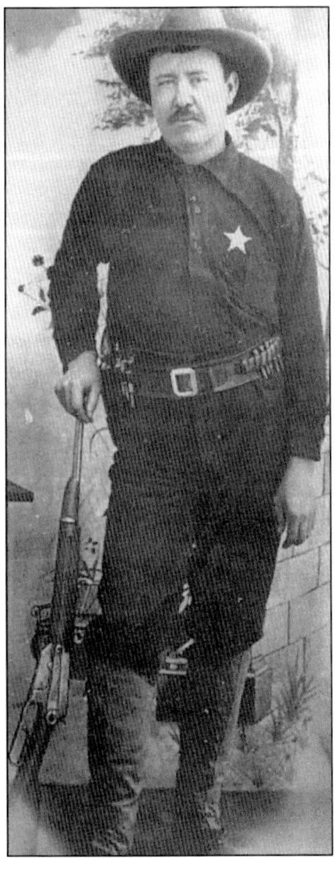

Paden Tolbert, shown at a later date, was in Sheriff Hub Sadler's posse, which brought in the gang that killed Conductor John Cain. The posse found the would-be robbers holed up in a cave in the Ozark mountains. The old log jail in Ozark served as their lock-up. The public defender mistakenly thought a change of venue to Clarksville would help. It didn't. The gang was sentenced to hang on June 22, 1883. A new gibbet was built and a large crowd gathered to view the exciting event. (Submitted Photo.)

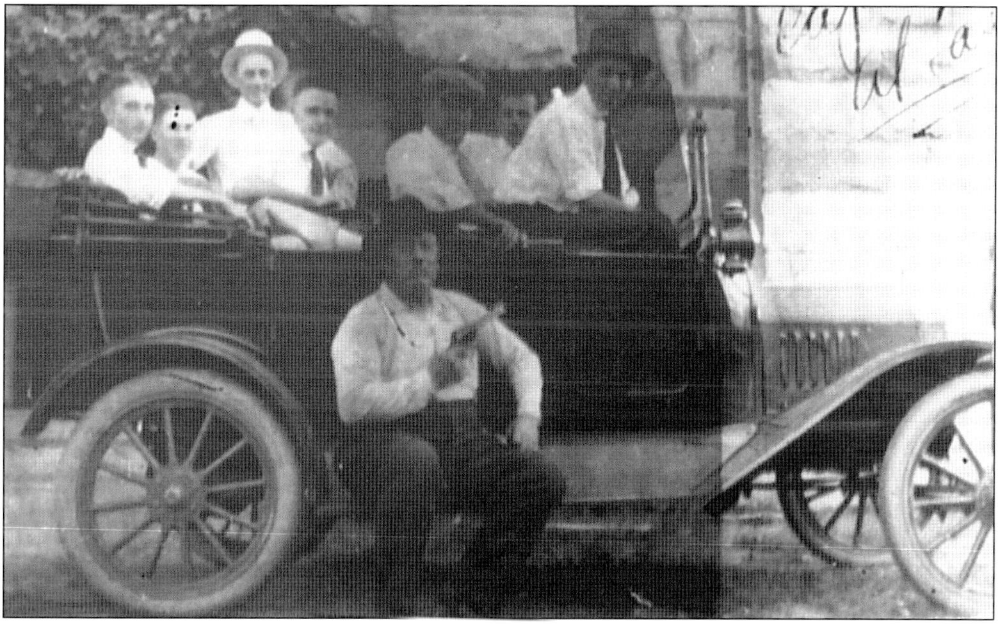

Shown in front of the colorful "new" jail is Hugh "Buck" McClelland, Franklin County jailer, c. 1929. The inscription reads, "Captured at last." Note the vintage automobile laden with animated tourists. Entrepreneurs in the historic, scenic town of Ozark posed tourists with local "celebrities." The tourists were then driven on a tour of Manitou Mountain, and along the Arkansas River. (Sadler H. Burrow Collection.)

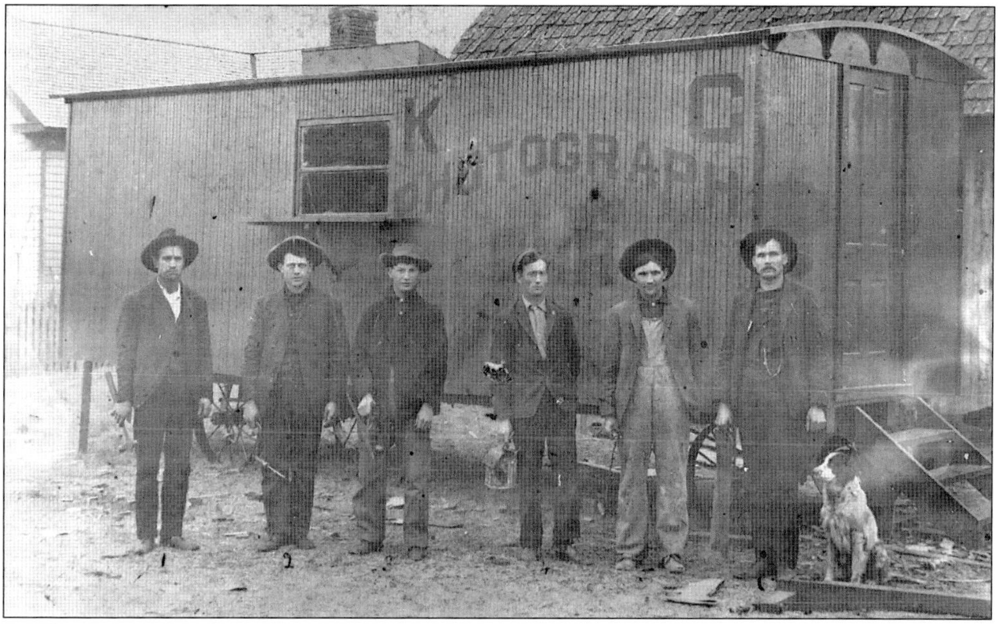

Workmen are posed in front of the K.C. Studio traveling photographer from Fort Smith. The men are holding objects of the trade of carpentry: a drawing knife, ball-pean hammer, brace and bit, wood-plane, paint brush, a bucket of paint, and a canine companion. K.C. is one of many studios that sent photographers throughout the area to record photo images of local residents. (Sadler H. Burrow Collection.)

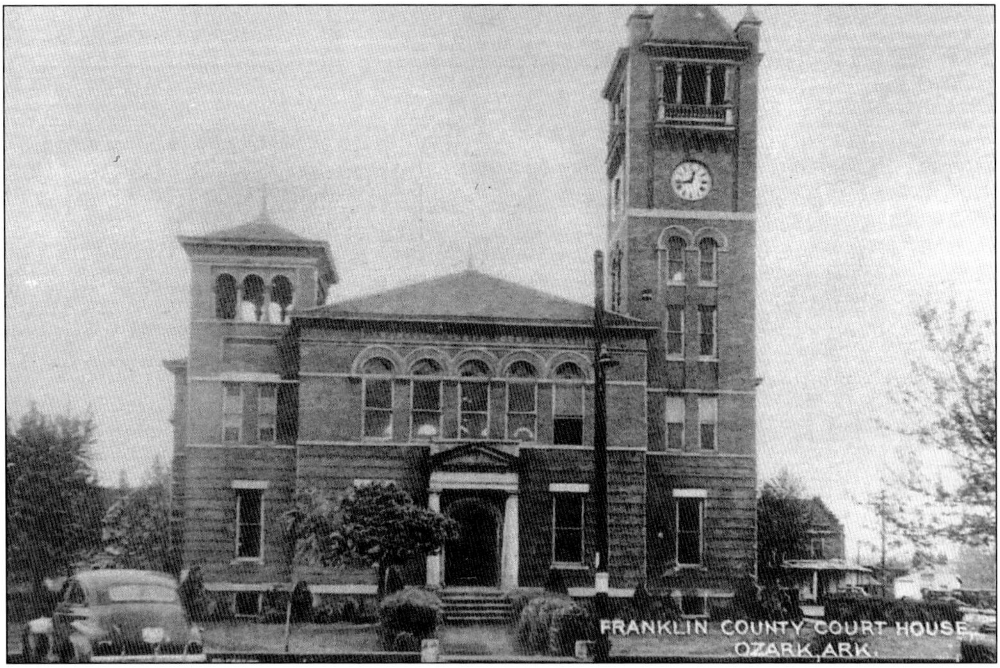

The Franklin County courtyard site, shown here in the early 1940s, was once a Cherokee peach orchard. The panoramic view of the Arkansas River and Ozark Mountains, from the second-floor courtroom, was once lauded as the most spectacular in the state. Coxey of "Coxey's Army" fame visited the square, John Phillips Sousa performed on the courthouse lawn, Carrie Nation once lectured here, concerning the evils of "drink," and in 1910, William Jennings Bryan "held forth" on the merits of Amendment Number Ten. (Sadler H. Burrow Collection.)

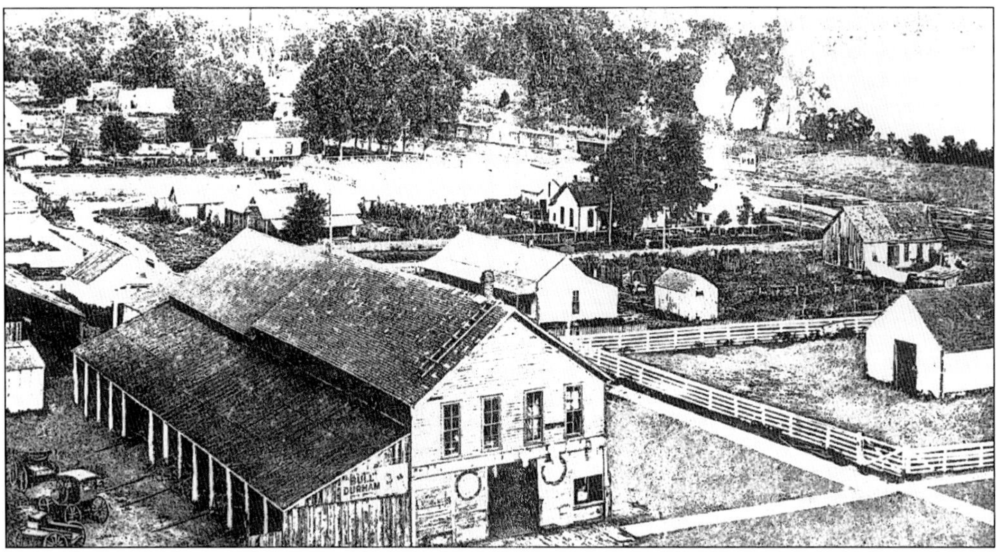

The large building shown is the Davidson Stable and Livery. Just southwest of this location, on February 27, 1880, 5,000 witnesses watched James Howard hang for the murder of his wife near Altus. A wagon picked up a coffin at the furniture store on the southwest corner of the square and, with Howard sitting upon it, traveled the short distance from the old log jail to the place of execution. The scaffold was made of new lumber. (Sadler H. Burrow Collection.)

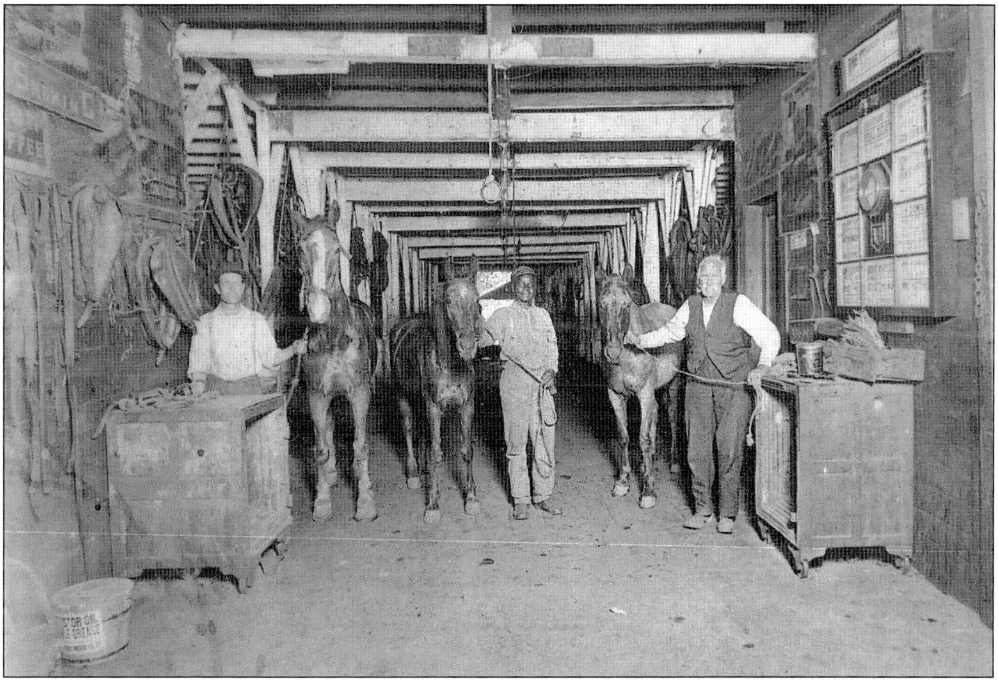

This image was taken of the interior of the Davidson Stable c. 1915. Note the old safes with doors removed to serve as a storage or work area. Horses and mules were shod here and wagons and buggies repaired. Hacks could be hired, by tourists, to ride along the river, or to tour the ever-popular Manitou Mountain. (Sadler H. Burrow Collection.)

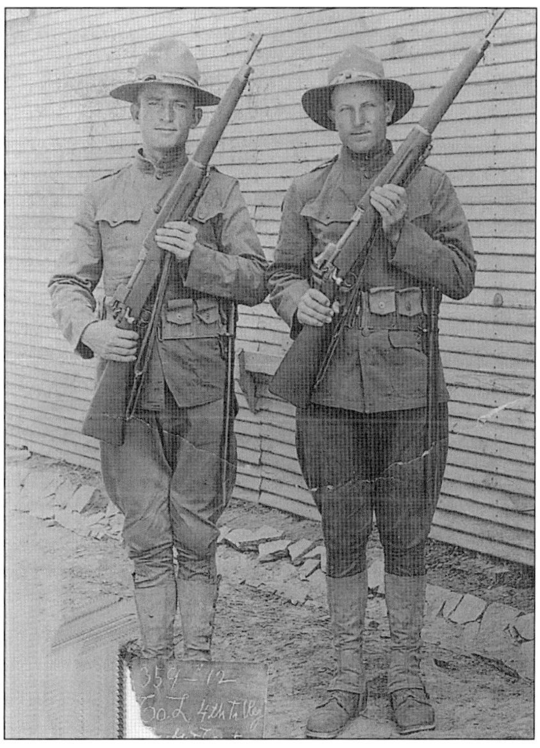

John Elliott Conatser, Franklin County's most decorated WW I hero, is shown c. 1917, on the left in this photo image, with an unknown soldier. At the Meuse Aargon, on November 8, 1918, just two days before Armistice, John threw himself over an exploding shell to save his platoon. He was so severely injured that he spent nearly all his remaining days in the VA Hospital at Fort Roots. On November 7, 1940, 22 years after his heroic deed, John was presented with the Silver Star and Purple Heart medals in a ceremony honoring him at Ozark's Legion Hut. (Ronnie and Sherrill Adams Cox.)

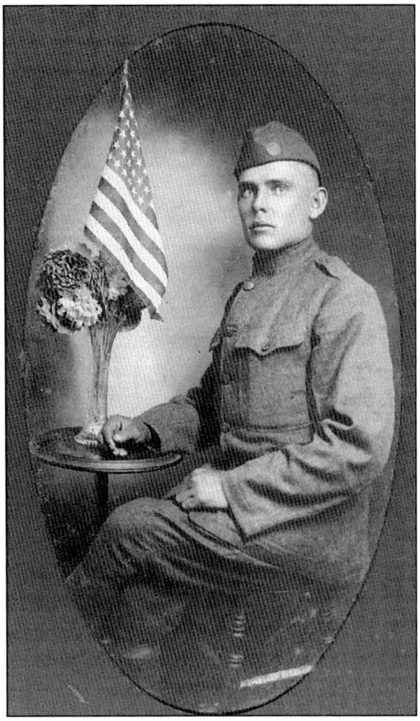

Garner L. Andrews, born in 1893, is shown during WW I at about 24 years old. At the time he joined the Army, he lived in Cecil, south of Ozark. In France, after the Armistice was signed, Garner and his buddies received an overnight pass. To get out of the weather they spent the night in a farmer's barn, and the farmer reported them. Their punishment involved marching with their packs for several hours. Garner witnessed Sergeant Alvin York, the highly decorated WW I soldier, receive his medals. York was in Garner's 82nd Airborne Division of the American Expeditionary Forces. (Latane Andrews Powell.)

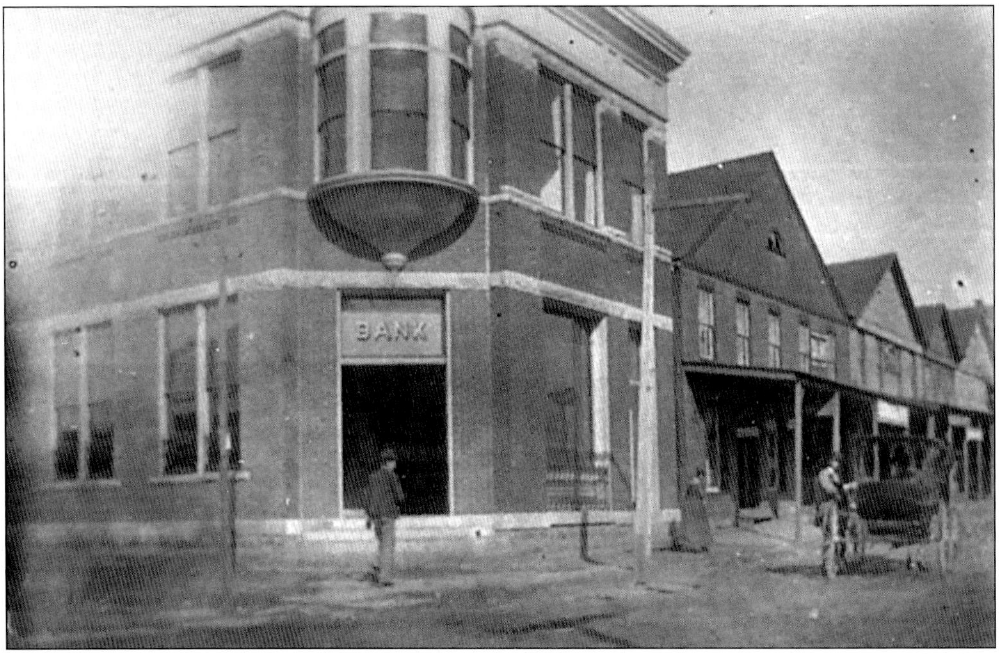

The Arkansas Valley Bank, in the foreground, opened in 1899. Sometime in the early days of the bank's establishment, Mattie Smith, owner of a boardinghouse located nearby, was awakened by a noise. She looked outside and began to see tigers, elephants, and monkeys. She thought she was still asleep and dreaming. She later discovered that a train carrying a circus had wrecked close to the depot. The handlers were taking the animals to Gar Creek to get them a drink of water. (Norman Powell.)

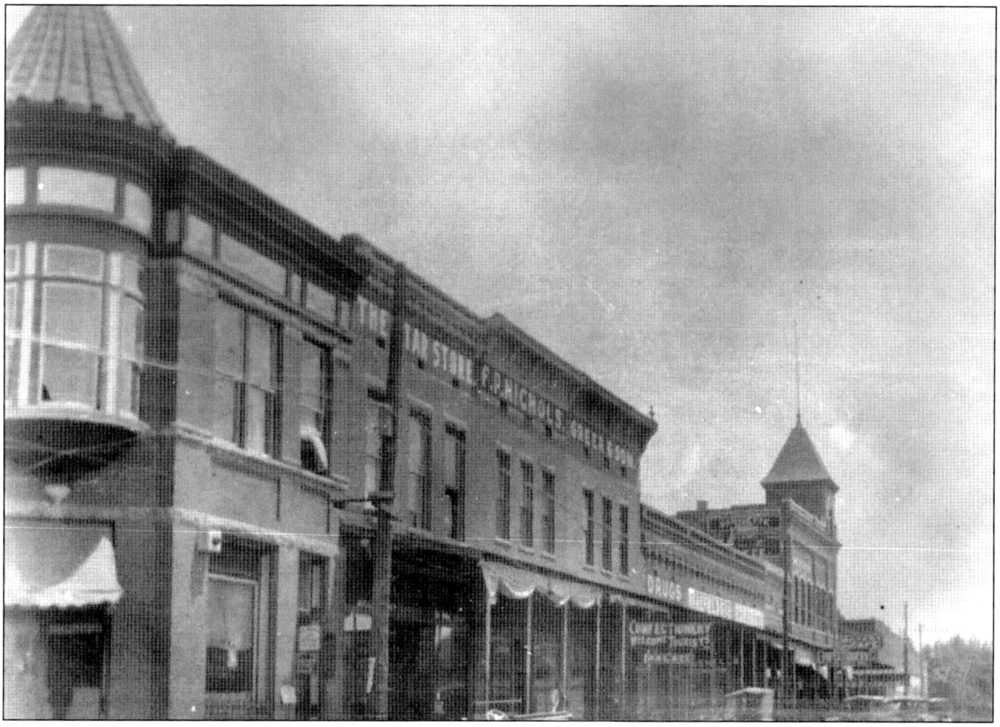

Mrs. T. Moore's diary states that before the Civil War she and her family lived in the Arkansas Valley Bank's location, shown in the foreground. Ozark had open saloons, and one was run by Bob Tweedy where the Roy Bell Confectionary was later located. T. Moore watched from an upper window, while men crowded around the saloon door and drank and fought like a pack of dogs. She also watched men shoot and kill each other. (Norman Powell.)

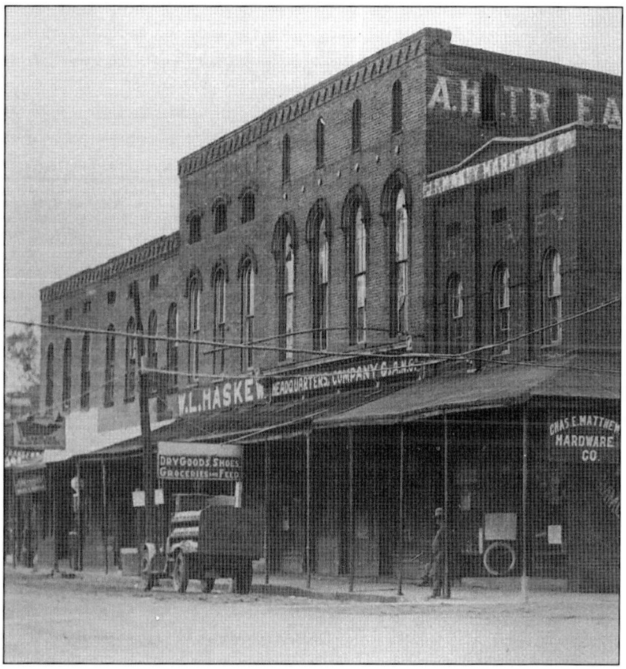

The YMCA was active in the old Ben Franklin dime store location offering boxing and basketball for young men, until 1910, when it disbanded. In recent times the dusty imprint of a basketball can still be seen on the ceiling. Holes where goals were attached to the walls are visible, along with names and the score of a long ago basketball game. A Coca-Cola truck is parked in front of Charles E. Matthews Hardware. (Norman Powell.)

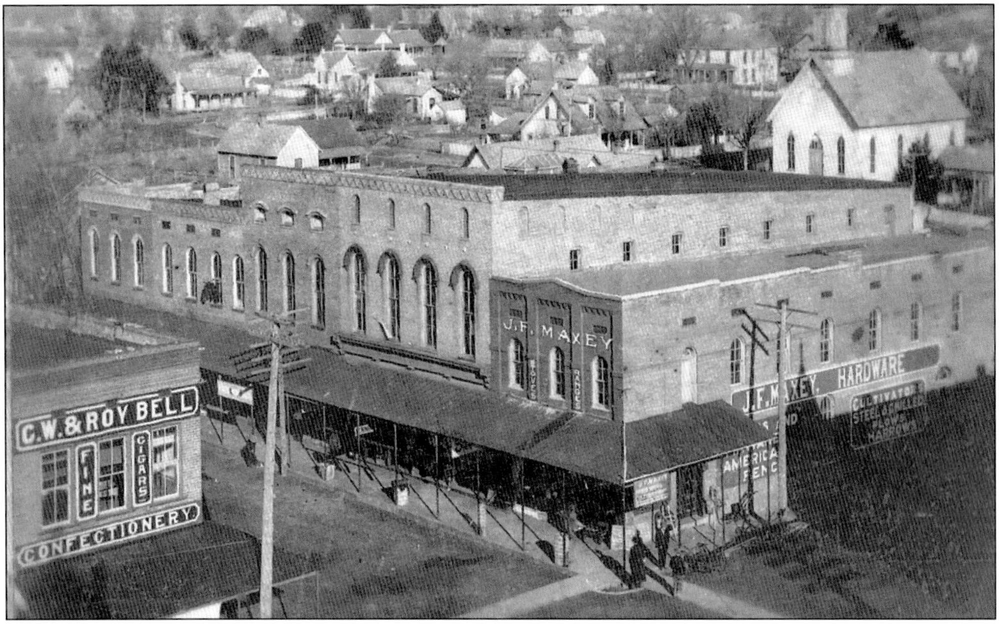

J.F. Maxey Hardware is central to this photograph looking northwest from the courthouse clock tower. In the early years, the dime store location was home to WW I's Company K, originally Company G, ANG (Arkansas National Guard). It was a sports gymnasium, a town hall, and had a public access stage across one side. J.F. Maxey was vice president of the YMCA, organized in Ozark in 1885. Maxey Hardware eventually became Matthews Hardware. (Sadler H. Burrow Collection.)

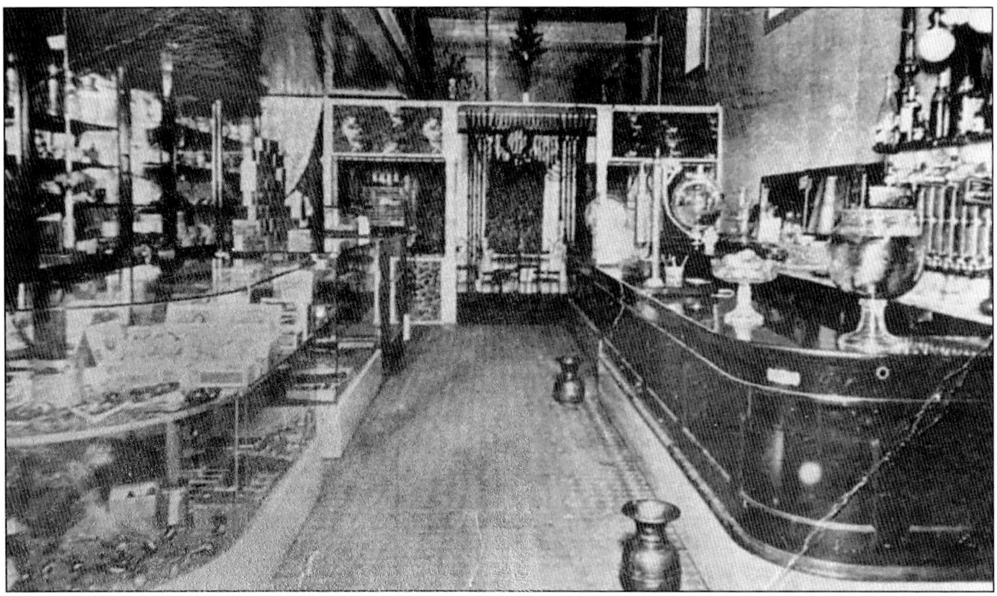
Shown is the interior of the Bell Brothers Confectionary. Note the old wrought-iron wire table and chairs to the rear of the building. On December 19, 1919, as a Christmas treat for the children of the community, Roy Bell sent up a paper balloon. He also arranged for Sheriff Ed Milton to dress as Santa Claus and ride the train into town. When the train arrived in Ozark, the delighted children were waiting for him at the depot. (Sadler H. Burrow Collection.)

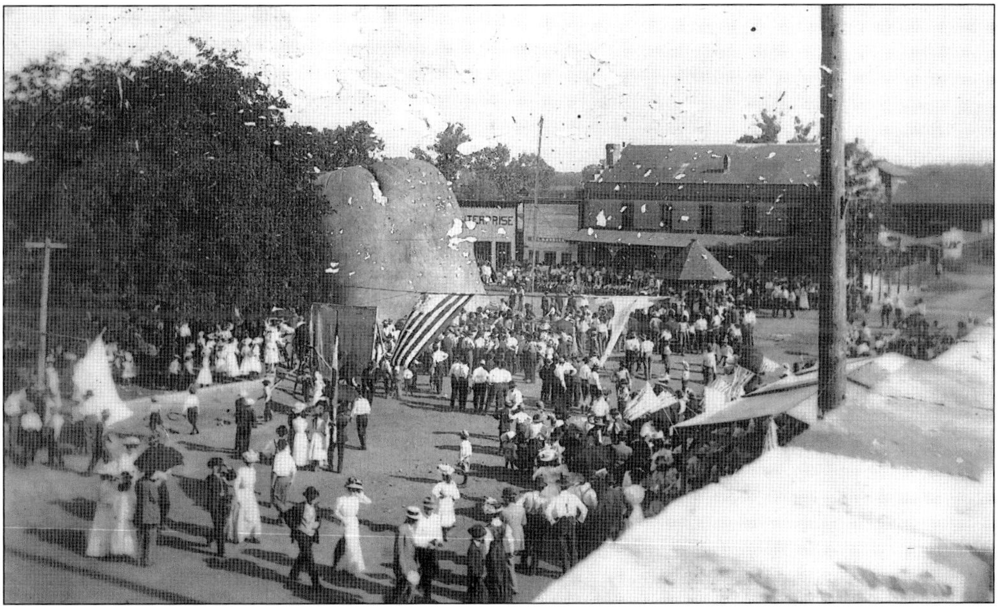

A parade, which appears to be over, is shown in this image. The photo, date unknown, was taken from the roof of Bell's Confectionary, looking to the southeast. Folks are gathered around the gazebo well-house, and a hot-air balloon is being deflated on the courtyard lawn. The large building to the right was the County Jail. The word Enterprise and an O.W. Barham sign can be seen in the center of the image. Note M.F. Greer Cording and Planing Mill in the right background. (Sadler H. Burrow Collection.)

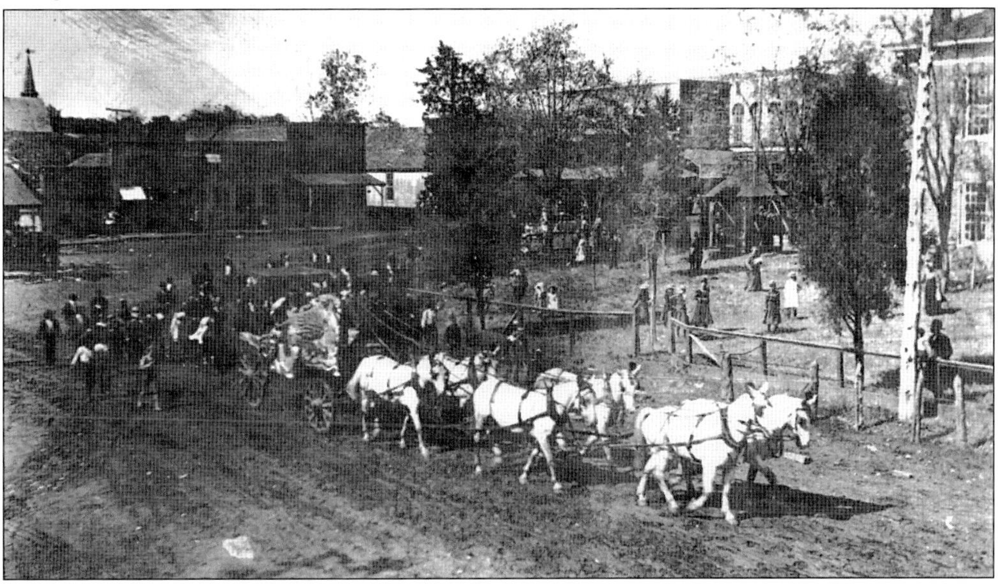

Shown is a circus parade, to the south of the courthouse, in 1898. The well-house west of the courthouse, dug in 1850, had the best water, but tasted of alum. The well on the extreme left was dry most of the year. The courthouse, torn down in 1904, was replaced with a new one by 1905. Sidewalks were rough, wooden boards and cattle and hogs ran at large. To keep hogs out of the stores, gates were installed on the doorways. (Dr. Thomas Douglass, Sadler H. Burrow Collection.)

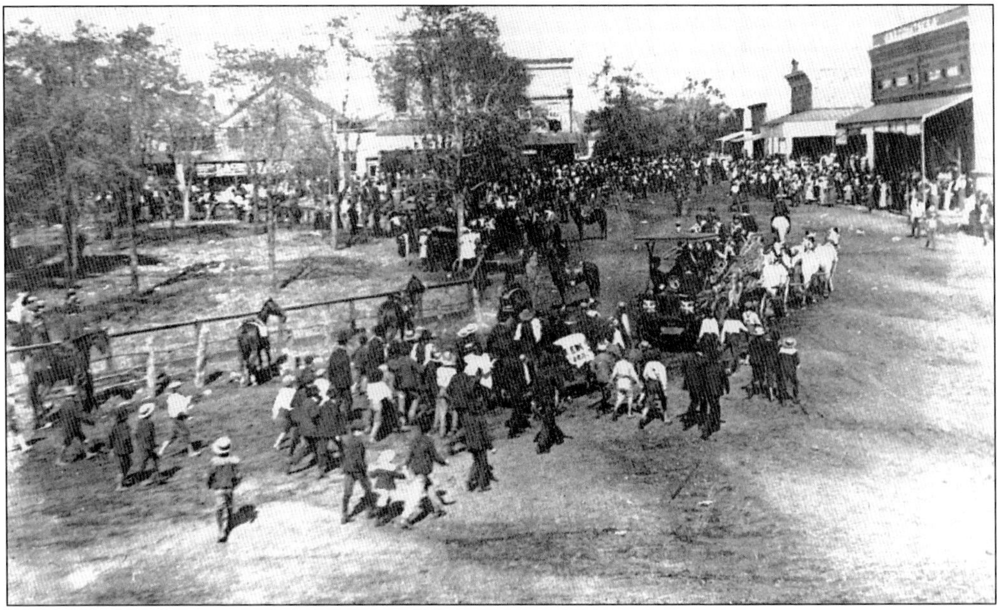

Pictured is a circus parade at the southeast corner of the courthouse square, in 1898. The east end of the northern section burned, as shown January 13, 1904, and caused one of the most restrictive fire codes in the nation to be adopted. Note the Conatser-Hill, Seaman Store building, seen at the right, and horses hitched to the courtyard fence. (Dr. Thomas Douglass, Sadler H. Burrow Collection.)

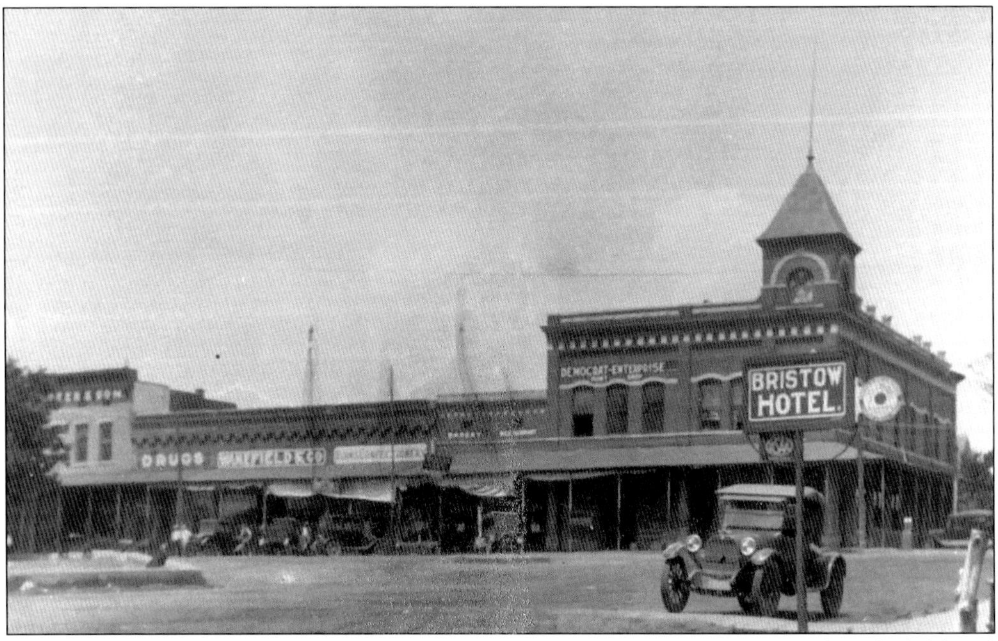

Looking north to the People's Bank is the *Democrat Enterprise* newspaper and Wakefield and Co. c. 1920. The north business section of the square burned February 14, 1926, except for the Arkansas Valley Bank on the west end, not seen in this image. Les McPherson confessed to robbing Wakefield and Company and setting the fire to cover his crime. He was sentenced to an 82-year term in the penitentiary. (Norman Powell.)

Seven

Ozark
Readin', 'Ritin', Religion

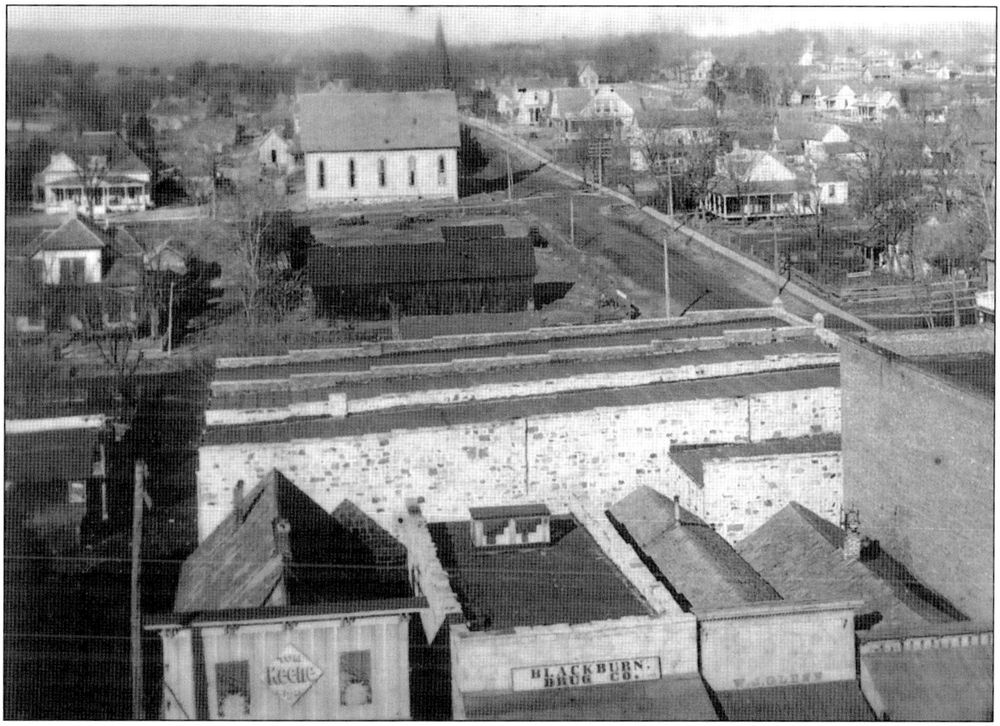

This c. 1909 photo image looks from the courthouse clock tower west to the white frame Methodist Episcopal Church, South. Ozark's churches and schools were among the state's best. Ozark had more miles of concrete sidewalk than any other small town in Arkansas. The little community once had an opera house for road shows, and was on the Chatauqua and Lyceum circuits. Note Dr. Blackburn's Drug Store sign at the bottom of the image. (Sadler H. Burrow Collection.)

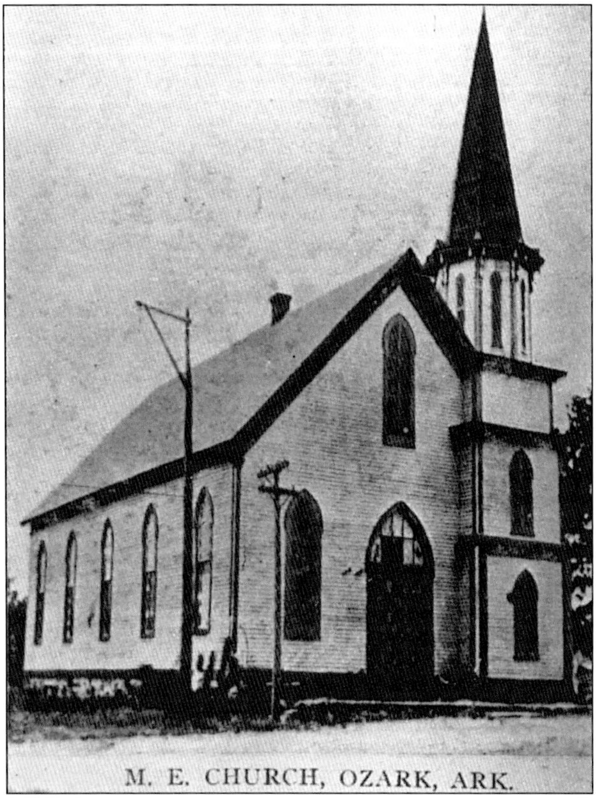

The Methodist Episcopal Church, South, in Ozark, was organized in 1871 by the Reverend Hastings Puckett. The frame building, shown, was constructed in 1876. After the last services were held in the little frame church they went out on the lawn and broke dirt for the new church. The next day Claud Talley tore the belfry down and began construction on the present stone structure. (Sadler H. Burrow Collection.)

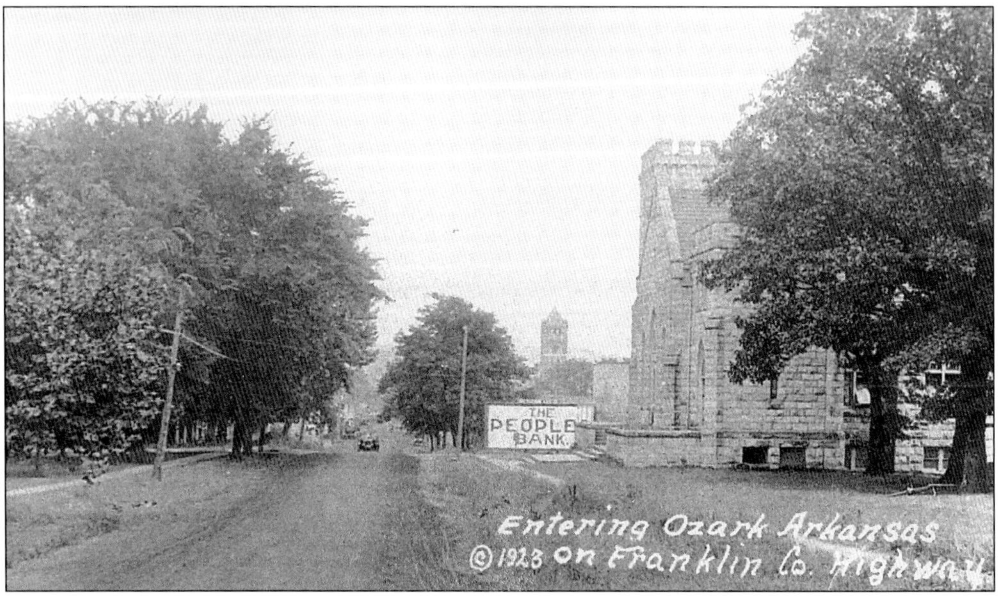

In 1923, visitors drove down this tree-shaded lane past the stone Methodist church shown, on Highway 64, into Ozark. Circuit-riding ministers brought Methodism to Franklin County long before the Civil War. The first assignment to Ozark, of record, is J.P. Hulse on November 10, 1852. The Methodist Church, South, in Ozark, was the largest Protestant church in Franklin County. The Ozark Methodist Church built in 1909 is a noted landmark. (Karla Rozell.)

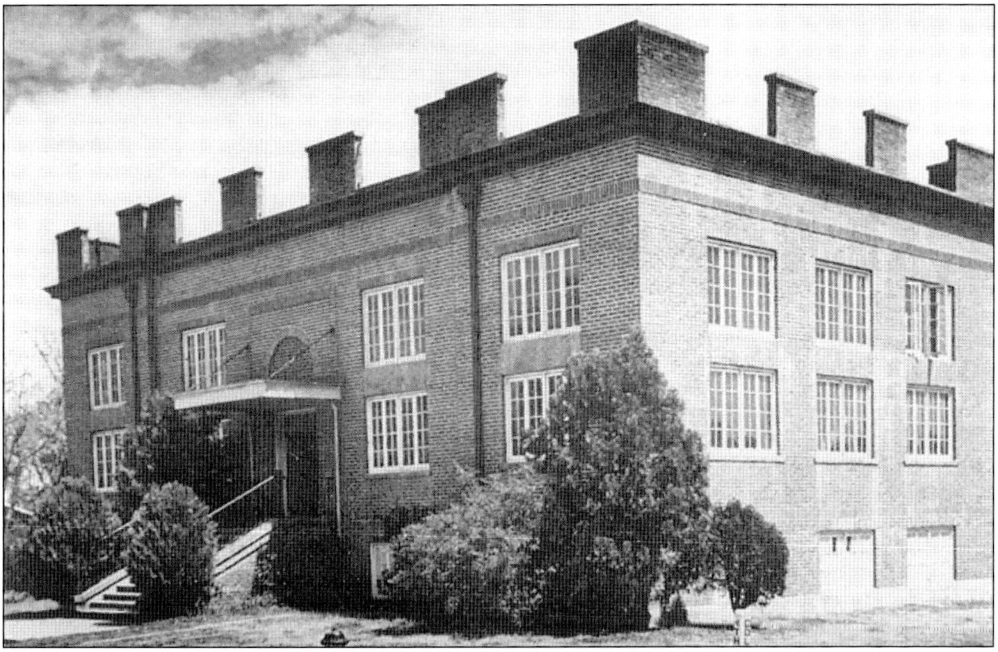

The Cumberland Presbyterian Church of Ozark is shown in this picture postcard from the 1960s. The church was organized in 1858 by Reverend John Buchanan. A brick church house was erected in 1859. A frame building constructed in 1876 burned c. 1925. By 1888, the membership was 120 souls. (Karla Rozell.)

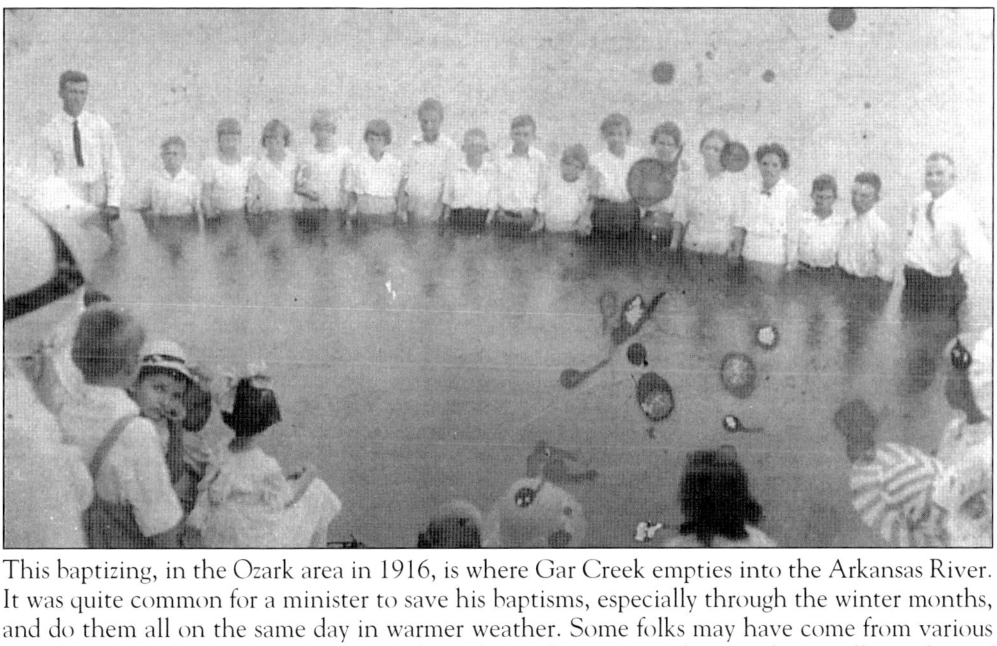

This baptizing, in the Ozark area in 1916, is where Gar Creek empties into the Arkansas River. It was quite common for a minister to save his baptisms, especially through the winter months, and do them all on the same day in warmer weather. Some folks may have come from various churches that the minister pastored throughout the year. Letha Smith Powell, mother of historian Norman Powell, is the tall girl, left of center. (Norman Powell.)

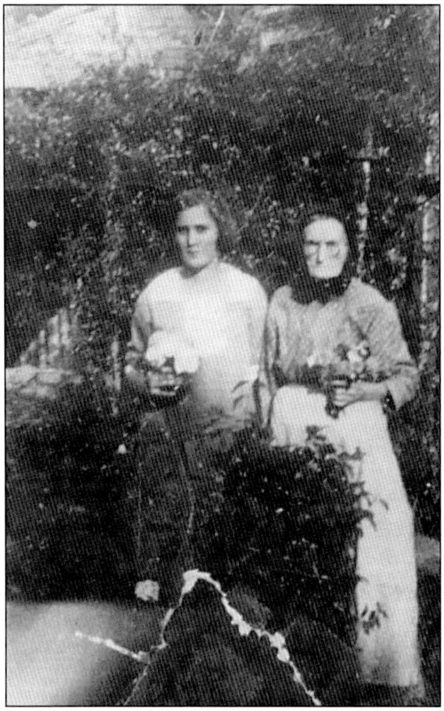

Shown in this photo image c. 1925 is Talitha Earp, at right, and Oma Smith, great-grandmother and aunt of historian Norman Powell. They appear to be holding bouquets of flowers near Talitha's floral and shrubbery covered house. Note Talitha's bonnet and long dress. (Norman Powell.)

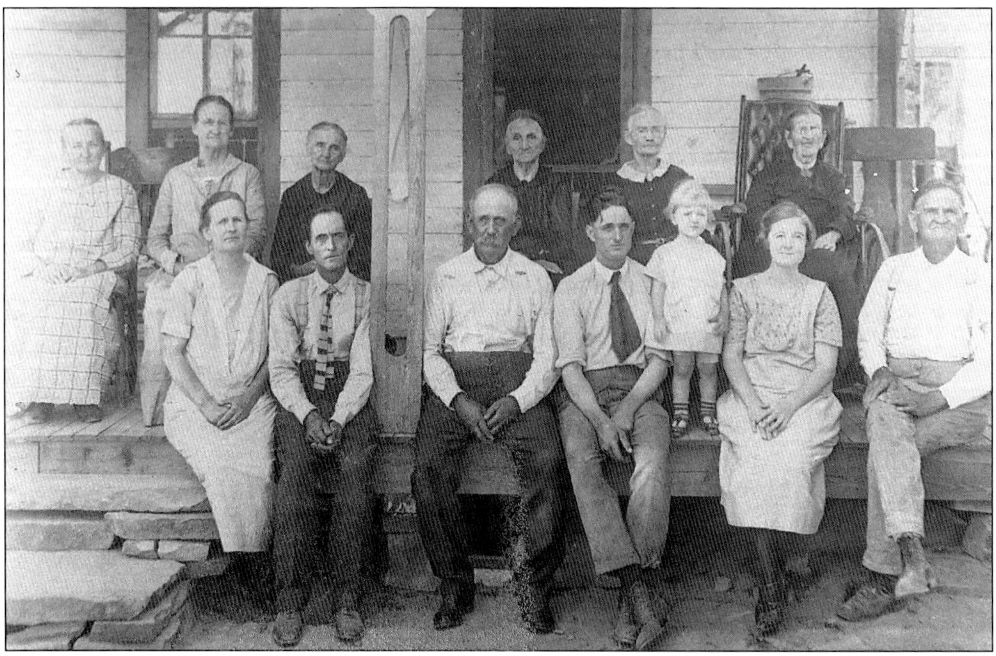

Vera Jean King is shown at David Hale's home, west of Cecil, with her seven grandmothers c. 1925. From left to right are (front row) Nancy and Tom Milam, James A. King, William King, little Vera Jean, Ethel King, Dave Hall, Mrs. James (Hester) King, Mary Catherine Hall, Nancy I. Milam, Mrs. Marge King, Mrs. Charles M. (Eliza) Price, and Ellen Jane Hall. Ellen Jane Hall came to the area with five families, each having five children, in five covered wagons. The women took in sewing that first winter to earn money for food. (Latane Andrews Powell.)

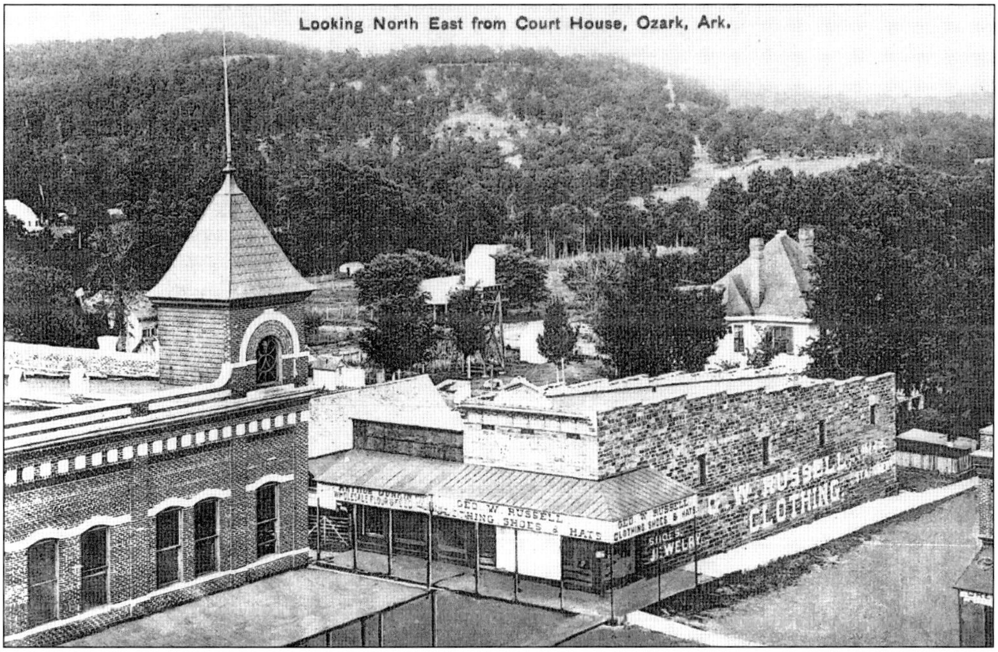

This photo image was snapped looking northeast from the Franklin County Court House clock tower c. 1909. In the foreground can be seen the Peoples Bank and G.W. Russell Clothing. During the Civil War Mrs. T. Moore wrote in her diary that Billy Bond and James Tweedy were killed on the side of Adams mountain northeast of town. She said she dipped a rag in the spring and washed Jim's face. There was a bullet hole in his forehead. He was son of her nearest neighbor. (Sadler H. Burrow Collection.)

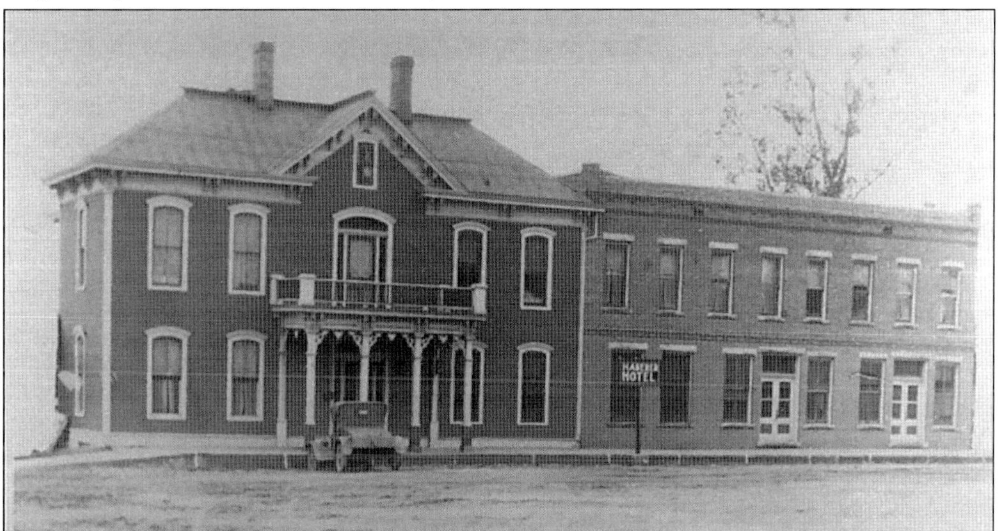

The Haberer Hotel is shown the way its exterior originally appeared. Stucco was applied between 1916 to 1920. At 3 a.m. on July 7, 1905, a passenger train, running too fast around the curve, wrecked east of the railroad cut. Sheriff Ed Milton was among the seriously injured passengers. The bell of the courthouse clock was rung to alert residents that help was needed. Many victims were taken to the Haberer Hotel until they could travel again. (Norman Powell.)

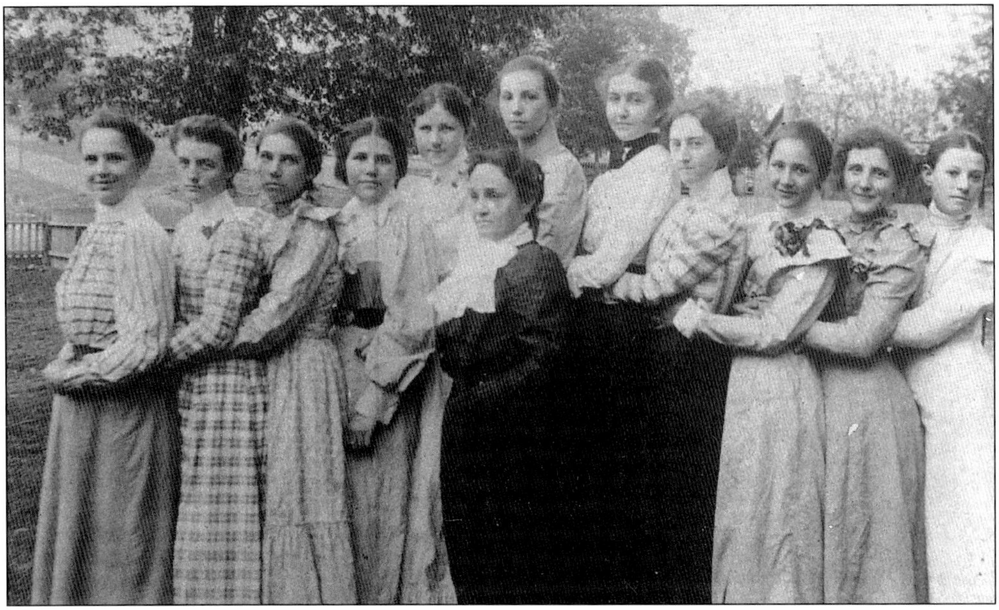

A group of unknown ladies are fitted snugly together so everyone can get in the photo. Their leader must be the short lady in front in the dark clothing. Some of the design of their clothing appears similar. Perhaps it is a sewing class. The faces of these young women who lived and loved long ago look pleased and non-stressed. (Norman Powell.)

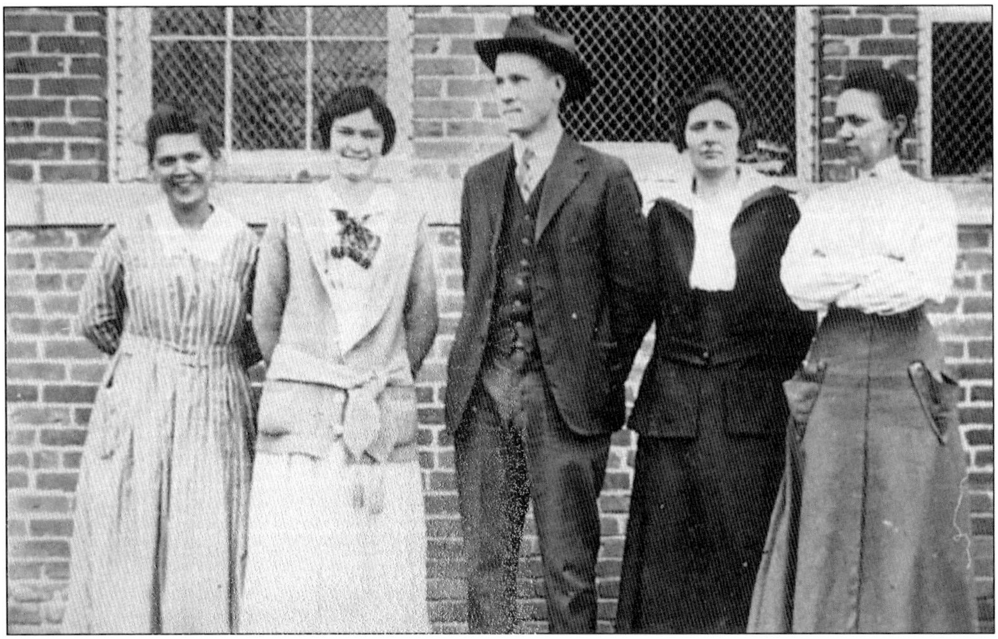

Ozark school teachers are posed beside the school building. Before the Civil War, residents were building a two-story school for boys, west of town. A Female Academy was located nearby. Civil War Soldiers took iron used in the construction and made shoes for their horses. Without support the upper story began to crumble. After the war the structure was made into a one-story building for both boys and girls, until a larger one could be built. (Sadler H. Burrow Collection.)

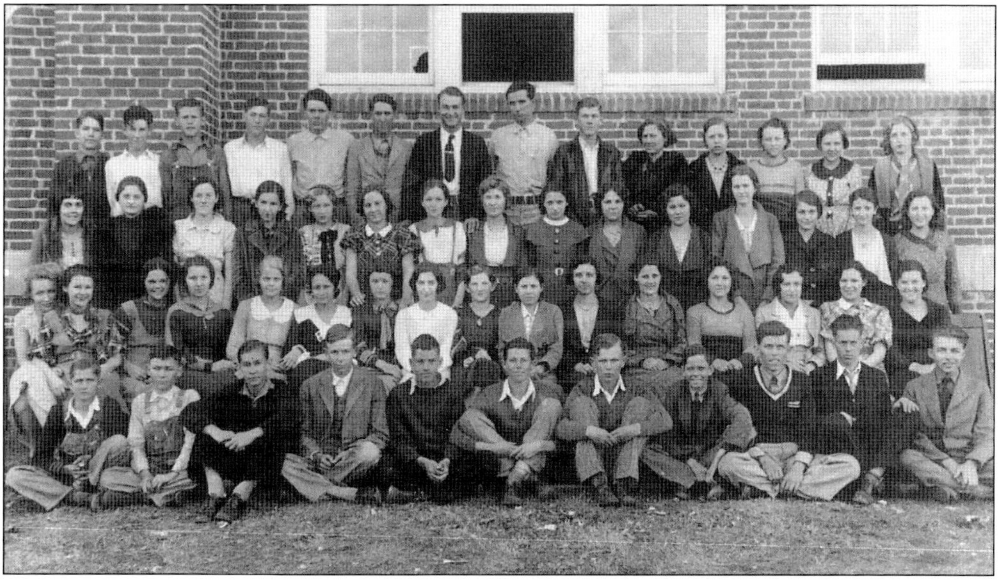

In 1920 and 1926, the primary and high schools burned. A large brick residence was purchased in 1922 to serve as a grade school, and in 1927, a new high school was built at a cost of $55,000. In 1929, Alix, Stone Hill, New Hope, Boston, Low Gar, and Cravens consolidated to the Ozark district. A Smith-Hughes building was erected by the N.Y.A. in 1937. Note well-dressed student Leon Rickard, shown on the top row in this Ozark High School photo. (Dollis Page Rickard.)

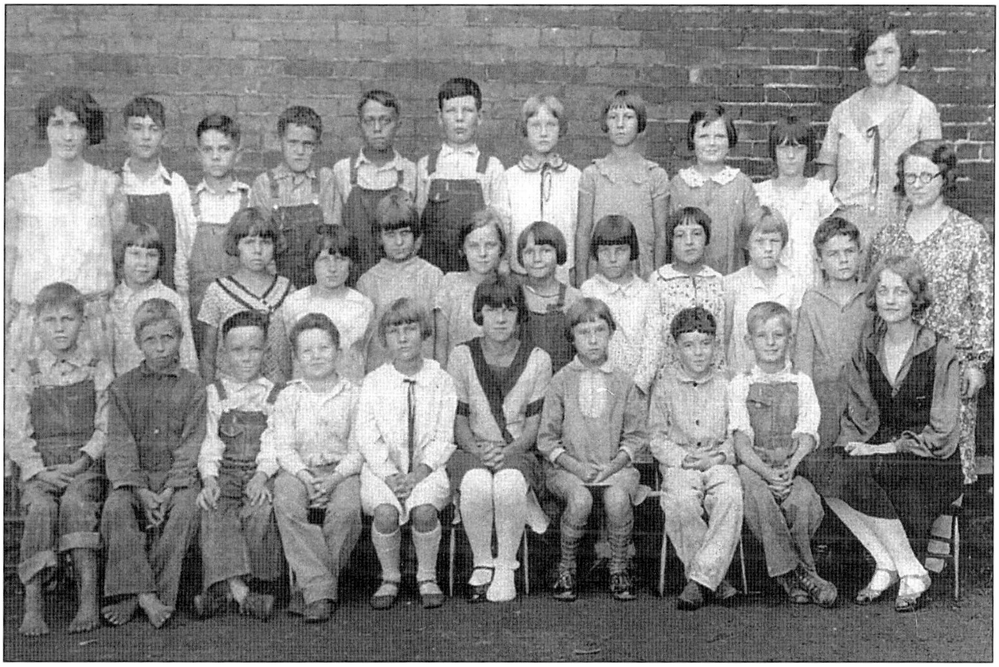

Four adults is an unusually large number of teachers for this student group of the Ozark Grade School, shown *c.* 1930. It could have been the occasion of a special activity. It must be warm weather, since at least two of the young men are shoeless. And, overalls were surely the most popular attire for the male students shown in this image. (Norman Powell.)

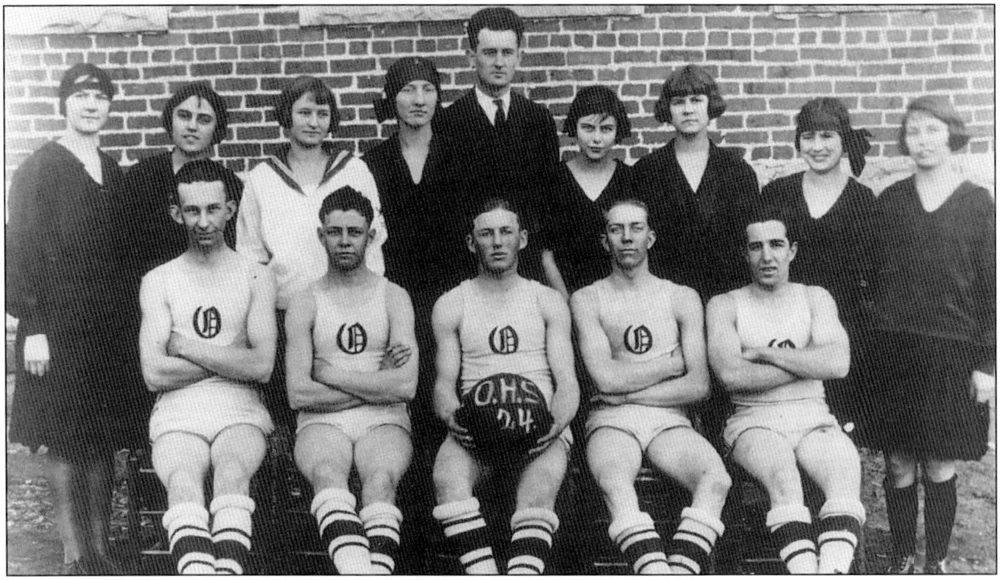

Shown here with the boys' team, the 1924 Ozark high school girls' basketball team, under the coaching skills of Luke Jackman, became the undefeated state champions. During the finals they won two games in the afternoon and one at night. Then, they defeated the College of the Ozarks and Arkansas Tech. These names are on the trophy: Hazel Phillips, Mary Church, Doris Hardgraves, Gussie Woods, Essie Faye Bailey, Ruth Moore, June Jeffers, Ruby Arrington, and Lucille Hardgraves. The first six players listed made all state. (Norman Powell.)

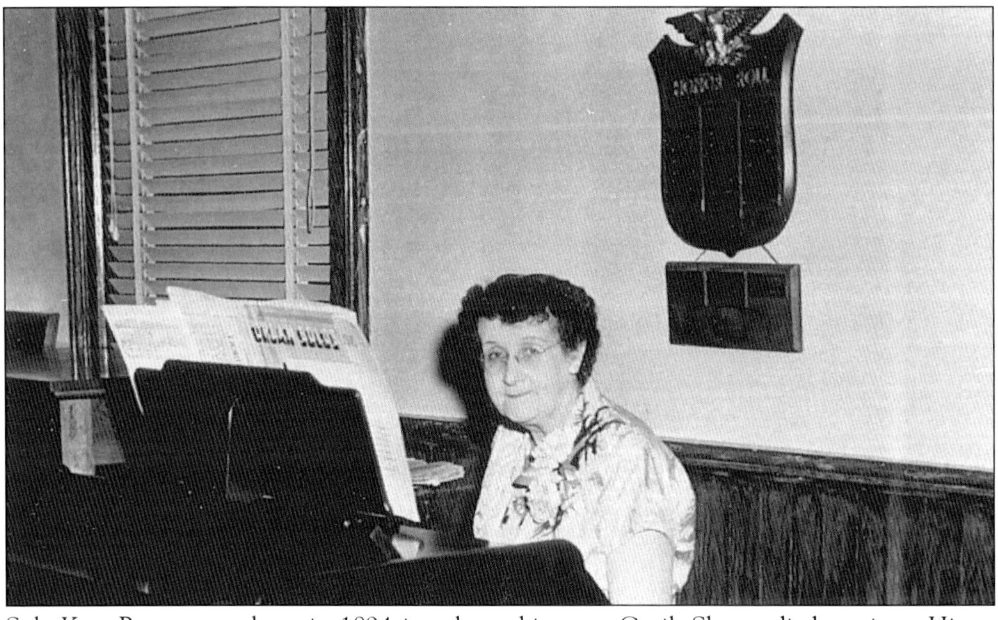

Sula Kate Benson was born in 1894 in a log cabin near Cecil. She studied music at Hiram and Lydia College in Altus and at Hendrix College in Conway. She also attended prestigious conservatories of music back east. Sula Kate played piano on the radio and travelled extensively to play in area concerts. She taught music in Ozark High School and was pipe-organist at the Methodist church. She also played for many weddings and funerals. (Sadler H. Burrow Collection.)

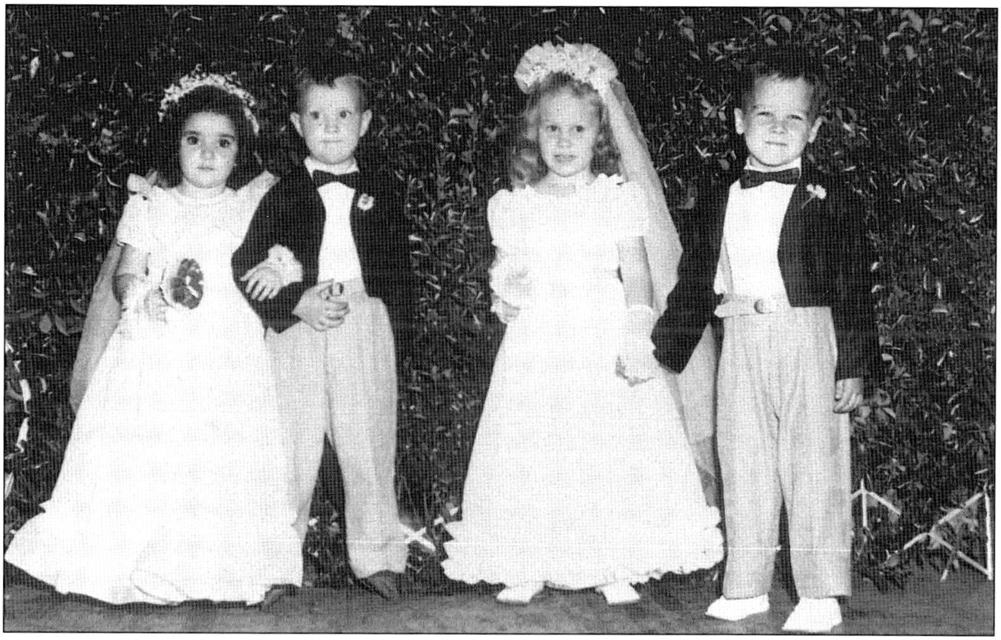

This Tom Thumb Wedding, in May 1950, was presented at a Parent Teacher Association program at Ozark's Carter Grade School. The handsome children involved are Billy John Grider, Kay Underwood, Sally Dangers, and an unknown little girl. (Sadler H. Burrow Collection.)

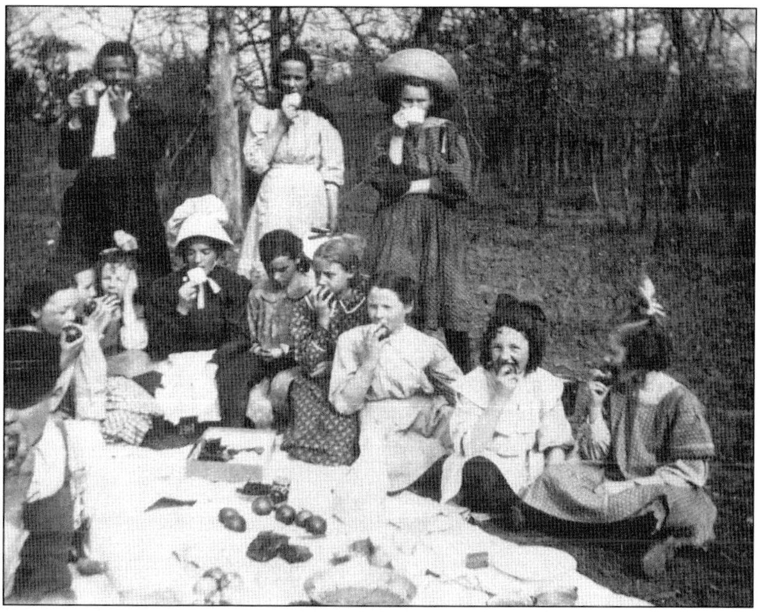

During a picnic outing on Manitou Mountain, these girls are preparing to bite into apples. In this beautiful setting was the Manitou Springs Resort for Health and Recreational Purposes in the late 1880s and a hotel, with a lovely bridal suite built in 1890, by J.J. Eichenberger. The hotel was torn down in 1942. The Methodists also built a Tabernacle Retreat here. Reverend A.H. Levine purchased the "log cabins" c. 1945 and established the Ozark Bible Institute, later renamed Citadel Bible College. (Sadler H. Burrow Collection.)

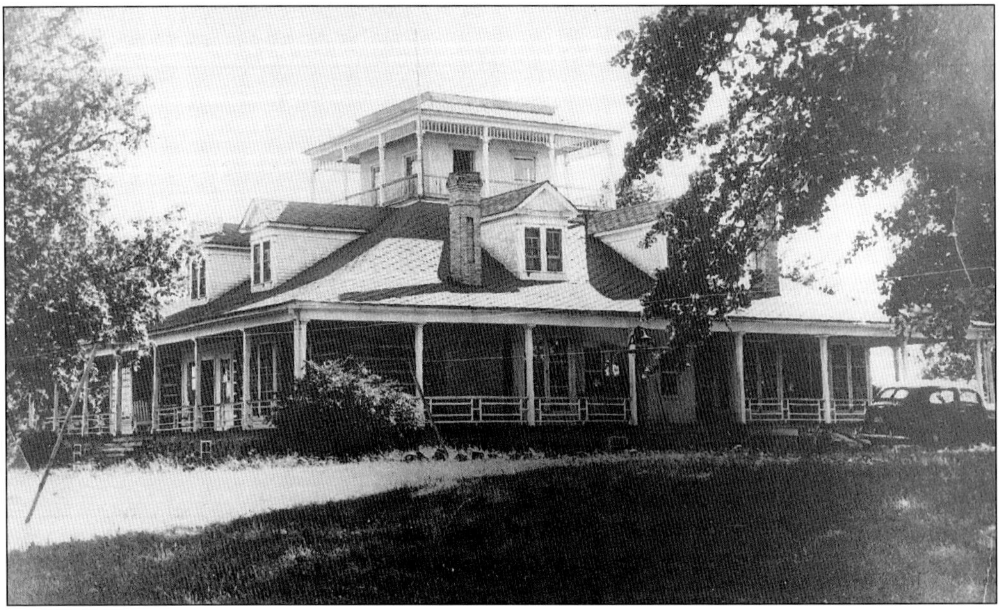

These log cabins, shown in 1937, were built by Colonel G.A.A. Deane as a country get-away. Deane, a Civil War lieutenant colonel, was a railroad land commissioner. The design included four individual log cabins, with a common roof, built in a square. The structure had an enclosed observation tower, with verandas on each side to view the river valley. The colonel had a Delco battery source for his electric light system. Tragically, this "historic treasure" burned in 1999 during renovations. (Norman Powell.)

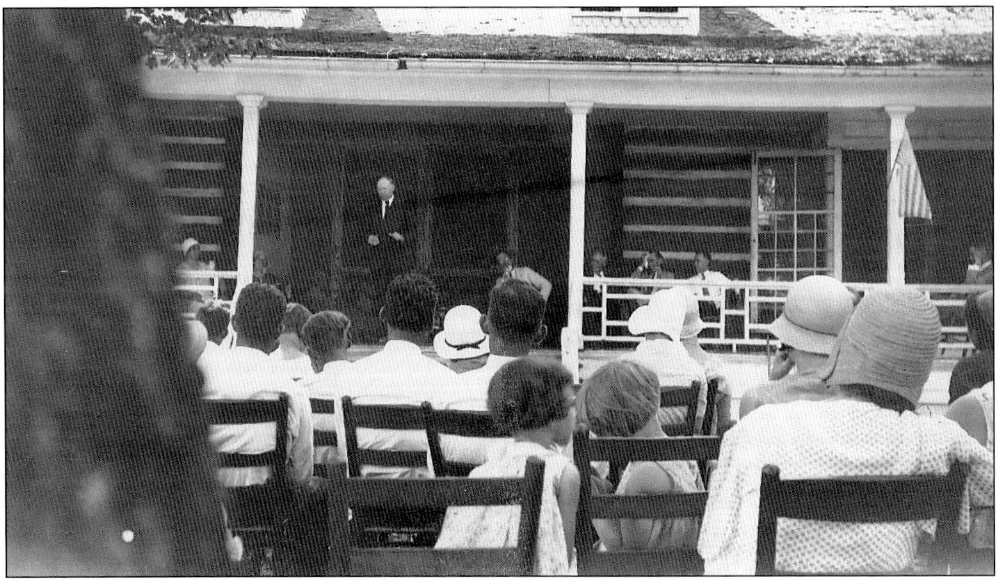

Manitou Mountain's log cabins are shown at the Bible College's dedication. This school made a great impact on Ozark and the surrounding area. Old-time Ozark residents recall ministerial students preaching on the corner by Matthews Hardware. On Saturdays they sent young men and women to witness individually to the crowds that surrounded the courthouse lawn. Most of the citizens were already "religious," but knew the young people were sent to "practice" on them, so they listened and encouraged. (Sadler H. Burrow Collection.)

Eight

Charleston
You Shall Know Them

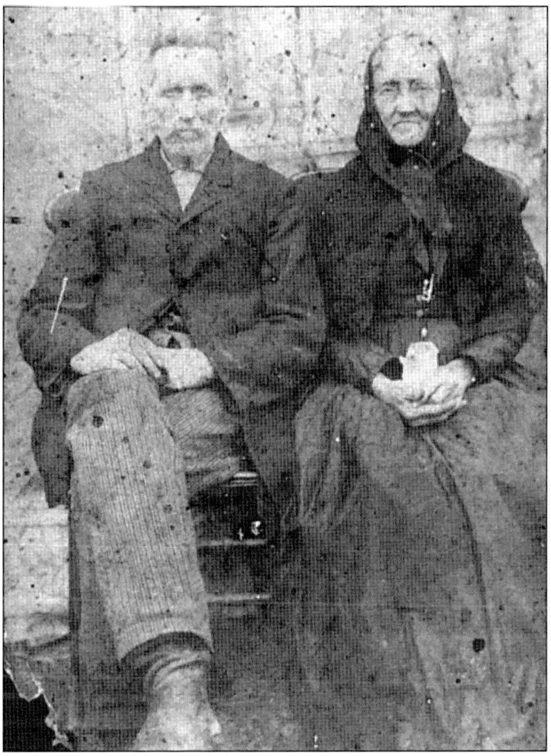

After the Civil War, S.S. Delaney came from Ohio by flat-boat with his family and all his belongings. He even brought his livestock, including two teams of oxen. A family named Patrick, whose destination was Ozark, owned a team of oxen which plunged into the Arkansas River and drowned. Aware of the family's great loss, Mr. Delaney gave Mr. Patrick one of his own teams of oxen. The Delaneys settled southwest of Charleston in 1868. (Belle Museum and Chapel.)

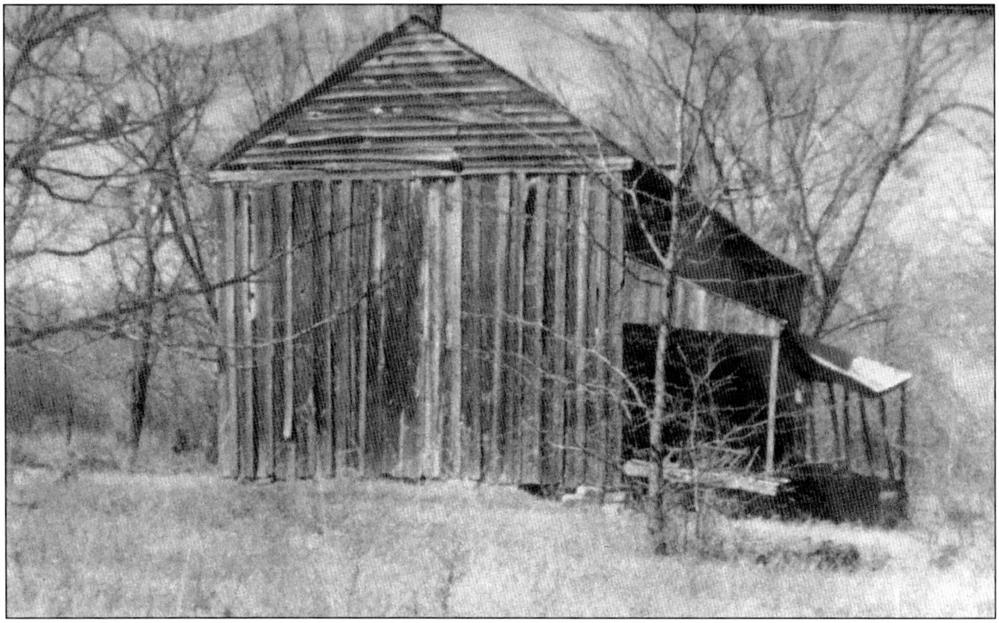

In this image is the Overland Stage Stop, west of Charleston. It was operated by A.J. Singleton. The stage delivered mail and goods to the stage stop store and blacksmith shop following the Civil War. In later years the kitchen was removed from the rear of the structure. This historic site is now Cormack property. (Cormack Collection at the Belle Museum and Chapel.)

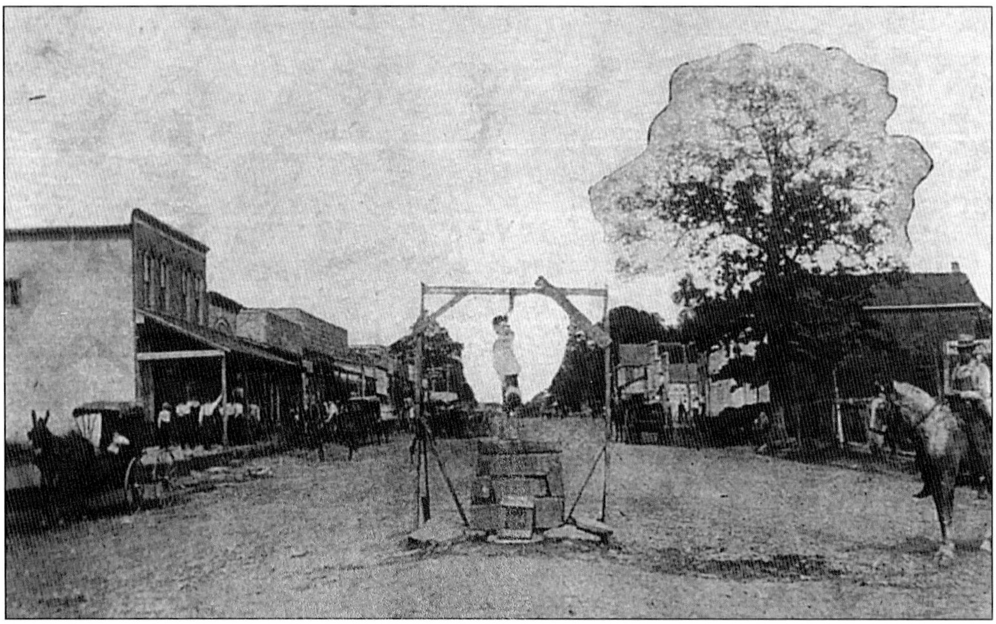

Shown is the city well in the late 1800s, on Charleston's Main Street, looking east. A young man is pretending to be hung. The date October 30, 1907, is written on the back of the picture postcard along with this message, "this will show how Charleston looks." Charleston, the largest town in South Franklin County, containing a square mile, was settled from 1843–44 by J.B. and R.C. Thaxton and Charles R. Kellum. The town was named for Kellum. (Belle Museum and Chapel.)

This photo image features Dr. Ralph Crigler beneath the Hotel Bollinger sign c. 1933. Also depicted is the merging of both types of transportation, the automobile, which was still fairly new to many households, and the horse and carriage. Note that the streets are already paved. (Belle Museum and Chapel.)

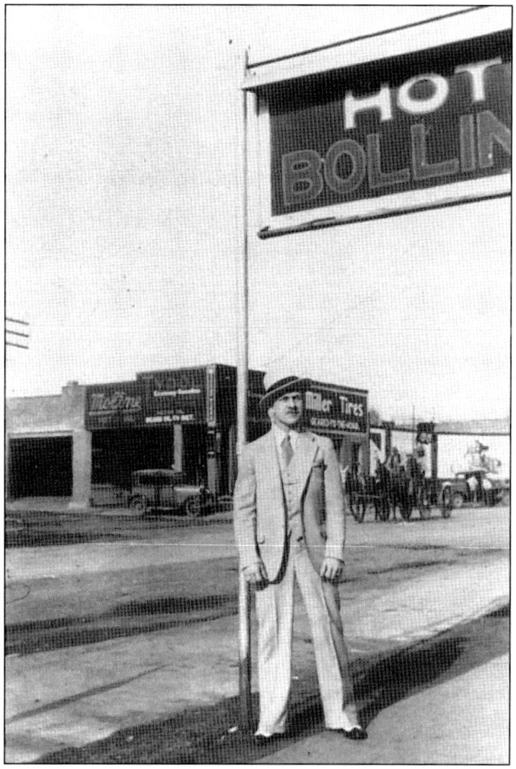

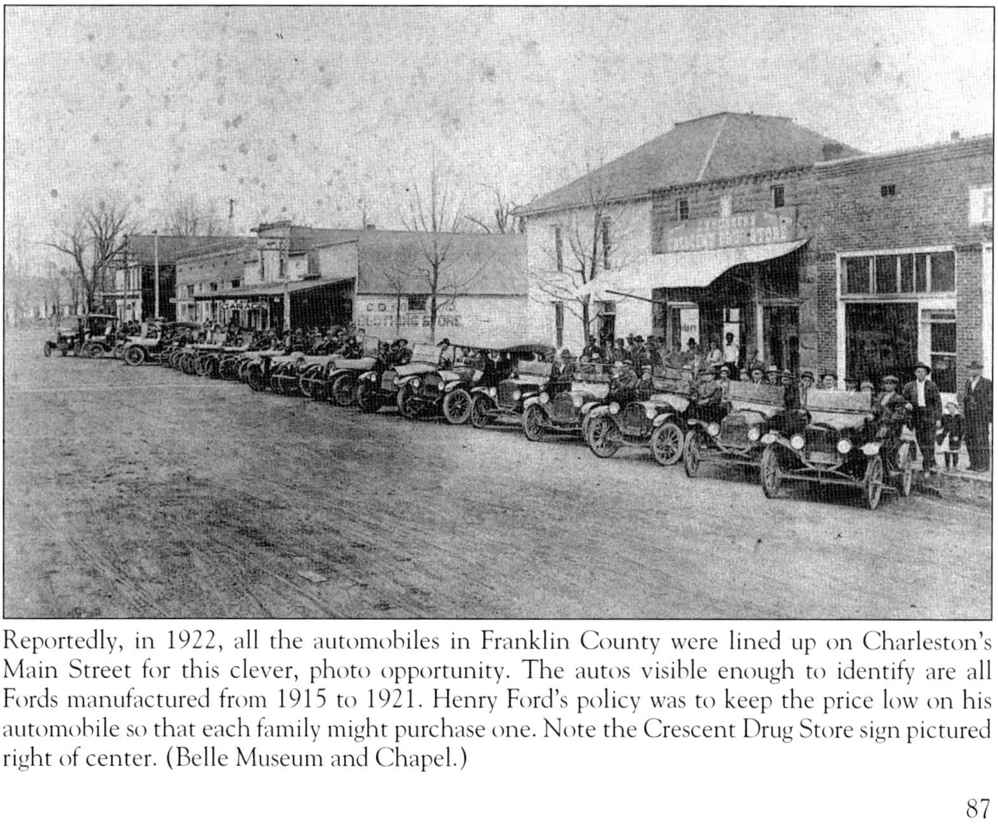

Reportedly, in 1922, all the automobiles in Franklin County were lined up on Charleston's Main Street for this clever, photo opportunity. The autos visible enough to identify are all Fords manufactured from 1915 to 1921. Henry Ford's policy was to keep the price low on his automobile so that each family might purchase one. Note the Crescent Drug Store sign pictured right of center. (Belle Museum and Chapel.)

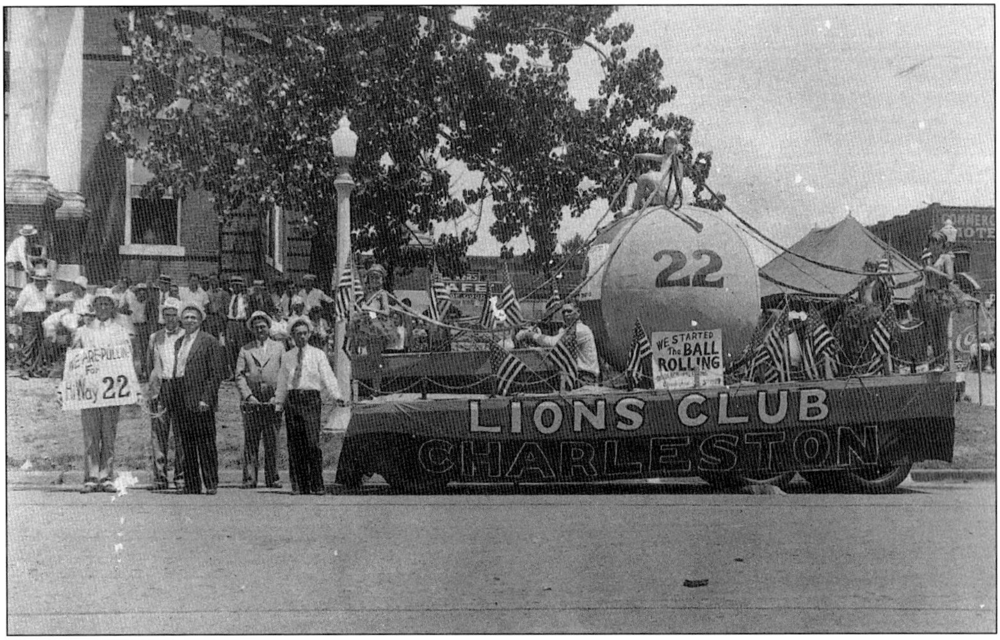

This photo image was made on the courthouse square in Paris, Logan County. It features a Charleston Lion's Club parade float celebrating the Highway 22, "hard-surface road" opening, in November 1929. The float proclaims to the community that the leaders of Charleston got the ball rolling for construction of the highway. Those pictured include Joe Lake, H. Clyde Hiatt, Luther Smith, and Sam Jamison. (Belle Museum and Chapel.)

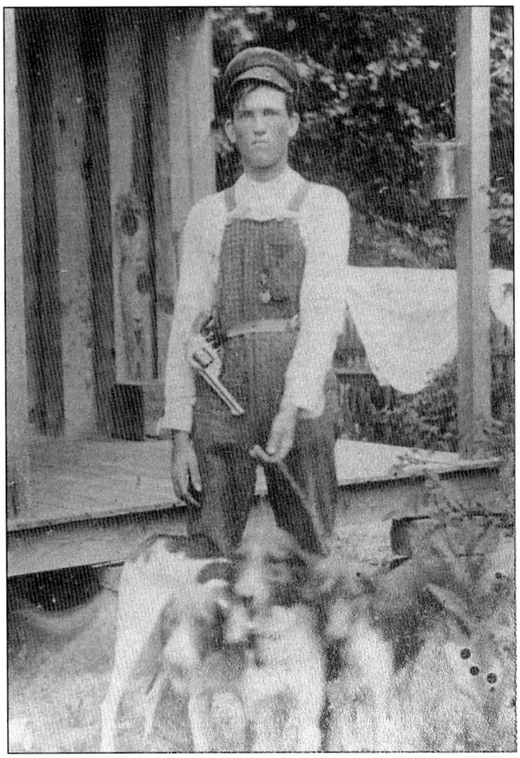

Homer K. Ervin is shown c. 1920 in the Vesta Community with his hound dogs. Homer's pistol trigger-guard is looped through his belt. A hole seen beneath the porch, next to the steps, is probably where the hounds slept. Hounds ate a lot, were very excitable, and had a long, loud howl. Note the feeder attached to the porch post and the paling fence, with sheets hanging on it. (Belle Museum and Chapel.)

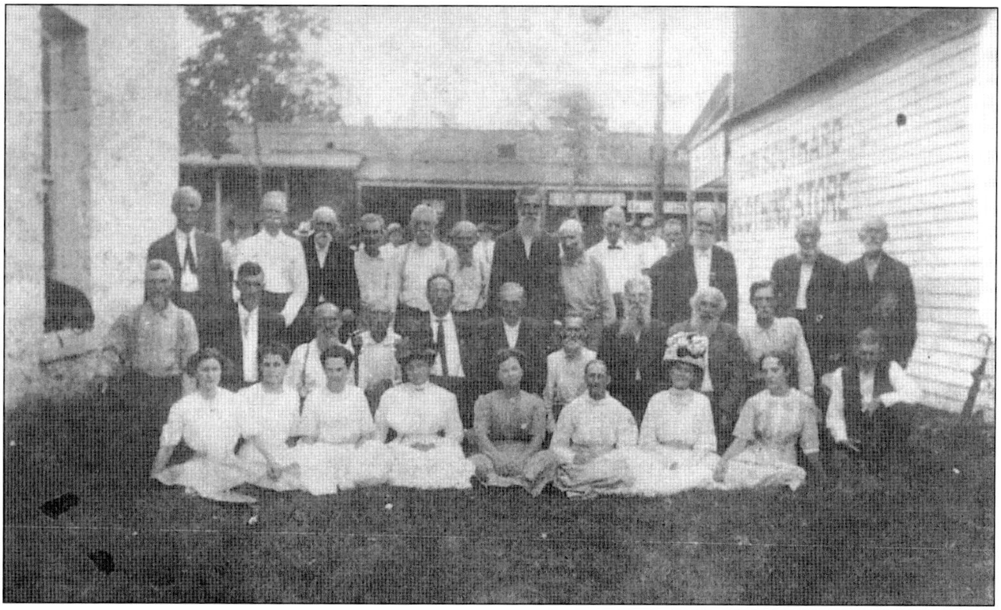

Among this group pictured by the native-stone courthouse on Main Street, may have been the last of the Confederate soldiers. For decades the soldiers held their annual reunion the last week of July at the 40-acre park east of town. About 1912, there were still around 60 veterans participating in the annual parades and activities. Over the years the gray ranks thinned until finally only a dozen or so old and feeble veterans were able to march in the parade. (Cormack Collection at the Belle Museum and Chapel.)

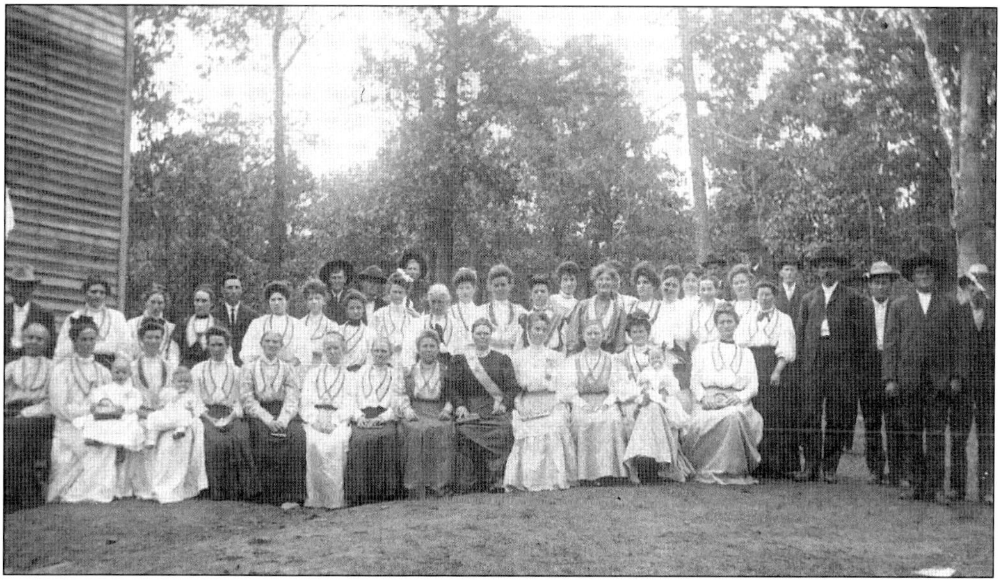

This group of ladies and gentlemen were photographed beside the Old Lodge Hall, built in the 1870s. Due to the women's similarly designed clothing it appears to be some type of club gathering. The Masons and various women's societies, the United Daughters of the Confederacy, and the Eastern Star, which was part of the Masons, participated in annual conferences and the Confederate Veteran's reunions and activities. Note the baby in the lap to the left, with mother's purse. (Cormack Collection at the Belle Museum and Chapel.)

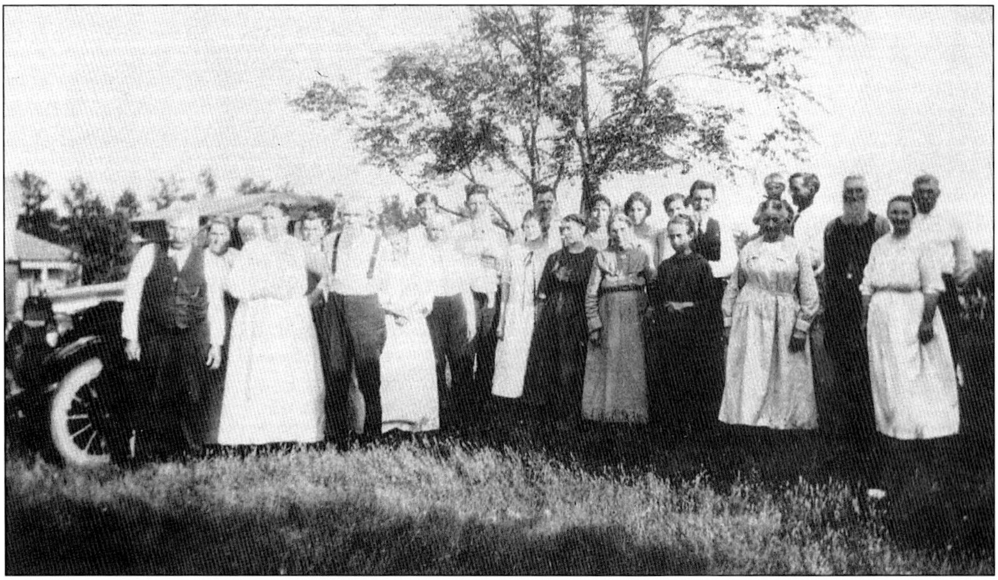

The Verkamp family is pictured at a Sunday dinner get-together at the Herman and Catherine Verkamp farm c. 1924. The special occasion was the visit of Herman's brother John Verkamp, an attorney from Indiana, and his wife. Also present were Mr. and Mrs. Moritz Adams, Mr. and Mrs. Alfred Schmucki, Mr. and Mrs. Lewis Verkamp, Anna Grover, Mr. and Mrs. John Meisner, and Mr. and Mrs. Rudolph Gramlich. Jerry and Regina Verkamp are holding their daughter Irene. Note also Father Alphonse Mueller, OSB. (Sister Irene Verkamp.)

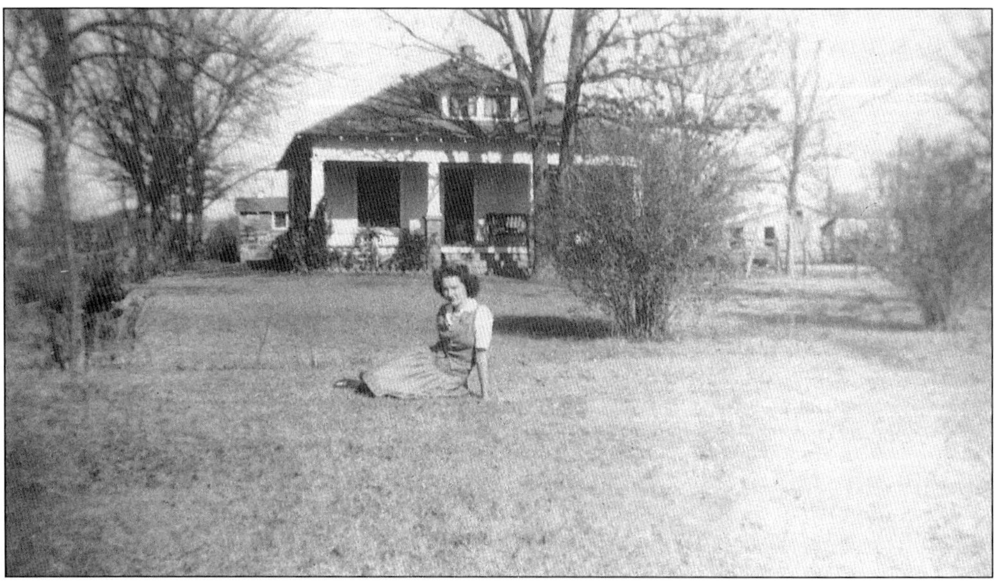

Years ago, Irene Verkamp listened raptly to her grandmother Katie Gramlich as they sat on the porch swing of the Gramlich homeplace, shown here. Her grandmother spoke of early-day events in Charleston and of the Greb and Maledon families. George Maledon was the hangman for Judge Parker's Court in Fort Smith. These conversations increased Irene's desire to learn more of the history connected with her family and with the area. Posing on the front lawn of the Gramlich homeplace is Imogene Verkamp Stec. (Sister Irene Verkamp.)

Irene Verkamp is in this photo image, with the notation "School Days 1955–'56." Sister Irene has never questioned living her life as a Catholic Nun. She feels blessed that she was chosen to serve God in this way. Sister Irene, in her youth, attended Charleston High School. The day after her 16th birthday she entered St. Scholastica Convent. She has had numerous duties and responsibilities over the years and remains a member of St. Scholastica. (Sister Irene Verkamp.)

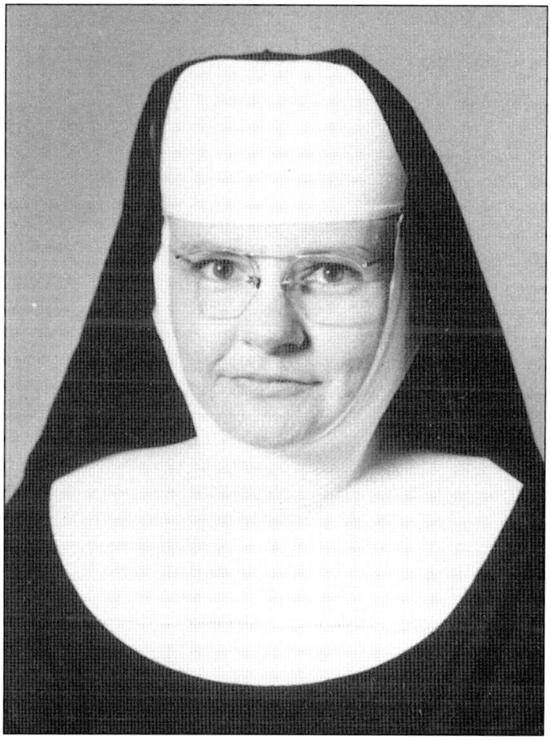

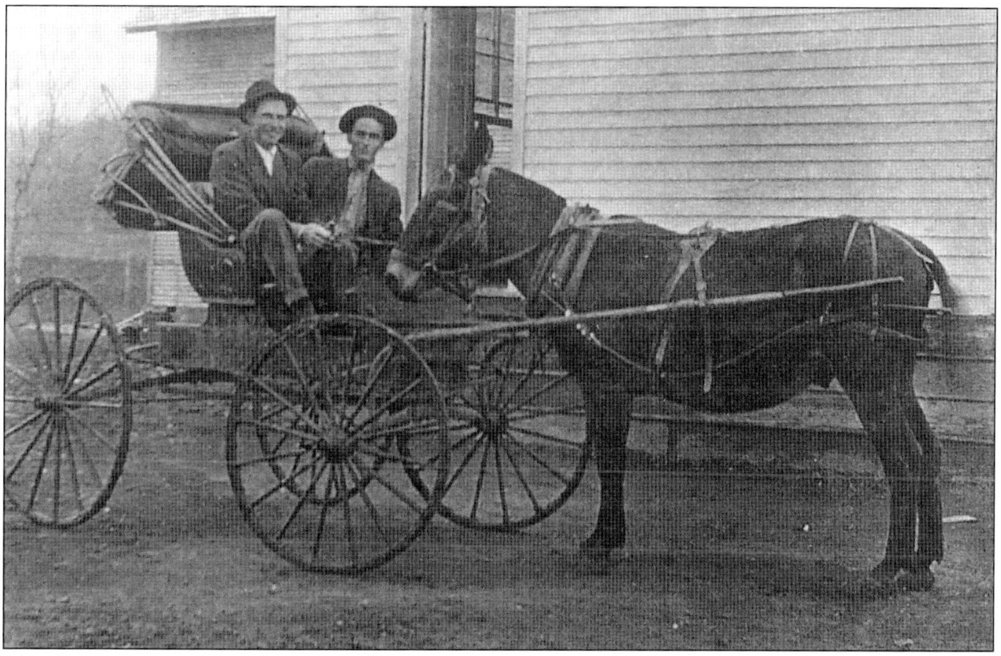

Charles C. Delaney and Ed Cormack are pictured *c.* 1913 in a little farming community, southwest of Charleston, in what eventually became Camp Chaffee Military Base. In a spirit of playfulness, perhaps sensing the Great War rumbling in their future, the young men hitched their mule backwards to the carriage. Charles became a county extension agent before going off to serve his country in the Army Air Corps. (Belle Museum and Chapel.)

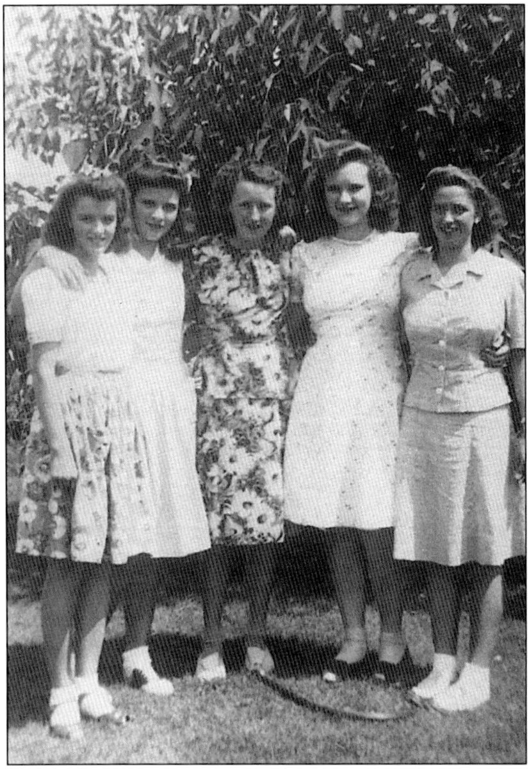

As if to usher in a kinder, gentler era, as WW II drew to a close, this group of lovely, fresh-faced young women posed for the camera in Charleston. They are: Mary Belle Delaney, Mona Lou Moore, Louise Kaylor, Bonnie Moore, and Zelma Rea Duvall. (Belle Museum and Chapel.)

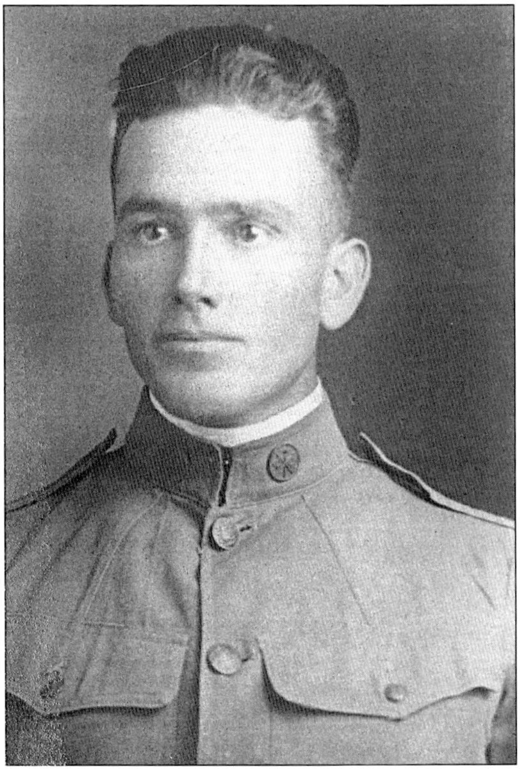

Master Sergeant Charles C. Delaney is shown during WW I. He was in the U.S. Army Air Corps of the 645th Aero Squardron. Turned down as a pilot due to a hearing problem, he worked with the ground crew. He met his wife Agnes Bain Thornton, in Scotland, where he had gone to take classes at the University of Aberdeen. Prior to WW I he was in the third graduating class at Arkansas Tech in Russellville, majoring in Animal Husbandry. (Belle Museum and Chapel.)

Beautiful Agnes Bain Thornton was working as a train conductress at the time she met Charles Delaney. He was attending the University of Aberdeen in Scotland when his landlady introduced them. Charles spoke so eloquently of the beautiful Dixie moon to Agnes that she laughingly wondered if a different moon hung over Charleston than over Scotland. They married at Prescott, Arizona, in 1925, and moved to RFD #1 Charleston. (Belle Museum and Chapel.)

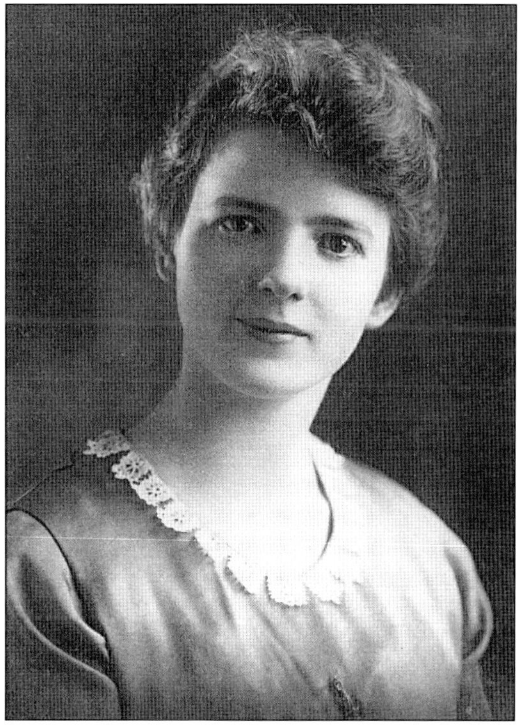

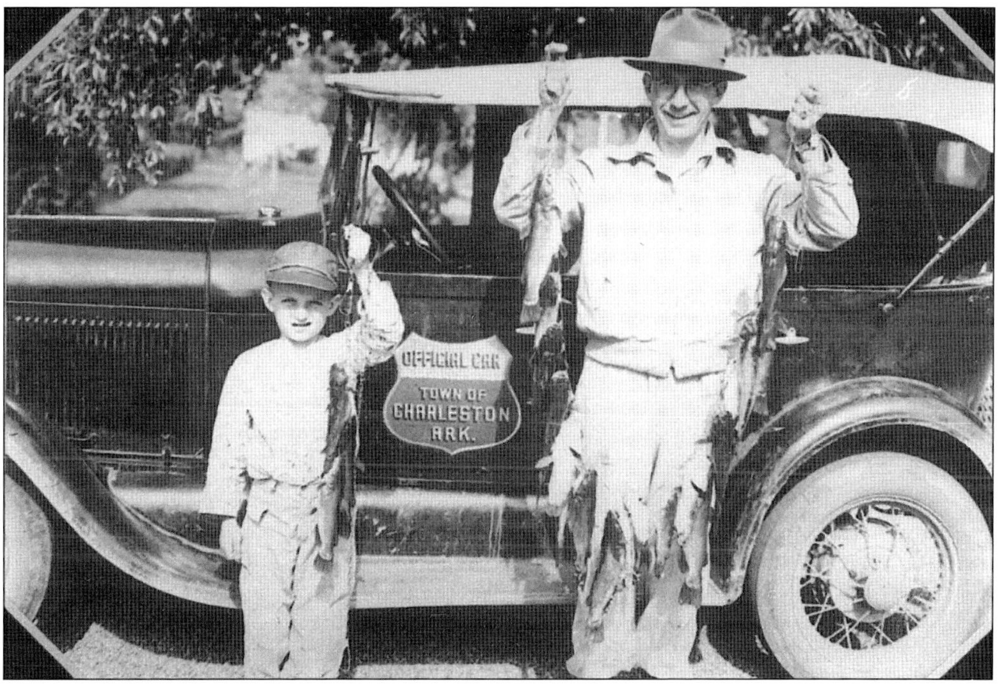

Posing for the camera, with their catch of fish, are A.R. Schaffer and his son Archie Schaffer III, in 1953. A.R., the mayor of Charleston, and Archie were fishing in the well-known coal pit fishing and swimming hole. Note the vintage, 1929 Model A Automobile. (Belle Museum and Chapel.)

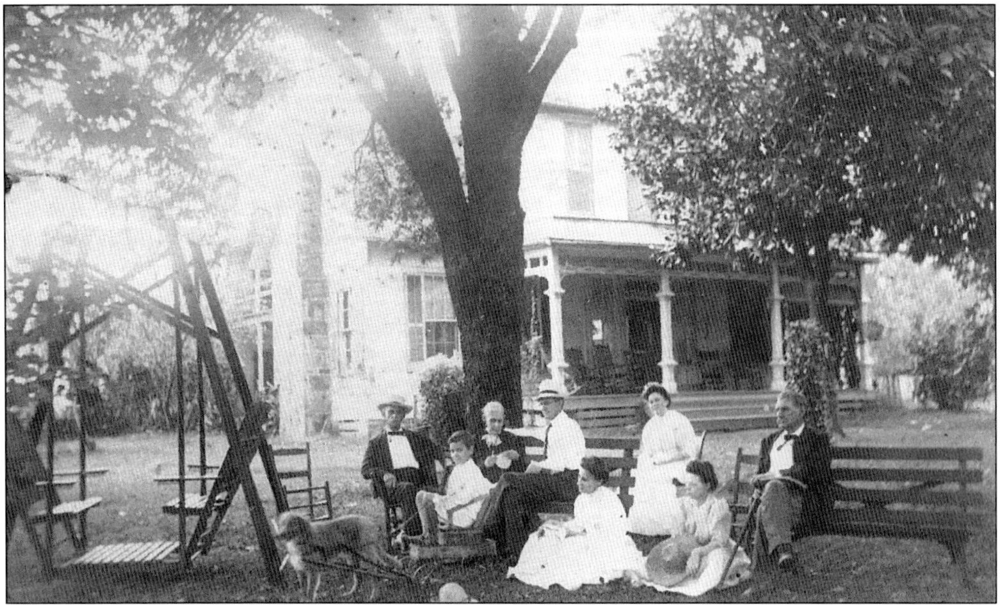

Shown are Colonel and Nannie Falconer in 1911. Also pictured are Mr. Ware, a son-in-law, and two daughters, Margaret and Bertie. Note the dog pulling the wagon with Falconer Ware in it. Colonel Falconer deeded the land where his home was to the county to build a courthouse. The house was cut in two and both parts moved one block south. (Mildred Ledgerwood Collection, Cormack Family Collection at the Belle Museum and Chapel.)

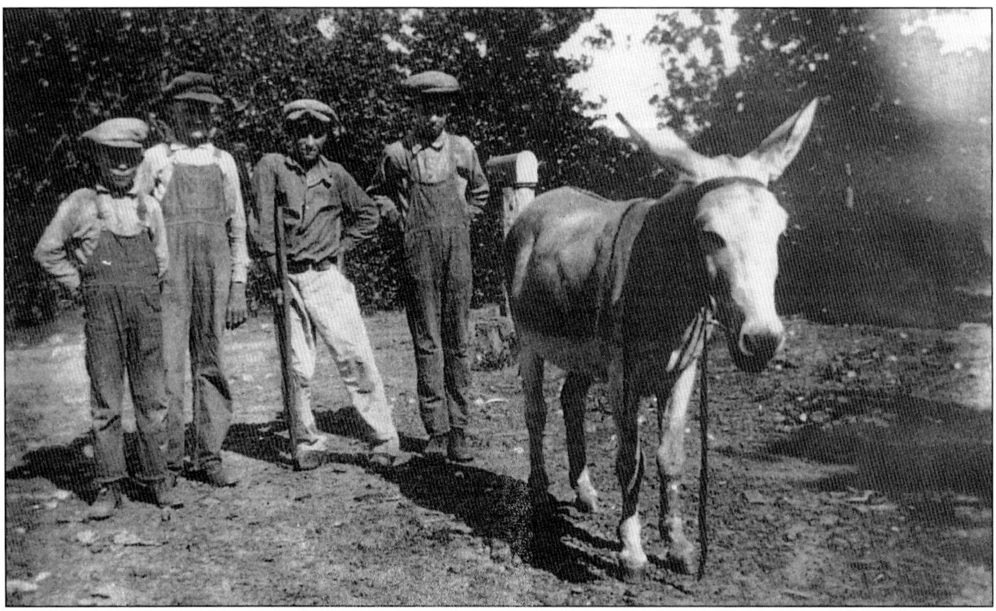

Ralph Norman "Doc" Rambo is shown c. 1926 with Clarence and Carl Harriman and Peter Flynn. At five years of age Doc contracted polio making it difficult to walk. Doc's donkey Blue Boy, his transportation, helped him as a child to become more self-sufficient. He refused to take disability so he worked at a canning factory in Iowa and was foreman for a local lumber company. He eventually bought 40 acres, north of Charleston, and raised cattle. He also made furniture, patio swings, cedar chests, and antique reproductions. (Belle Museum and Chapel.)

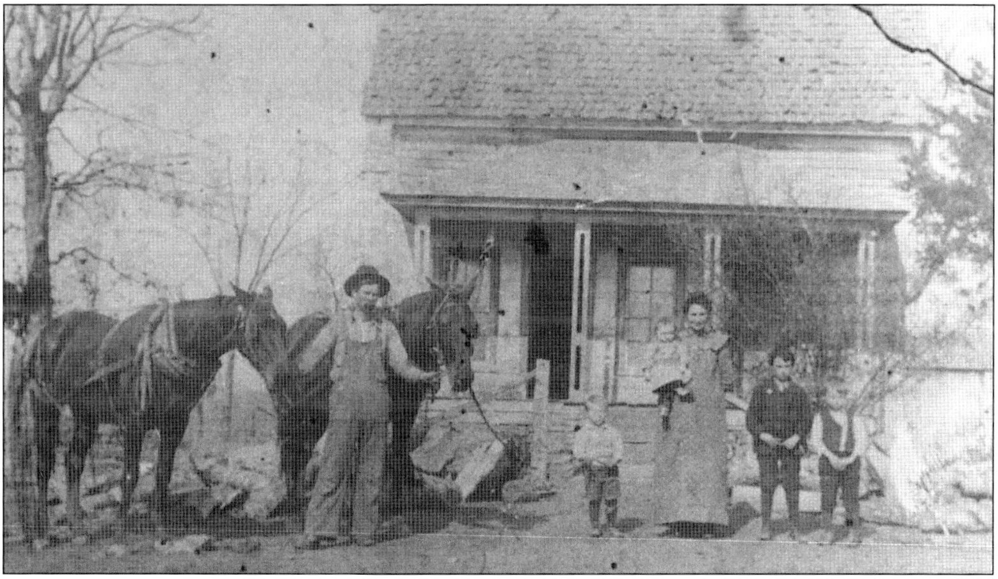

Homer and Effie Flynn Rambo, parents of Doc Rambo, are pictured c. 1900 in front of their home, with their older children. The farm was located 1 1/4 mile south of Hwy 22 on the Sebastian/Franklin County line. Doc Rambo was born years later on October 8, 1914. This homesite eventually became part of the Camp Chaffee military base. Note Homer holding the reins of the fine team of horses. (Belle Museum and Chapel.)

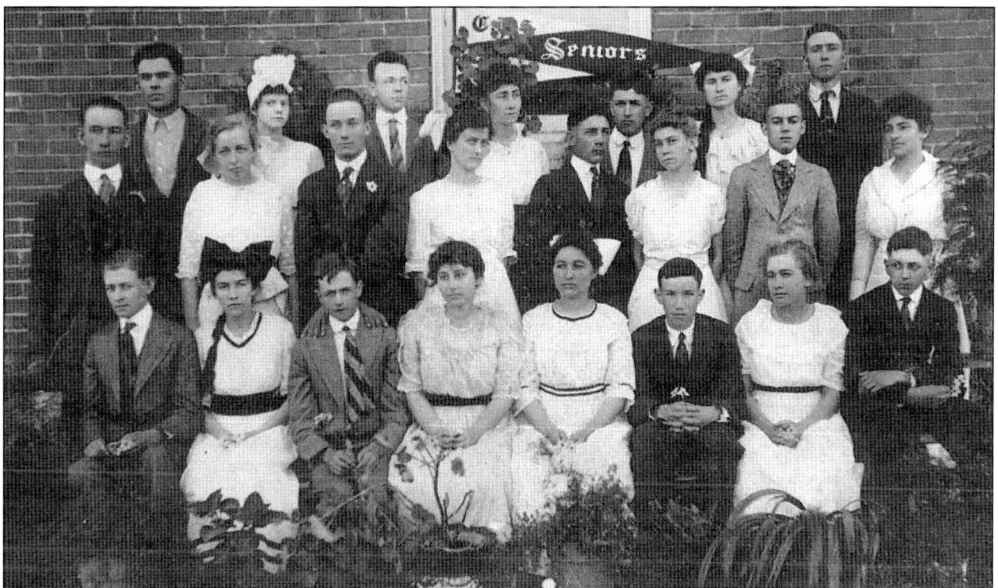

A well-dressed Charleston Senior Class of 1916 is shown at the brick school built in 1909. Picture-taking day at school included using available potted plants and greenery to dress up the photo. The present high school building was constructed in 1930, and the gymnasium was built in 1938. The log school, established by Professor Northrum, was built in 1855, but had to close during the Civil War. It reopened in 1867. The first woman teacher, Julia Singleton, was hired in 1869, and the Masons built a school, lodge combination in 1870. (Belle Museum and Chapel.)

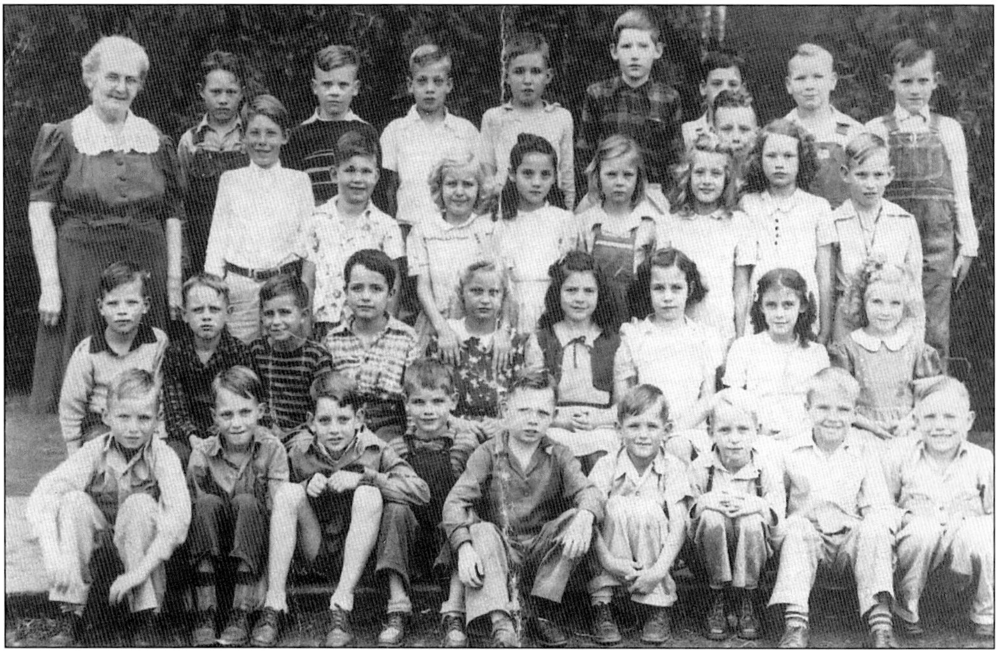

Shown is Charleston's fourth and fifth grade classes in the early 1950s. The teacher was Mrs. G.L. Amos. Some of the boys are dressed in overalls and one young man, before dress codes were stringently enforced, even had on shorts. Note the Pressed Arbor Vitae, a flat type cedar, located directly behind them. (Belle Museum and Chapel.)

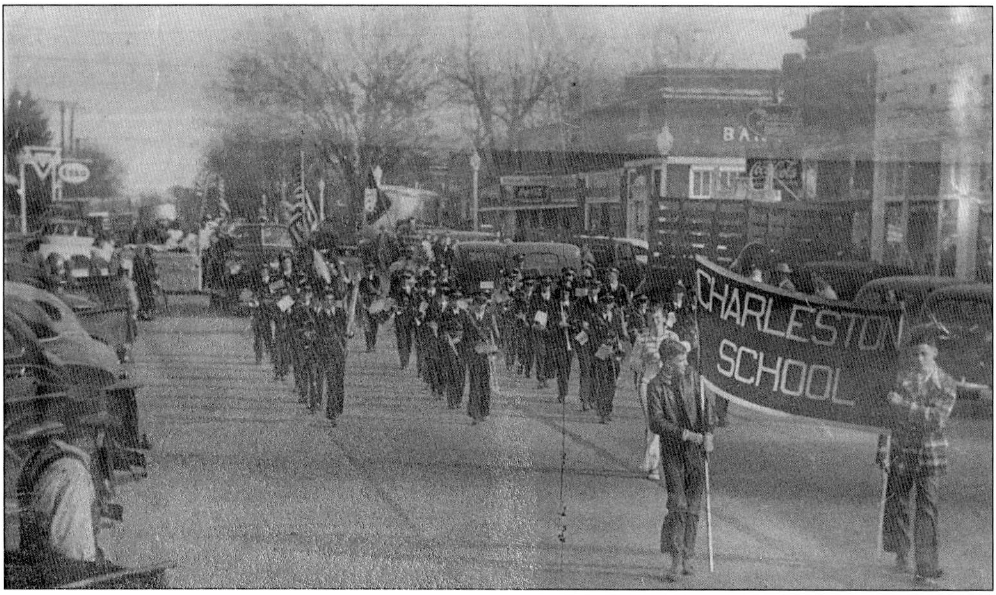

The Charleston High School Band is featured in a parade in downtown Charleston c. 1950. Locally owned cars and trucks were used to transport people and items in the parade. Forming a nice backdrop is the American State Bank. After more than 80 years, the bank's name has been changed for the second time. The first time it changed from German-American Bank to American State Bank, during WW I. Again in 1999, the name was changed to Simmons First National Bank. (Belle Museum and Chapel.)

Nine

CHARLESTON
HARD TIMES MADE US STRONG

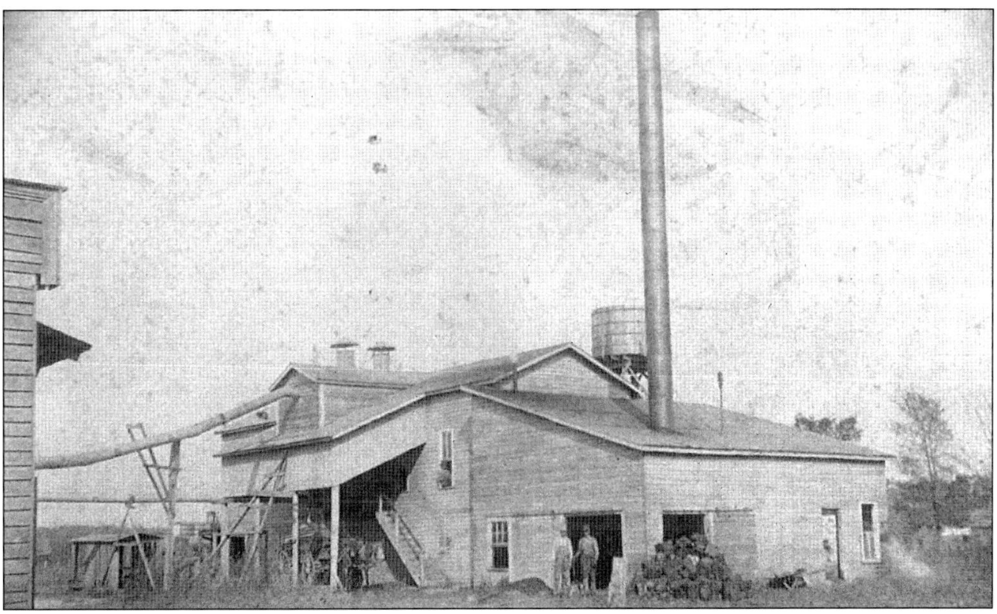

This photo image shows a cotton gin which operated in Charleston in the 1920s. Located in the northeast part of town near the old nursing home, this cotton gin was one of three in the Charleston area. It was also a gristmill, grinding corn and wheat. W.P. Cormack and Hamp Floyd, shown in the doorway, sold this cotton gin to two gentlemen named Bishoner and Heinricks and purchased another mill. (Cormack Collection at the Belle Museum and Chapel.)

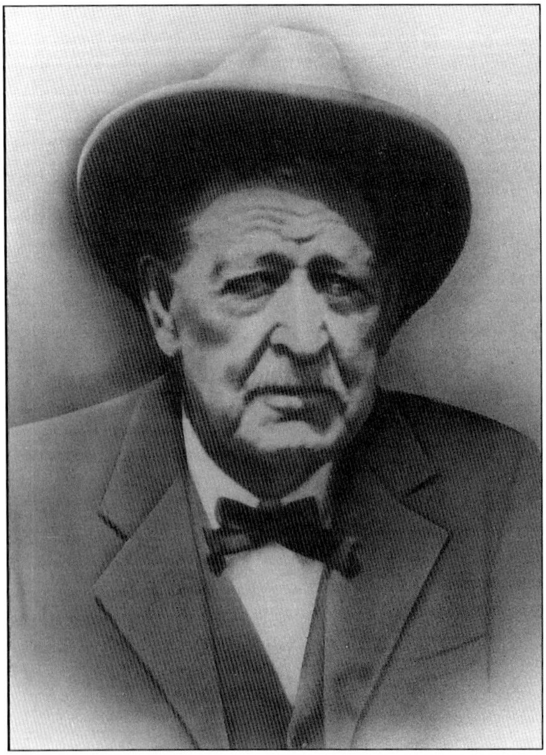

The American State Bank's first president, 1910–1911, was P.C. Mays, shown here. The German-American Bank was chartered on June 10, 1910. During WW I, the bank's name was changed to the American State Bank. The great flood in 1927, which wiped out the cotton crops of Charleston and surrounding communities, and the stock market crash of '29 were devastating to the bank. However, they survived these potential disasters, thanks to sound business management. The American State Bank is now Simmons First National Bank. (Eula Hiatt.)

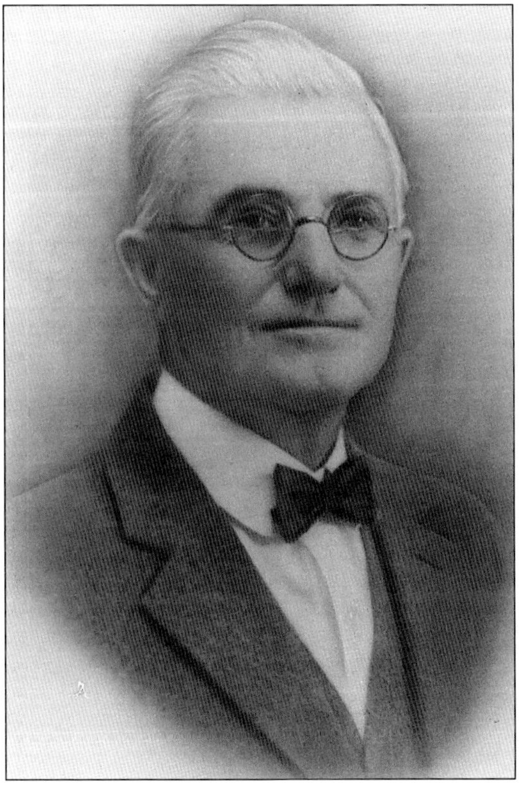

C.H. Charlie Hiatt, as pictured, served as president of the American State Bank from 1919 to 1952, establishing a family and business presence in the community that exists today. During Charlie's tenure as president, the bank survived the closure by President Roosevelt of all U.S. banks. Roosevelt declared a holiday from Monday, March 6 through Thursday, March 9, 1933. Many banks did not reopen. Early day banks operated for the benefit of the individual rather than to make money for stockholders. (Eula Hiatt.)

Former bank president Charlie Hiatt's son was H. Clyde Hiatt, shown here. Clyde was president of the American State Bank from 1952 until 1967, when he died. He was married to Eula. Involved in many civic endeavors Clyde also served the Masons as Worthy Patron of the Charleston Chapter Order of The Eastern Star, in 1936 and 1937. He was Master of Charleston Lodge No. 155 from 1929 to 1931 and again in 1935. Clyde was on the building committee that constructed the new Masonic and Eastern Star Hall. (Eula Hiatt.)

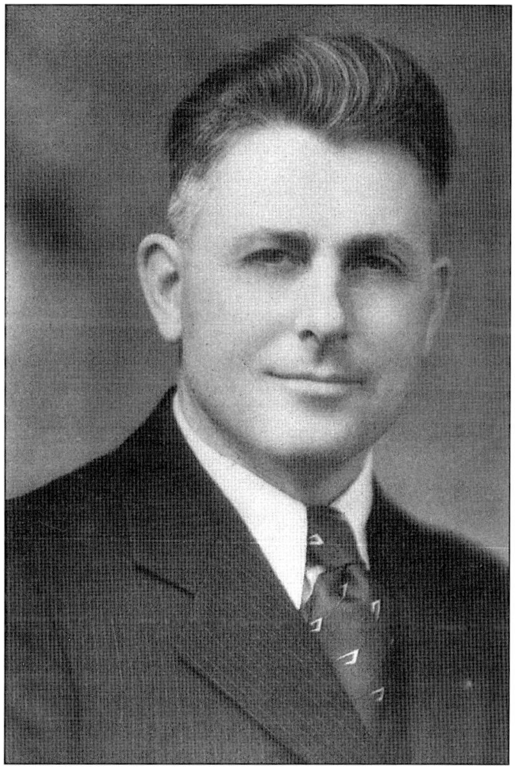

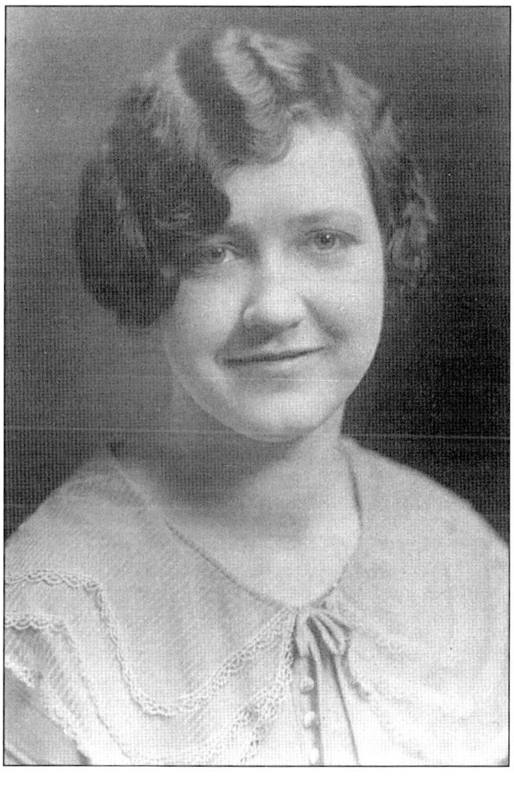

H. Clyde Hiatt's wife Eula, at age 95, still resides in the house which she and Clyde shared and raised six children. Eula, shown here, is a member of the Eastern Star and served as a Worthy Matron in 1934. The Charleston Chapter Order of The Eastern Star was chartered August 31, 1906. Members of the order, in the early days, felt a responsibility within the community to help children, widows, and those who were sick. They are still an active group and will help whenever they see the need, or they are called upon. (Eula Hiatt.)

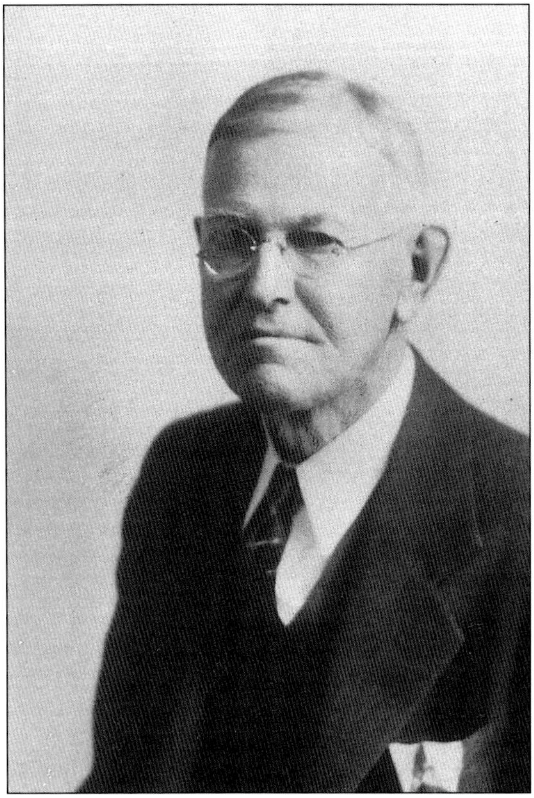

"Uncle" Orr Sherman and brother-in-law C.H. "Charlie" Hiatt first became business partners in Vesta. They bought several buildings and used them in combination as a general store and supply business. They were located in Vesta for around 20 years. In Charleston, as well, a number of businesses on Main Street still visibly bear the Hiatt and Sherman name on their buildings. After going blind Uncle Orr lived out his years at the Milner, formerly the Main Hotel, in Fort Smith. Here he was often seen entering with a young woman on each arm. If spoken to, he would reply "have you met my nieces!" (Eula Hiatt.)

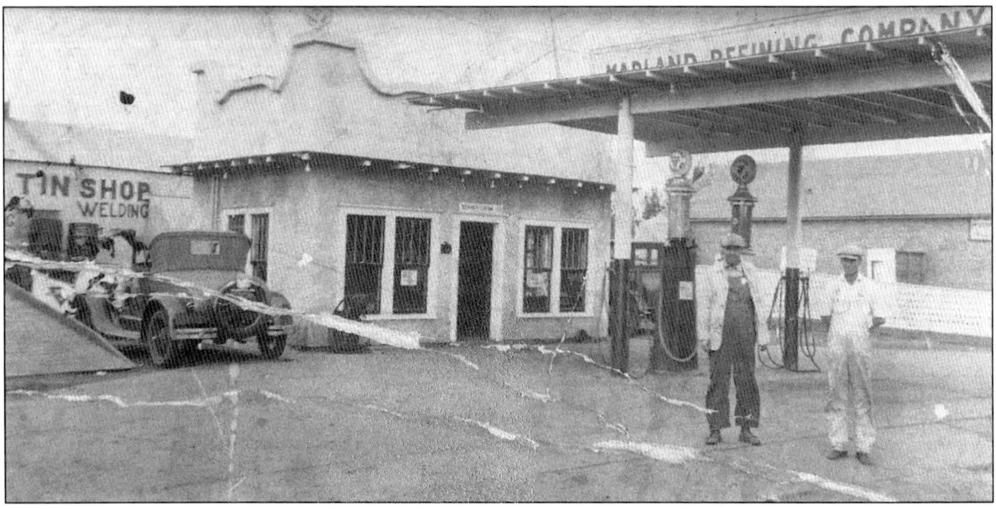

Shown is Marland Filling Station and Refining Company in 1928. George Mullins is on the left and Uel Shelby on the right across from the present courthouse, now the Farm Bureau location. The Marland name is associated with big Oklahoma Oil companies. Note the interesting old gasoline pumps and the antique car. (Belle Museum and Chapel.)

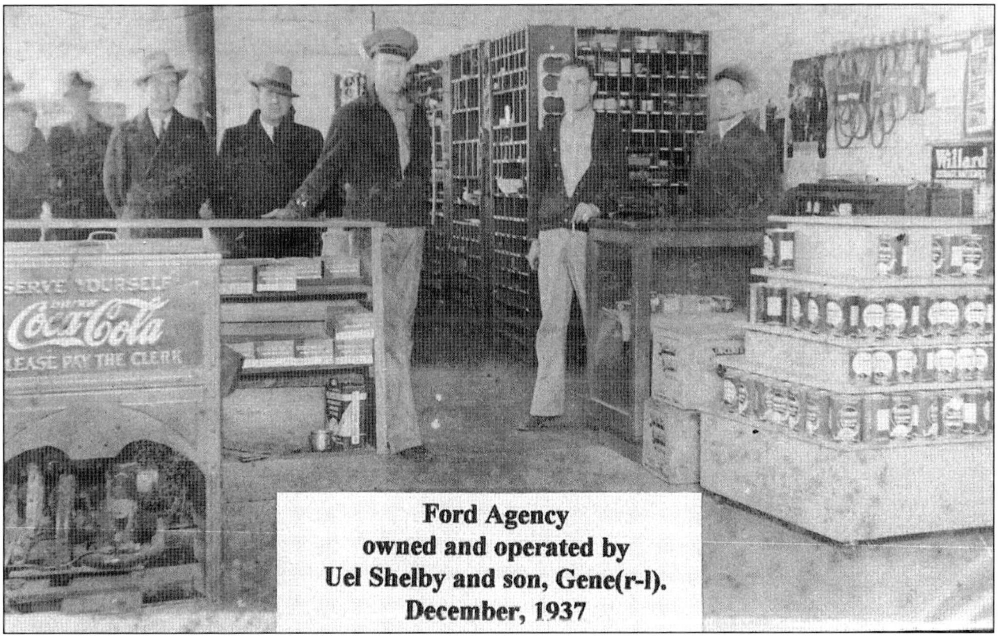

These Ford Motor Co. Officials are pictured in December 1937. Uel Shelby, in the center, and son Gene were the owners and operators of the Ford Dealership Agency in Charleston. It was located on the south side of Main Street. The oil cans say Sinclair Oil. Note the Coca-Cola box urging customers to "serve yourself and please pay the clerk." (Belle Museum and Chapel.)

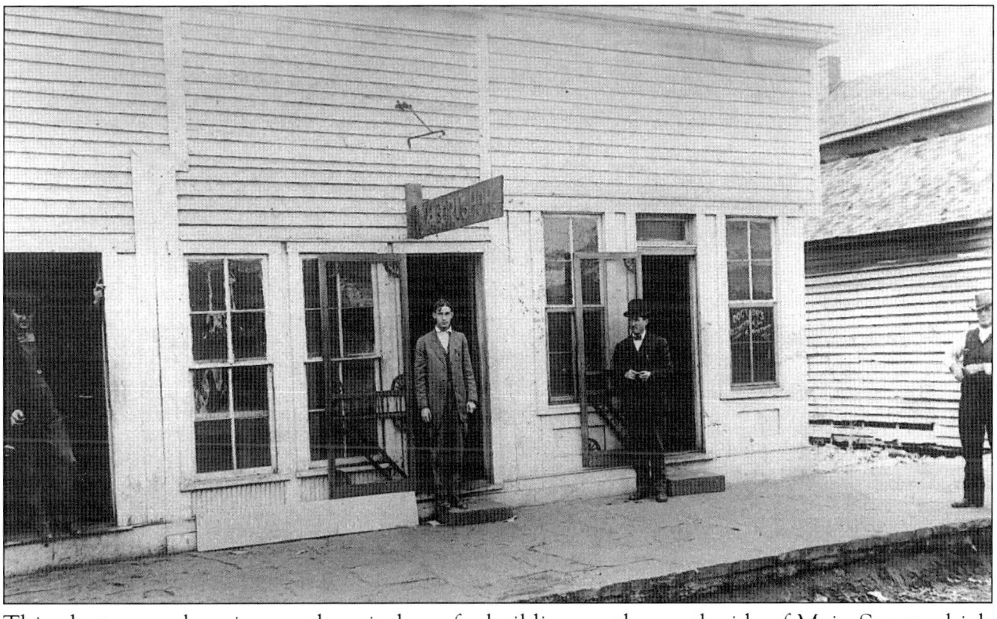

This photo reveals a sign on the window of a building on the south side of Main Street which says "Bollinger and Northum Doctor's Clinic." Dr. Bollinger is to the right, and Dr. Northum is in the doorway of this 1907 image. Dr. Bollinger was licensed in 1907 and he married Ollie Hiatt that same year. Their home became the first unofficial hospital in the area. Dr. Bollinger put extremely ill patients to bed in the upstairs of his home. Note the Victorian screen doors and the paved sidewalk. (Isaac Bollinger.)

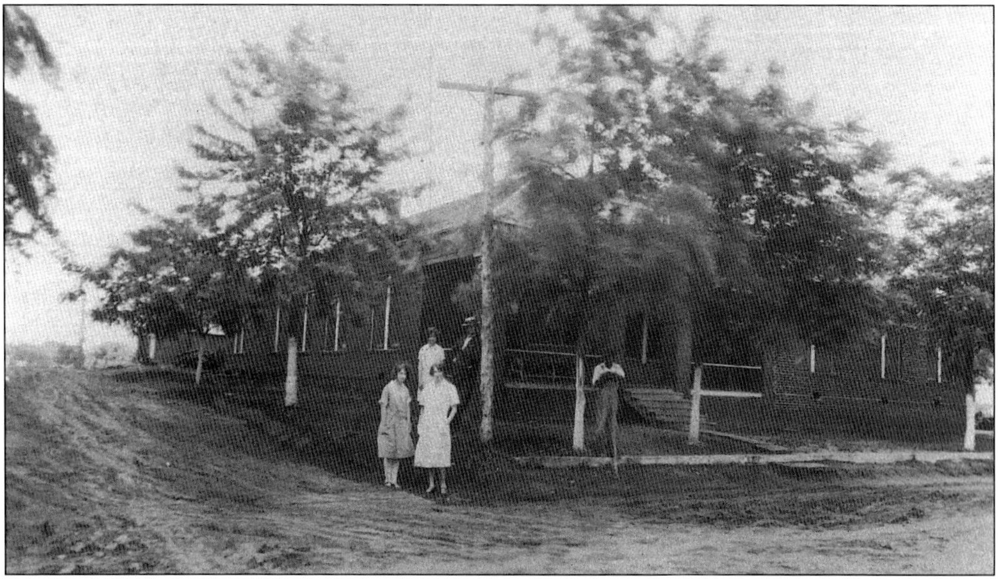

Dr. Bollinger, shown here in a straw hat c. 1925, established the Bollinger Hospital in 1917. It was the first hospital in the area. He later built a north wing. One year he and Miss Willie, his nurse for 35 years, delivered 120 babies, 60 girls and 60 boys. Over all he delivered 35 sets of twins and one set of triplets. He served in excess of three generations of patients working up until just a few months before his death. He died at age 84 in 1966, after almost 60 years of practice. (Belle Museum and Chapel.)

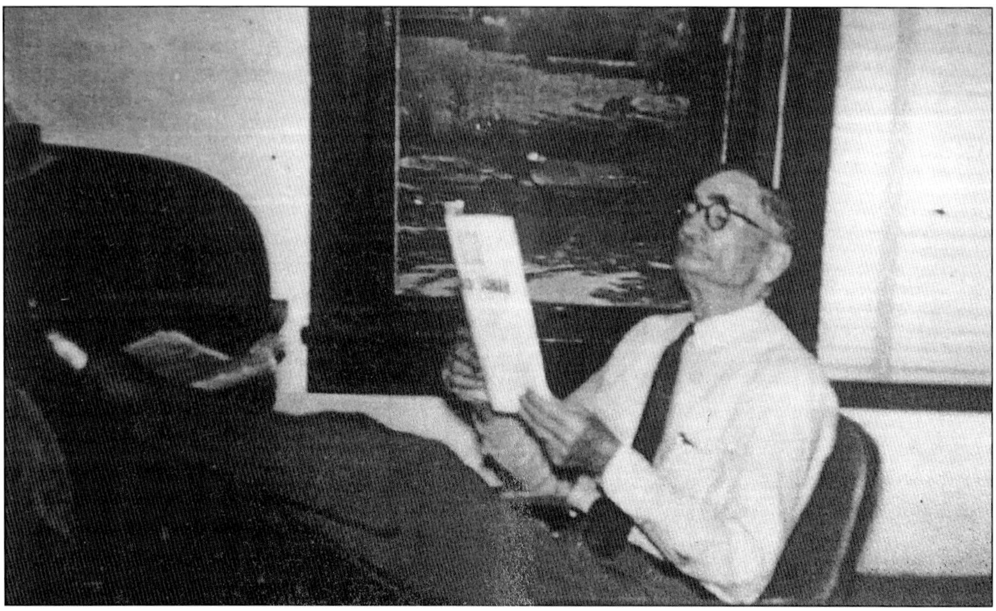

Dr. Bollinger, shown here before retirement, received his medical education at the University of Arkansas. Much of his time was spent at Mt. Sinai Hospital in New York City and Cook County Hospital in Chicago. Doctor Bollinger was born November 27, 1883, the son of Isaac Wesley and Nancy Hunter Bollinger. He was the grandson of Armistead and Margaret Bollinger, who settled southeast of Charleston 30 years before the town was incorporated. (Belle Museum and Chapel.)

Seemingly against all odds, Dale Bumpers, a Charleston attorney, defeated Orval Faubus in the 1970 Democratic primary election for governor. In another upset he vanquished the incumbent Republican Governor Winthrop Rockefeller. After two terms in the governor's office, he ran for the senate seat held by the popular William Fulbright. In 1998, after a distinguished career, Senator Dale Bumpers, of the little town of Charleston, Arkansas, retired. (Ezra Skinner Photographer, A Closer Look Photography.)

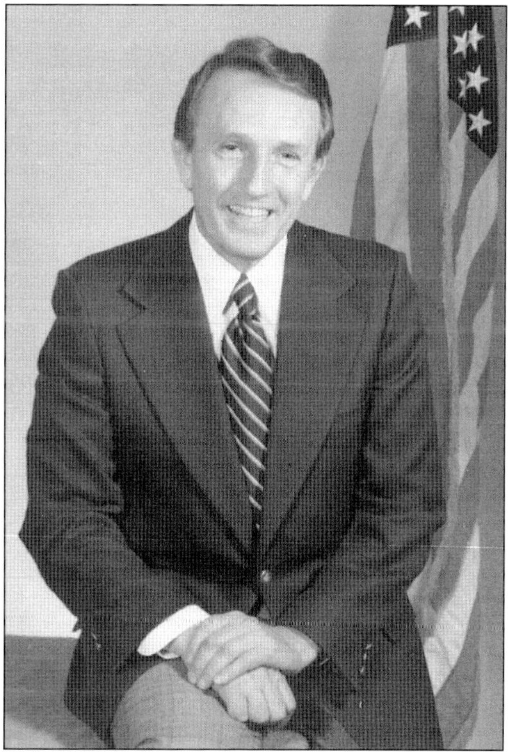

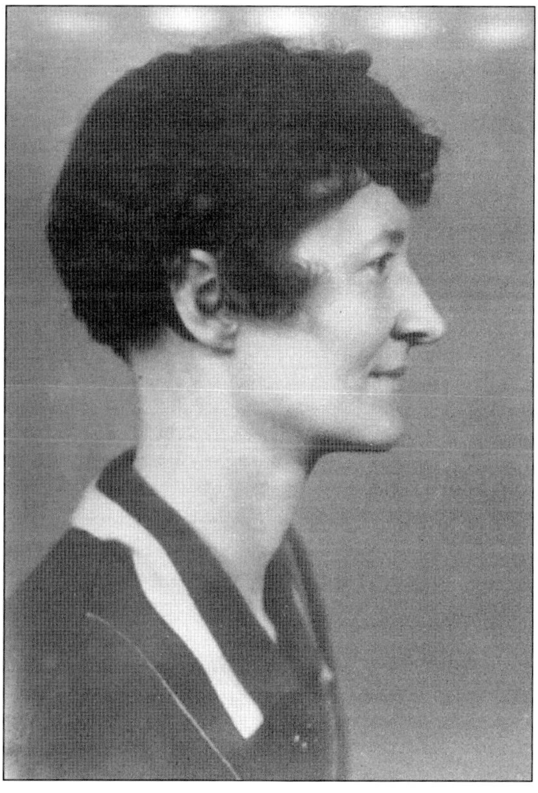

Helen Pettigrew's profile is shown in this unusual pose in the 1920s. A fun-loving person, she wrote verses for greeting cards and stories for Jack and Jill. She also wrote plays for children, Bible crossword puzzle books, and literature for Sunday School Quarterlies. She belonged to the Presbyterian Church. She never married and carried on in her mother's place, taking care of her ailing father. (Belle Museum and Chapel.)

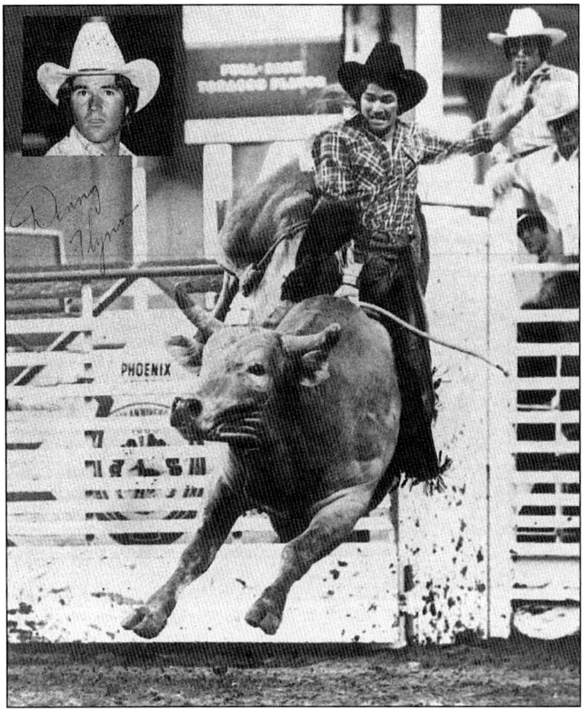

Charleston's Championship Cowboy, Denny Flynn, is a six-time National Finalist Rodeo contestant. He compiled the highest score ever recorded, 98, on the bull "Red Lightning" at Palestine, Illinois, in 1979. That high score was given recognition in the 1984 Guinness Book of World Records. The book states that he amassed the most points as a Rodeo Bull Rider during a single ride. (Belle Museum and Chapel.)

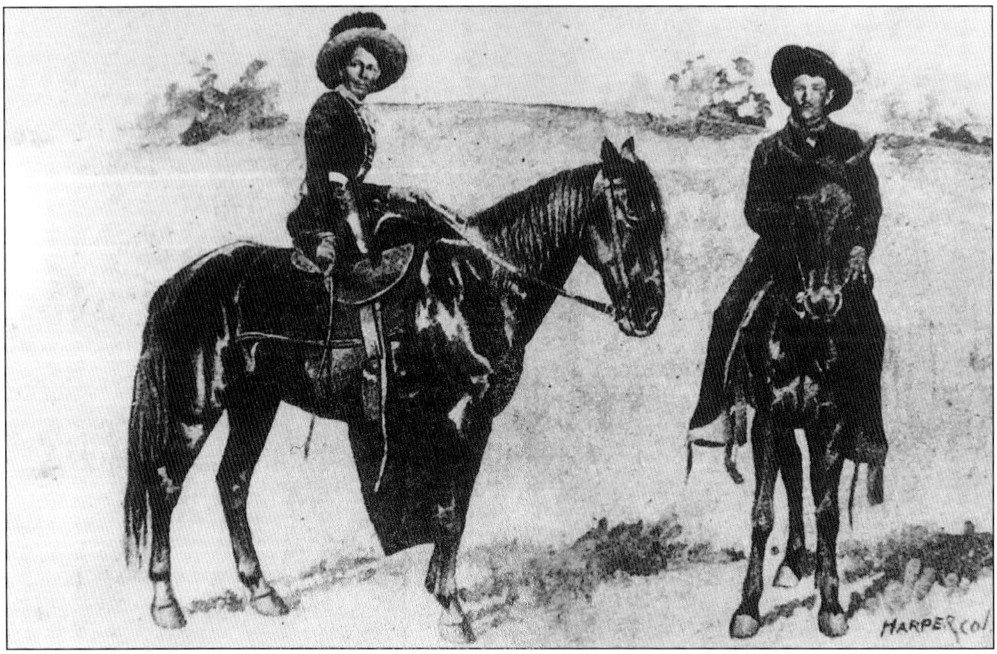

On Saturday, May 28, 1886, Belle Starr had a photo made on her horse at Rhoeders Gallery in Fort Smith for the *Globe Democrat* newspaper. The photo shown, of an oil painting of Belle and Sam Starr, was probably painted from that photo. *The Globe* reported the night before, on May 27, that Belle bought a pair of black-handled, short-barrel .45-caliber revolvers at Wirsing's for $29 cash. Everything Belle did made news. Belle stayed with family and friends in Charleston when visiting or passing through the area. (Fort Smith National Historic Site.)

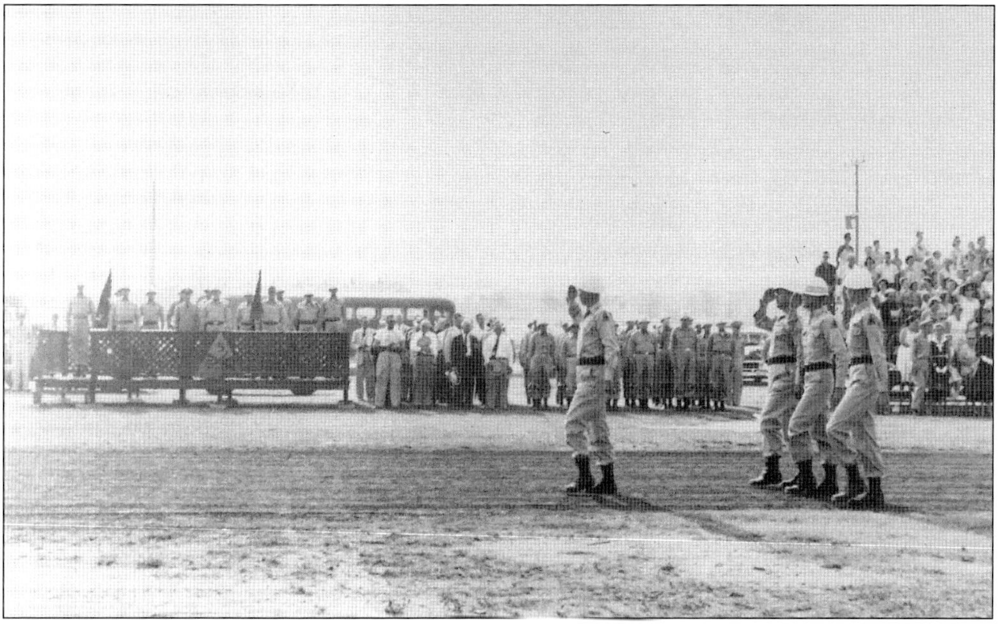

Camp Chaffee soldiers passing in review are pictured here. In 1940 the federal government began acquiring land for the military post that was to become Camp Chaffee. The land purchased was in an area from south Fort Smith to Charleston and from Arkansas 22 south to Arkansas 10. Twenty-five percent of the folks who traded in Charleston lived on land taken for the camp. Many displaced families, finding themselves without a place to call their own, left the area. Some sought work in defense plants in other states. (Fort Smith Chamber of Commerce.)

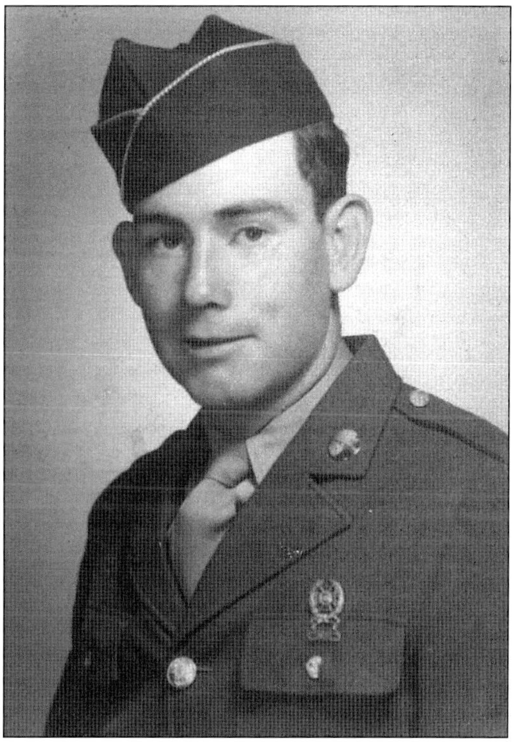

Joseph N. Pritchett will remain forever the 20-year-old lad shown in this photo image. He will never grow old. War has a way of doing that to young men. Joseph, who served under General George Patton in Patton's famed Third Army during WW II gave his life serving his country. Like many other young men, he was killed in action. He made the ultimate sacrifice. (Pritchett Collection, Belle Museum and Chapel.)

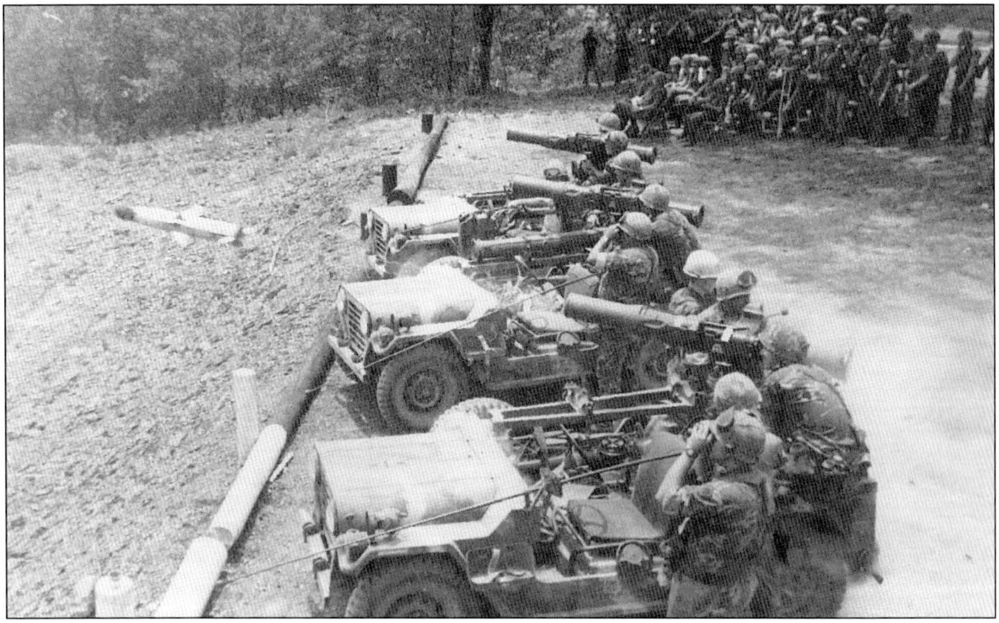

The shell can be seen as it's fired from a cannon-type weapon in this dramatic shot at Camp Chaffee military base. The photo image was taken during a weapons training exercise by the U.S. Army Signal Corps c. 1945. Note the group of soldiers to the far right and the one who appears to be on crutches. (U.S. Army Signal Corps, Fort Smith Chamber of Commerce.)

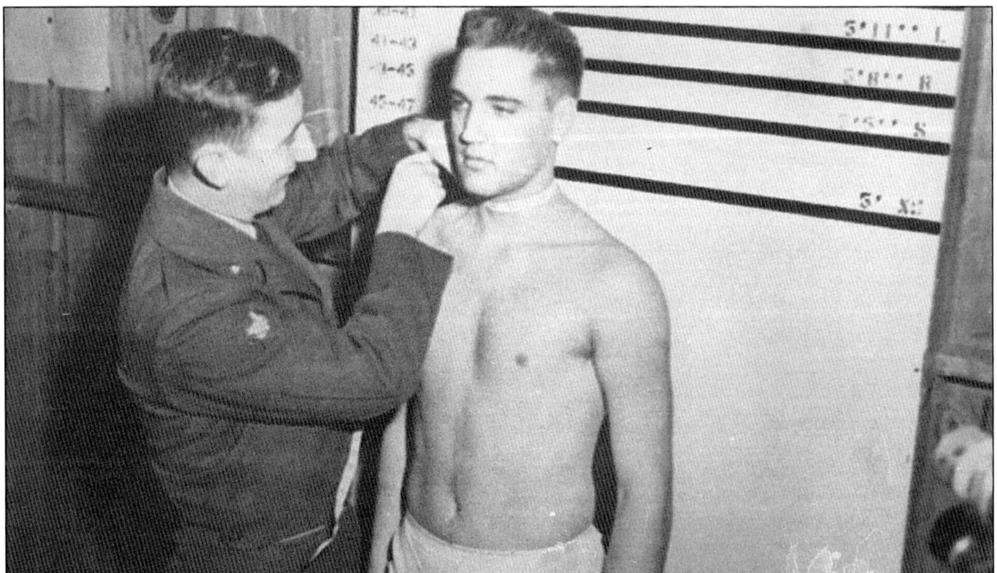

Induction into the Army c. 1958, a well-publicized haircut, and a portion of basic training are what Elvis Presley took from Camp Chaffee military base. In this famous image of Elvis posing in his underwear, he appears to be just over 5 feet 11 inches. The other recruits were so distracted by him that they could not fulfill their basic training requirements. And, the group of screaming teenagers who visited the gate each day was demoralizing to the other men. So, Elvis was transferred to Texas where he finished his training. Elvis' Army Unit was the 32nd Armored Battalion, 3rd Armored Division. (U.S. Army Signal Corps.)

Ten

North Franklin County

That Sad Old Road

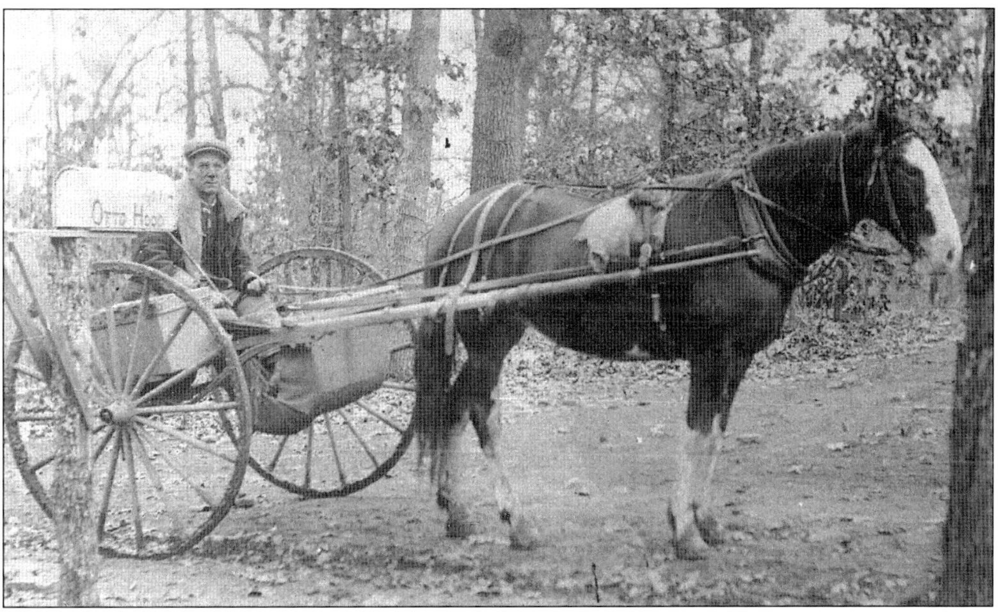

The U.S. Postal Carrier shown, with horse and buggy, is Henry Foster. The mailbox on Highway 64, west of Ozark, was Otto Hood's. Postal carriers had to contend with muddy roads, freezing rain, snow, and long hours. The carrier checked on old folks in remote areas, helped them write letters and checks, and delivered their prescriptions. In the early years the postal customer could "hitch" a ride into town with the carrier. (B.L. Spaulding, Sadler H. Burrow Collection.)

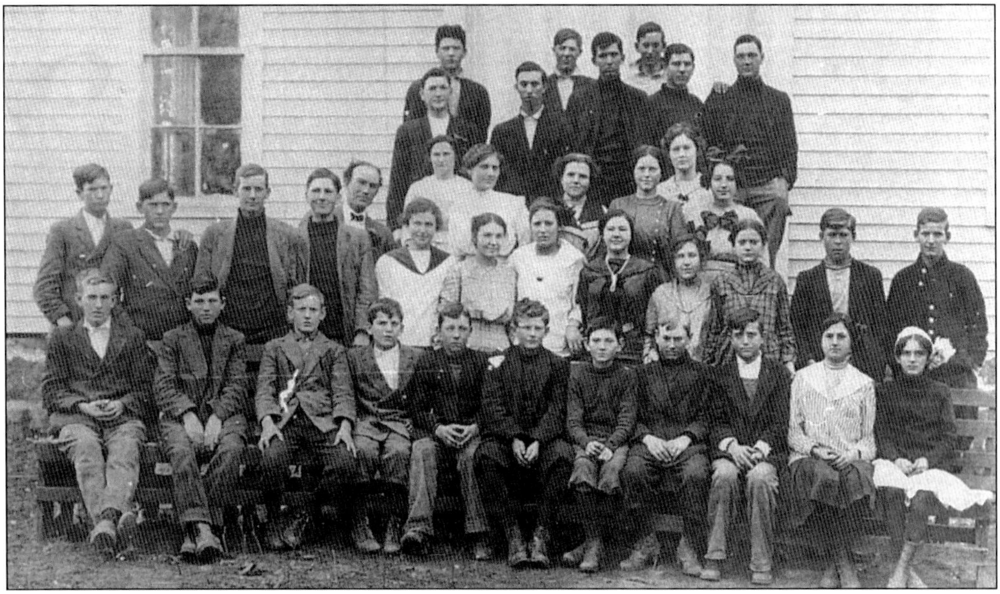

This photo image was taken at White Oak School in 1913. On cold winter mornings, before the school bell rang, the students would crowd around the cold, pot-bellied stove until the teacher, or an older student, could get the fire going. Hardy students also beat a path to outside toilets. Before Franklin County was formed, White Oak was created in 1838, from parts of other townships, and was split up later to form additional townships. (Norman Powell.)

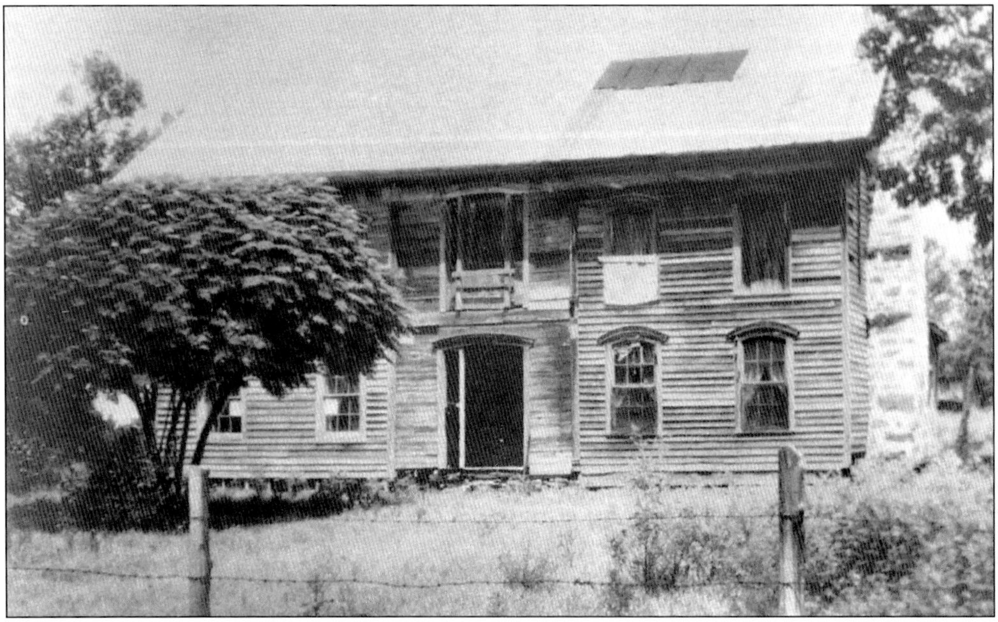

The old structure, shown c. 1939, was known as the White Oak Changing Station and Tavern. Others called it the Jesse James Hotel. Jesse's holdup money was, reportedly, buried in a cave farther north. The hotel was located along the old Wire Road, of Civil War days. The two opposing armies met in a skirmish about ten miles west of the hotel. The beautiful old building, once said to be the second oldest structure in the county, has been gone for many years. (U.S. Forest Service.)

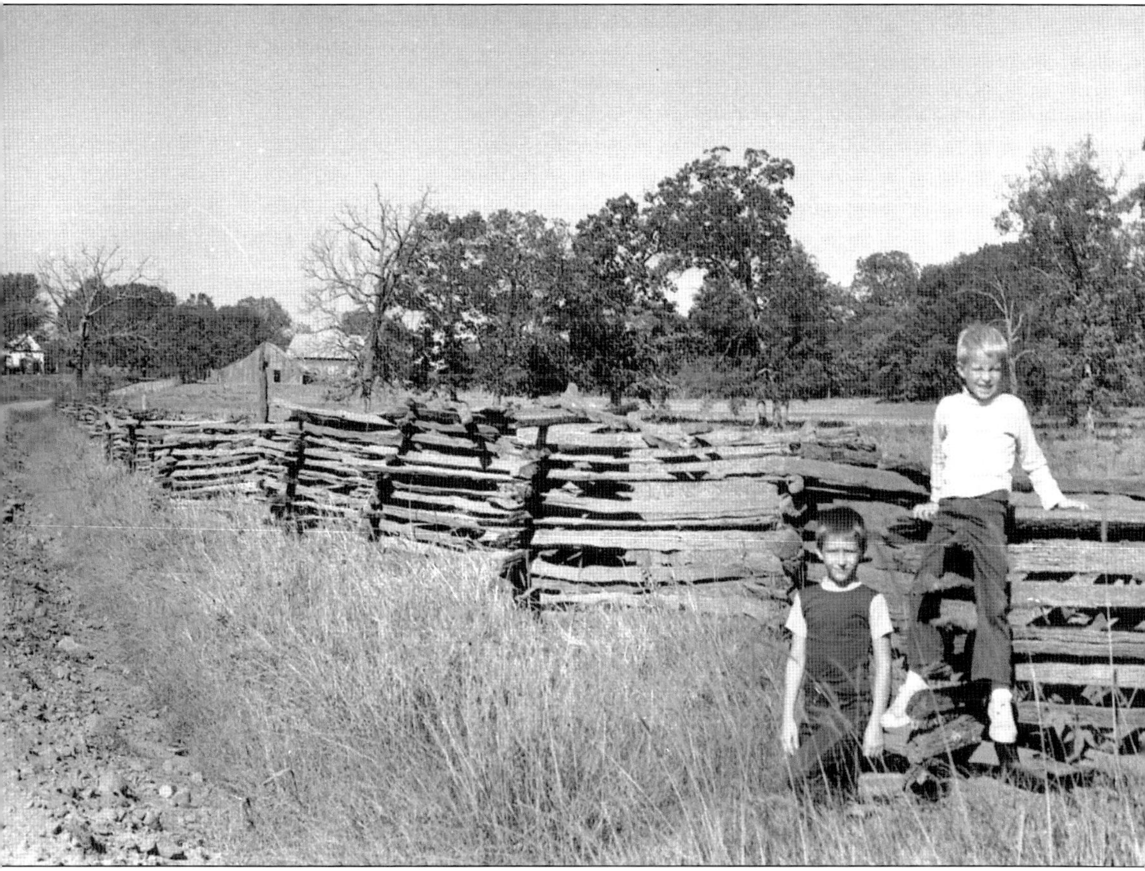

Colin and Brent Shropshire pose at a split-rail fence in 1977 between White Oak and Cravens, on the Confederate Wire Road. The first telegraph wire into Ozark was the Confederate wire, strung in 1862, and from which the Wire Road takes its name. There are certain characteristics of the road that have remained the same since Civil War raiding parties rode their horses here. (Author.)

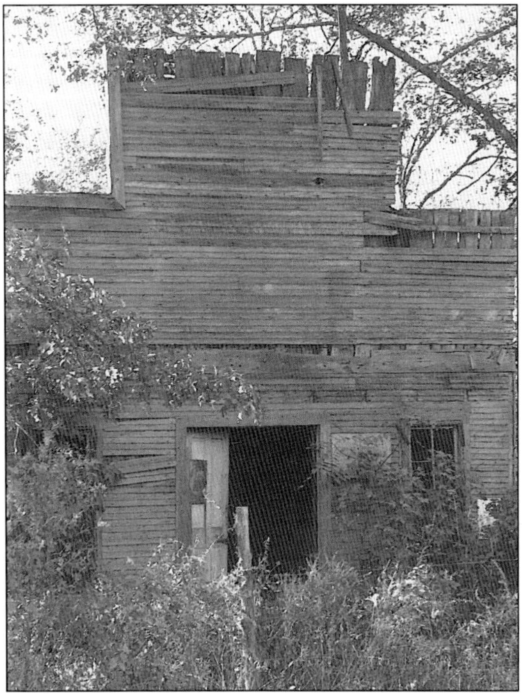

Cravens Store, appearing not unlike an abandoned movie set, is shown in 1977. In the 1940s, to learn about crops, when to kill hogs, and the price of corn, old men sat around the pot-bellied stove and traded information. The store was run by a plucky Chester Bowles. Although legally blind, Chester not only ran a successful business, but did it by himself. To read written material, and to make change, Chester held it near the light, about one inch from his good eye. (Author.)

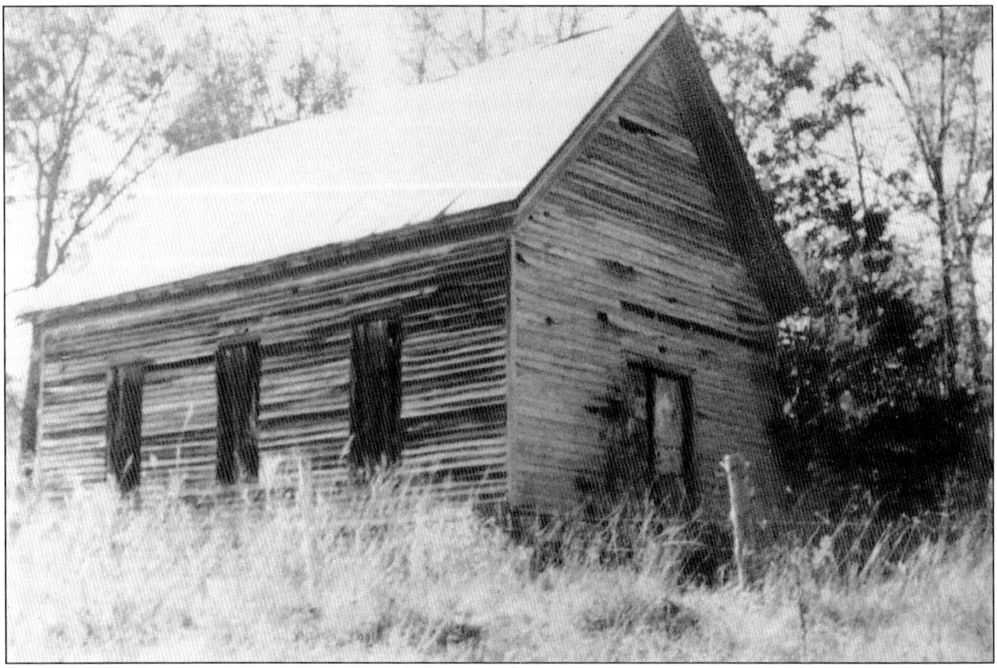

Woodlawn School, pictured here c. 1980, sits today, after all these years, along the old Wire Road between Cravens and Lone Elm. Trees, bushes, and the road have encroached upon the building and playground. Here, young children once played dodge ball, hide-and-seek, and keep-away during recess. The building has not been used, except as a home for field mice, in decades. The one-room schoolhouse serves as a reminder of Franklin County's vanishing, pioneer heritage. (Norman Powell.)

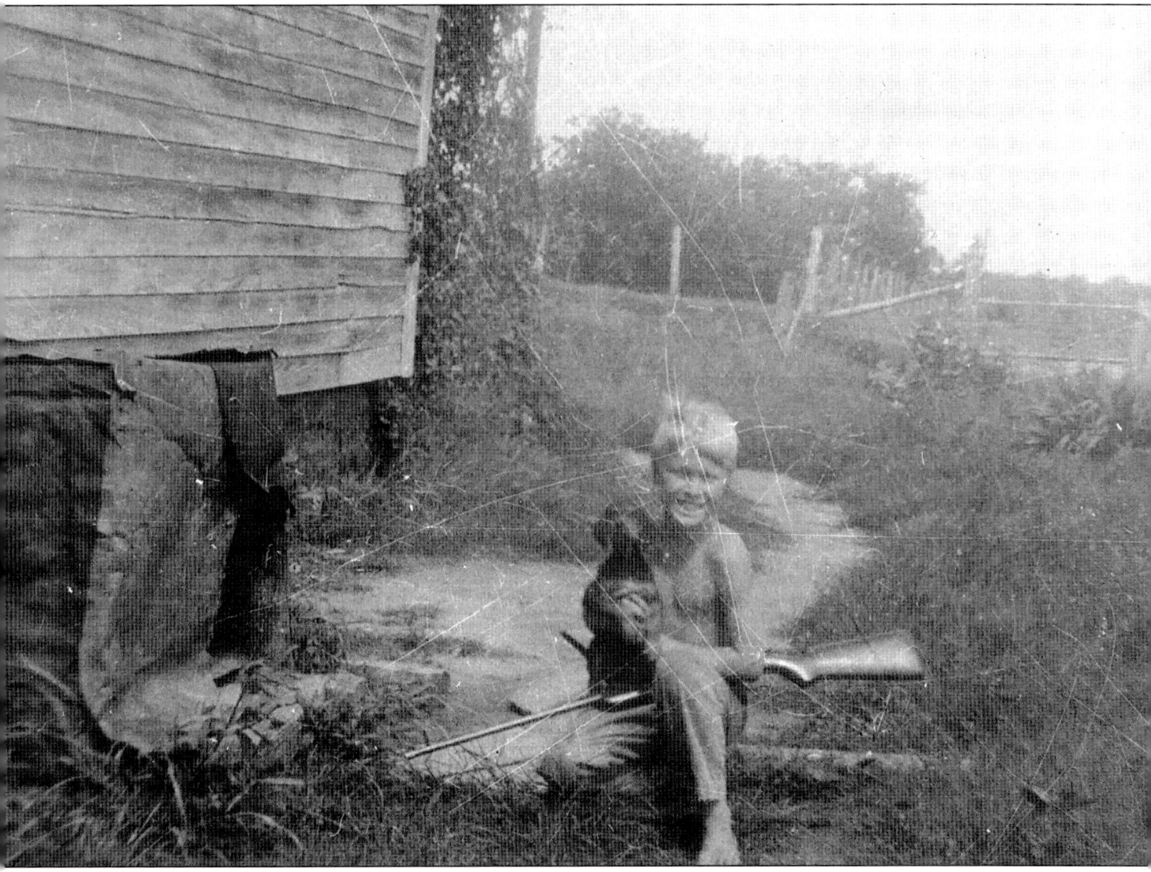

Shown is J.W. Brewer c. 1948 with a hound dog named Chief. A .22-caliber rifle and a good hunting dog were necessary to the livelihood of country folk. Pre-teens and teenagers were usually the best shots. For food, they killed squirrels, rabbits, and an occasional Opossum. The unwritten code was if "you killed it you ate it." Many people chose to live in remote areas, despite the strenuous life, because they preferred the solitude. (Elizabeth Muchmore Page.)

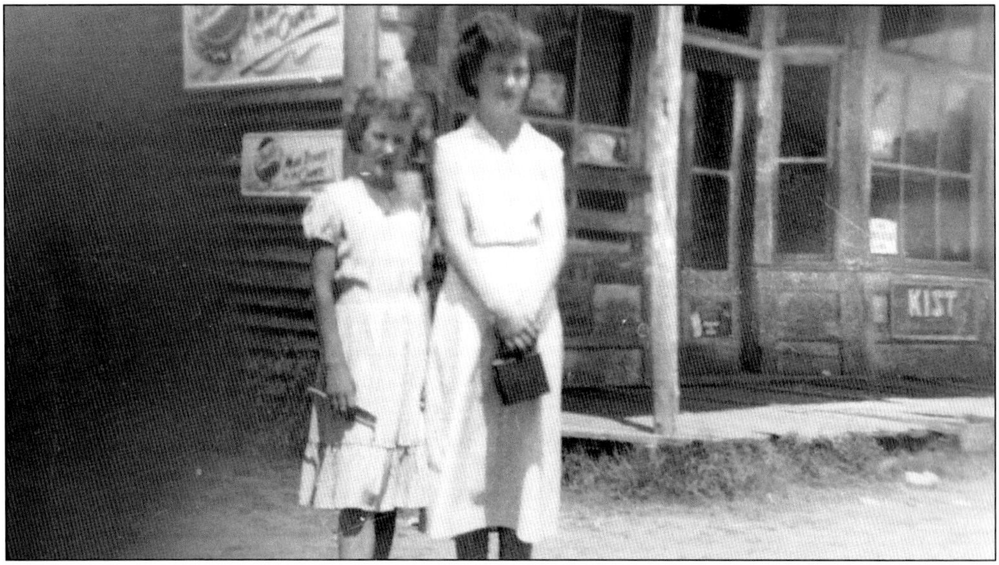

Charlene and Pauline Henry are shown c. 1949 at Dick Peters White Rock Store. The store carried household staples, livestock feed, and sported a beautiful Coca-Cola ice box. Nearby was a Church of Christ, a cemetery, and a large, two-room schoolhouse. The older students "found" nests in the woods belonging to Dick's chickens. They sold his own own eggs to him for a penny each to buy bubble gum. Dick, with a twinkle in his eye, resold the eggs to the students' parents. (Elizabeth Muchmore Page.)

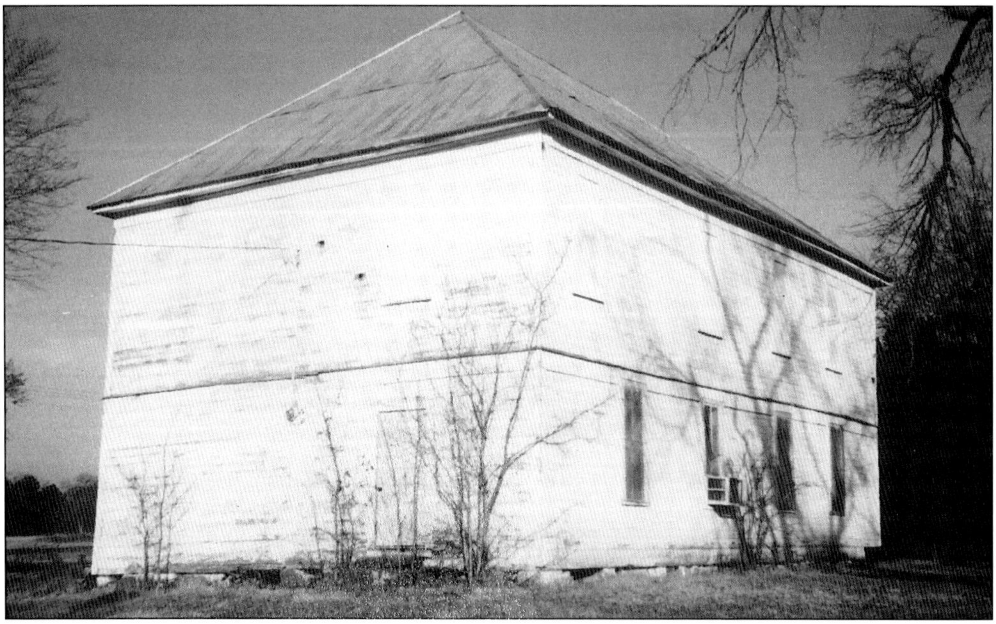

Shown is the Lone Elm Schoolhouse and Masonic Lodge, all boarded up. Lone Elm Missionary Baptist Church was formed in 1882. They never constructed another church building, preferring for years to meet in the old schoolhouse. A Confederate soldier, who had been in the army for only six months, was hung at this location after the Civil War was over. They were bushwhackers and wanted his money. His wife came along and took him down in a wagon and buried him. (Author.)

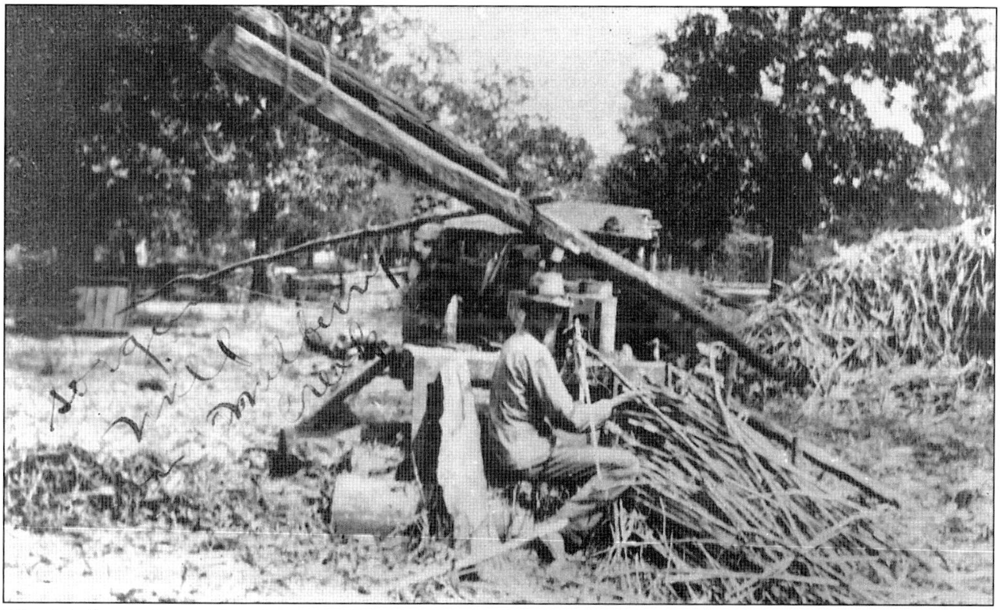

The Mulberry River Sorghum Mill is shown in this photo image. As the mule pulls the wooden, cross-pole in a circle, the farmer stuffs sugar cane into the center of the mill, where it is ground up. The product, a sweet, pulpy juice, is poured into a container to be boiled until it becomes thick, black Sorghum Molasses. The Mulberry River, flowing through the Ozark-St. Francis National Forest, is considered a part of the Wild and Scenic Rivers System. (Sadler H. Burrow Collection.)

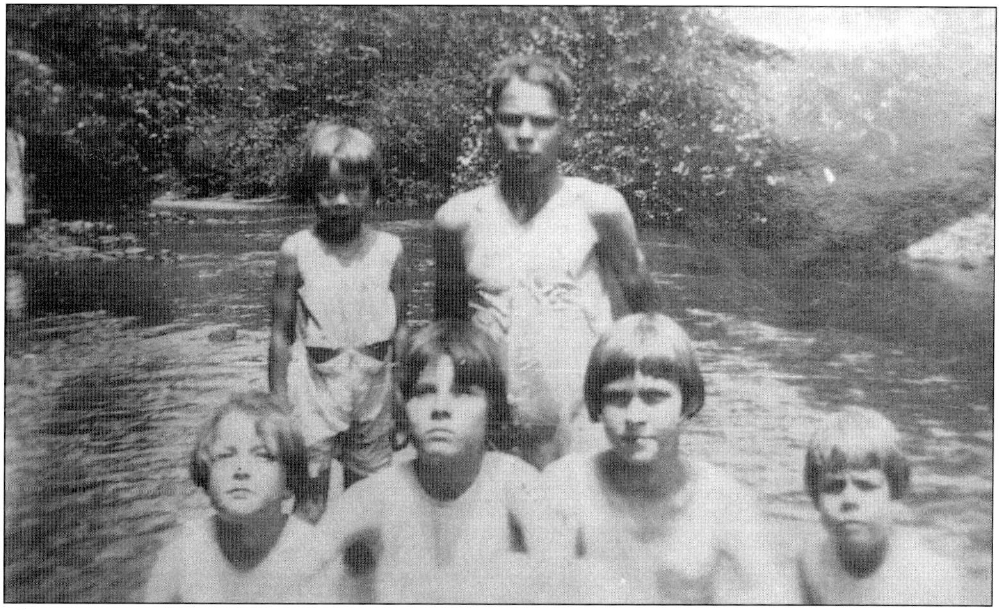

Shown are Walter Mason, on the back row, his sister Grace, third from the left on the front row, and their cousins, sisters Gladys, Edith, Jean, and Ina Page. The photo was made c. 1924 at Turner Bend recreational area, near Cass. They made the trip in Wallace Page's Baby Overland Automobile, which weighed around 6 or 7,000 pounds. It had lots of flats, but made it fine that day. (Elizabeth Muchmore Page, Grace Mason Watts.)

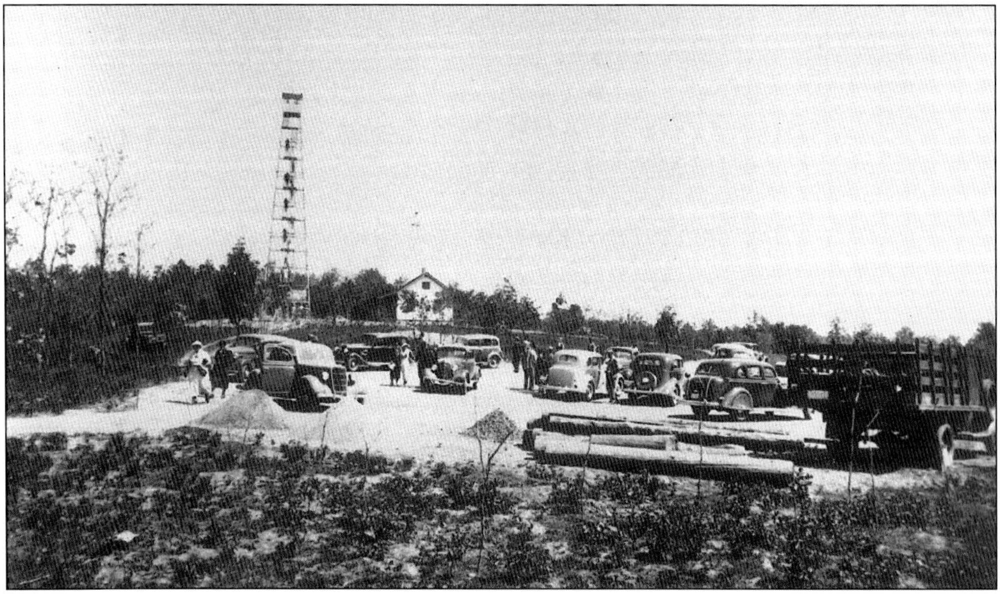

The White Rock Mountain parking lot and look-out tower are shown c. 1937. Hiking trails, which go all the way from Lake Fort Smith to the Boston Mountains, wind throughout the Ozark Highlands. Hikers are treated to some of the most spectacular scenery in the United States. The Ozarks have waterfalls, crystal-clear streams, moss-covered boulders, dramatic bluffs, and outstanding, geological formations. (Ozark Branch, U.S. Forest Service.)

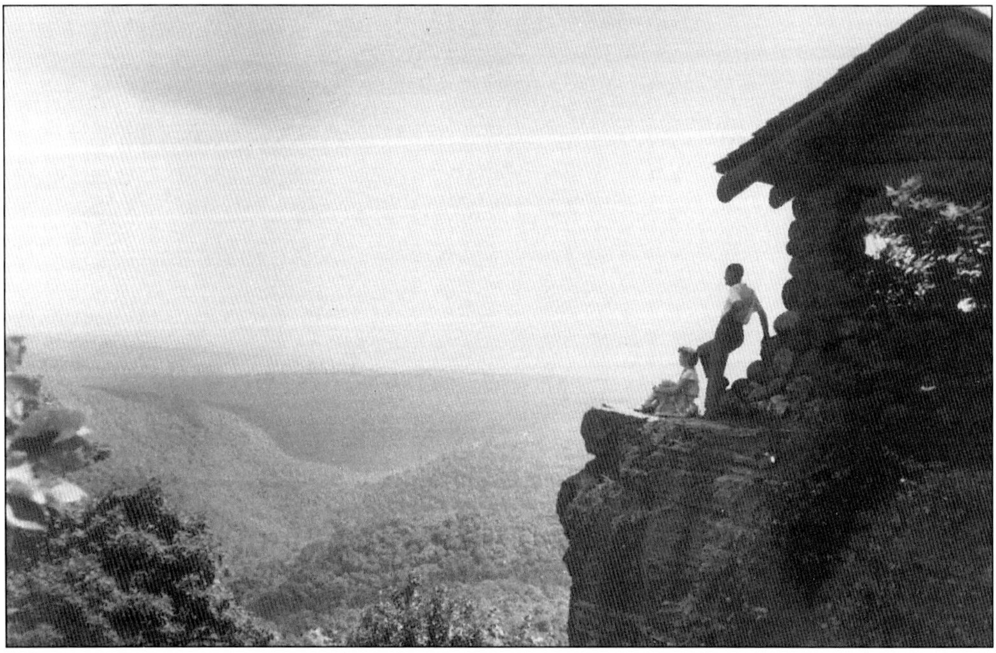

White Rock Mountain Overlook is shown c. 1937. Thousands of tourists visit the site each year. At this point one can see up to 40 miles on a clear day. It is a wilderness showcase. Nearby is a portion of the 181-mile Ozark Highlands Trail system, which intersects the White Rock Mountain trail system. Connected to the White Rock system is the 13-mile Shores Lake Spur Trail loop. (U.S. Forest Service, Russellville.)

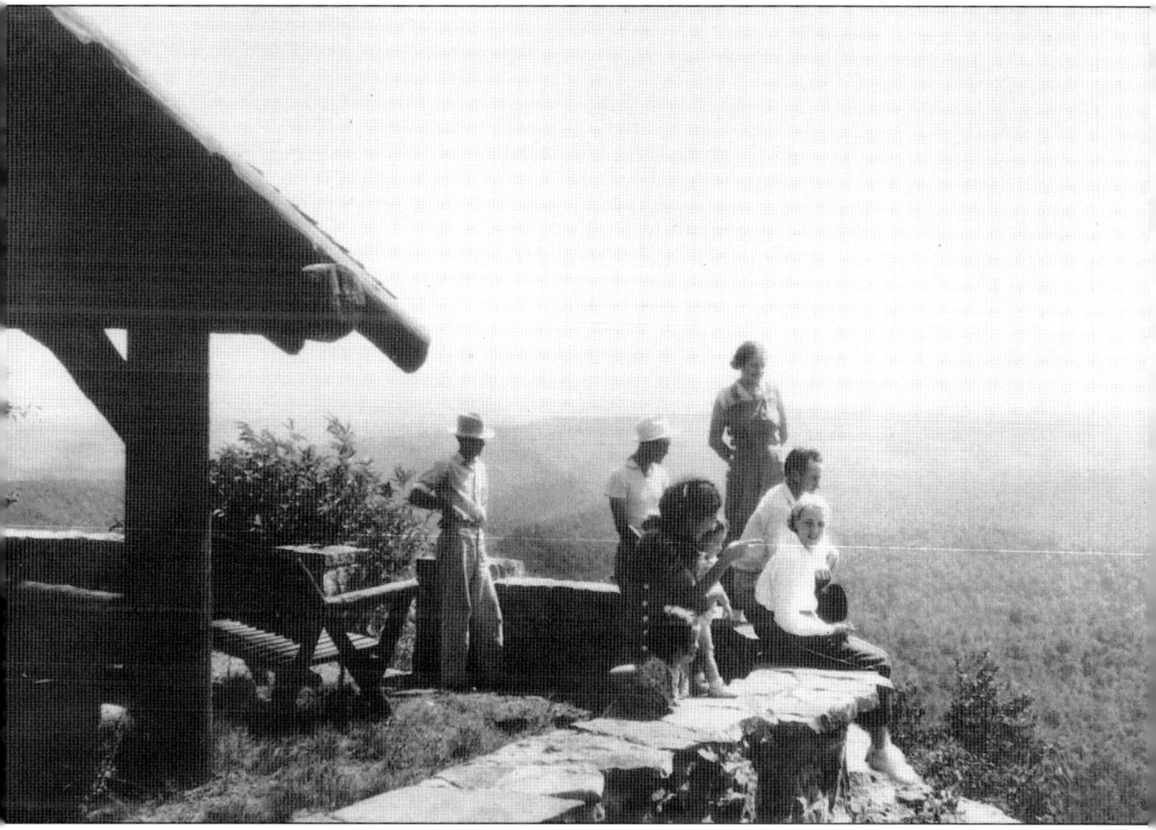

A spectacular vista is shown c. 1937 at the sheltered overlook on White Rock Mountain. Nearby are natural-stone cabins and a lodge, built in 1937 by the Civilian Conservation Corps. The CCC was organized during the Great Depression by President Franklin Roosevelt. The buildings had greatly deteriorated by the time a volunteer group, Friends of White Rock, began renovating them. The cabin and lodge restoration was completed in 1991. (Ozark Branch, U.S. Forest Service.)

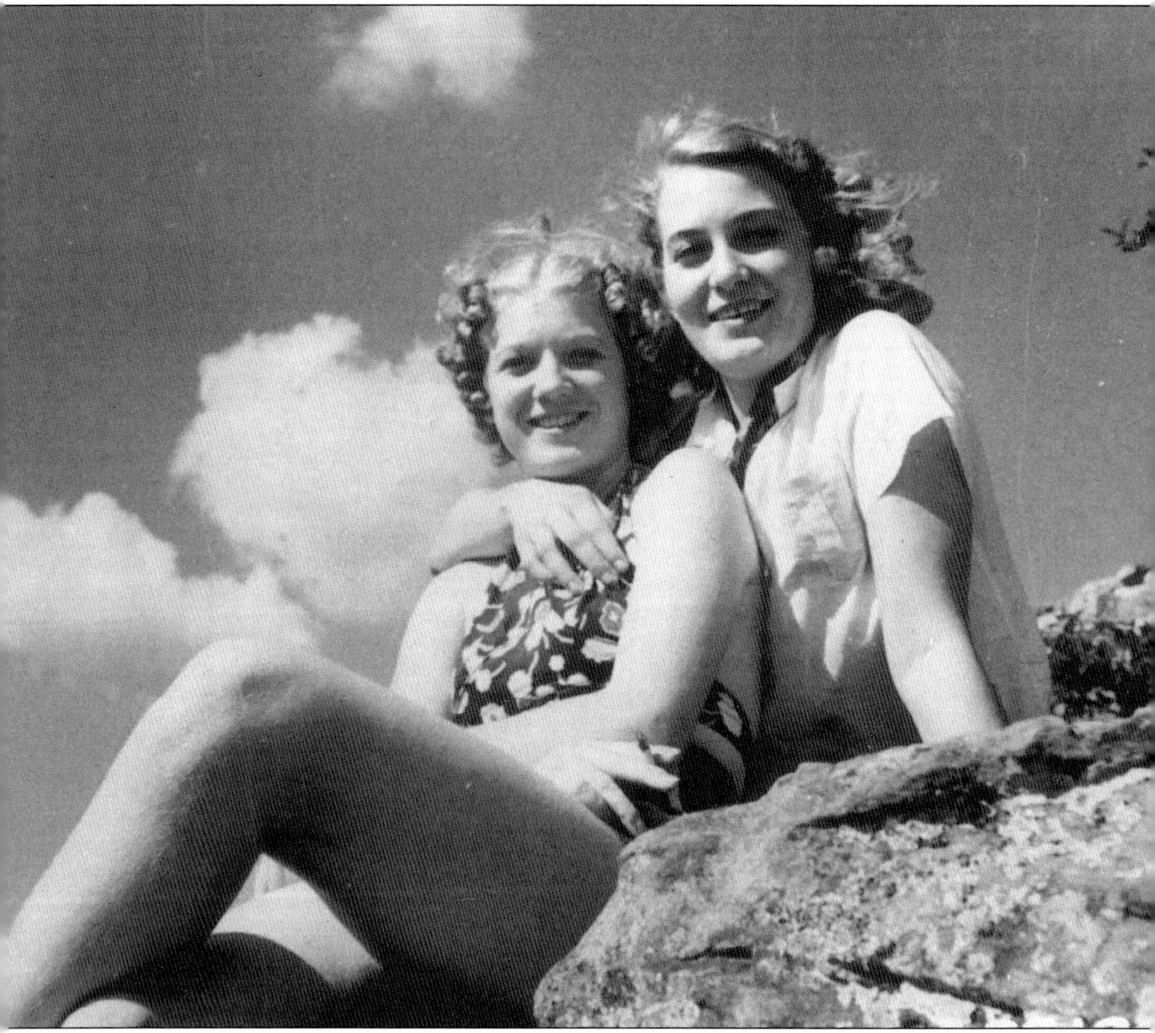

Two young ladies in July 1938 are shown at the White Rock Mountain overlook. With few guard rails to spoil the beauty, the scenic area is surrounded by potentially dangerous high bluffs. Walking and climbing with great care are necessary for safety. The mountain is 2,260 feet above sea level. White Rock Mountain is maintained by the U.S. Forest Service and is part of the Ozark-St. Francis National Forests, United States Department of Agriculture, Southern Region. (U.S. Forest Service, Russellville.)

Eleven

North Franklin County

Remote, Mysterious, Beautiful

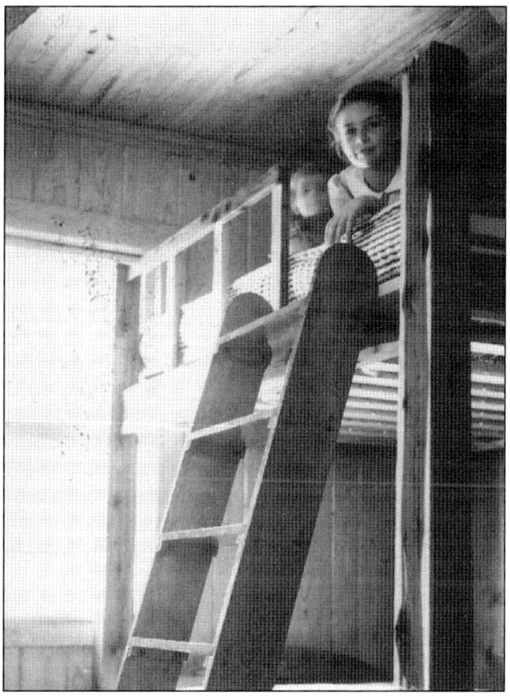

Two girls peer out the bedroom door in the Forest Building's Cabin B at White Rock recreational area, in 1937. Three historic cabins and a lodge, restored in 1991, can be rented at reasonable rates by individuals or by a group. Hiking, picnicking, and horse-back riding are possible, recreational pursuits of those who visit the area. (U.S. Forest Service, Russellville.)

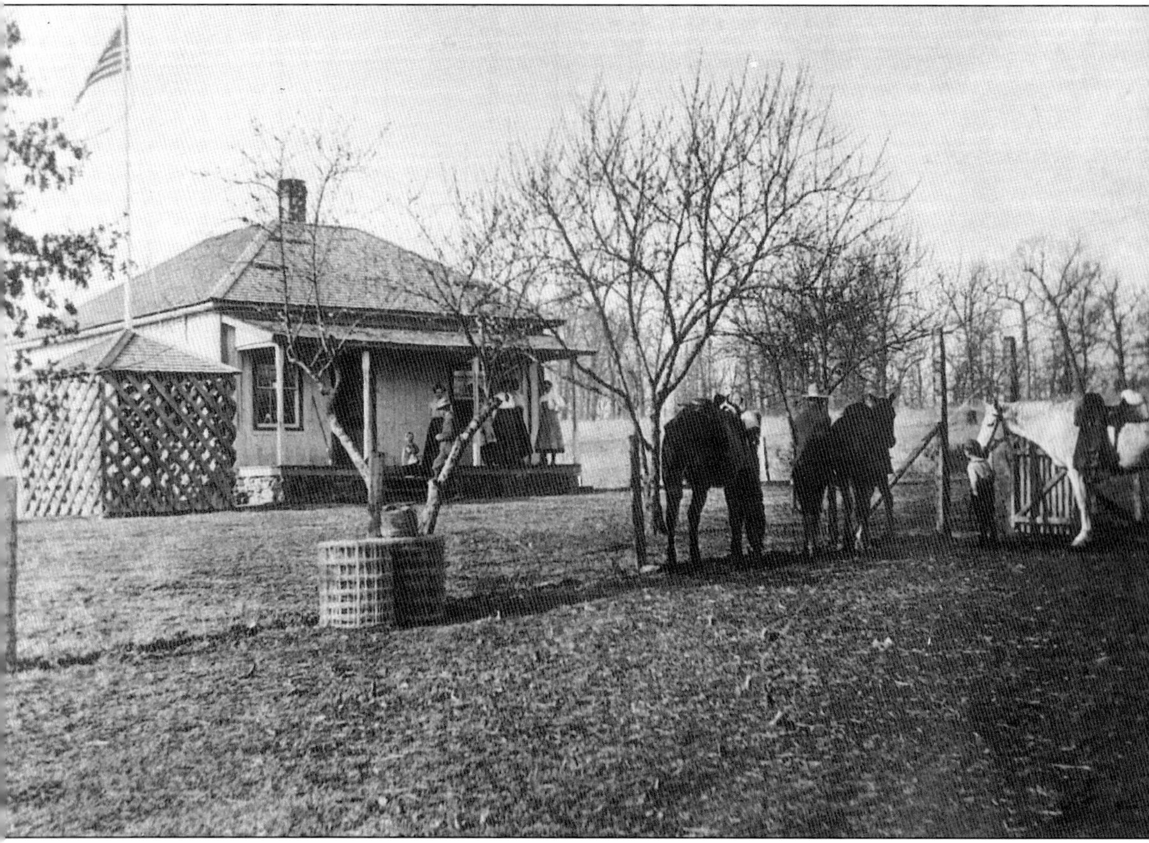

People, probably former residents, pose on the front porch of this Ranger Station. In the beginning, the U.S. Forest Service purchased property already on the market in the Ozark National Forest. Those homesteads became Ranger Headquarters or Stations. The Ozark National Forest covers more than one million acres, mostly in northwest Arkansas. It was established March 6, 1908, by Presidential Proclamation. (Ozark Branch, U.S. Forest Service.)

Many residents of White Rock Mountain opposed the idea of a government-protected forest. In protest, they wrecked the White Rock look-out tower in 1912. Shown is a Ranger attempting to climb the leaning tower. Residents eventually agreed that everyone benefits by conservation, and preservation, of the forests. Pilots use the Arkansas River when flying east and west and the White Rock Forest Tower when flying north and south. (U.S. Forest Service, Russellville.)

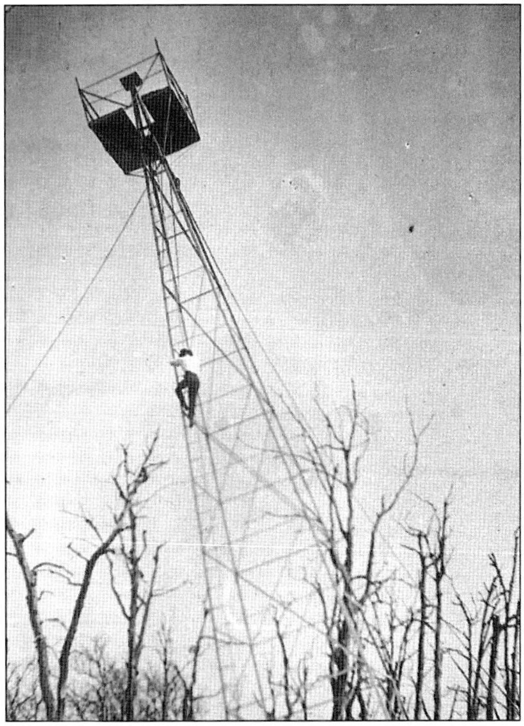

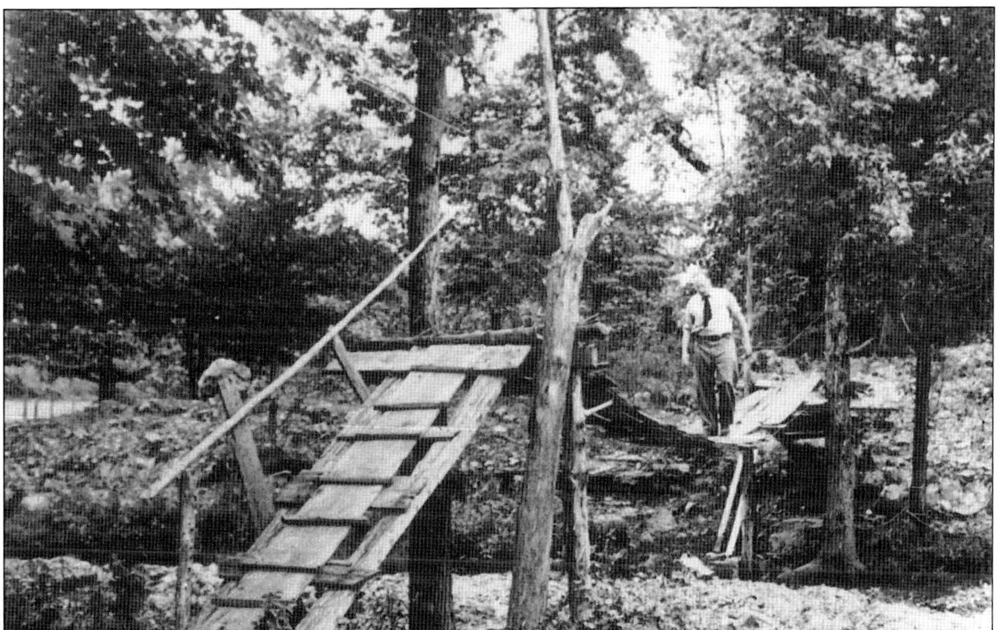

A forest official, as shown in July 1938, walks along Sneed Creek Footbridge and trail. One old trail crossed a nearby river seven times within a five-mile stretch. In rainy weather the trails were impassable for the small farmers who hunted and fished and kept a few cattle. In 1938, under forest supervision, an all-weather road was built down Big Mulberry River to east of Cass. (U.S. Forest Service, Russellville.)

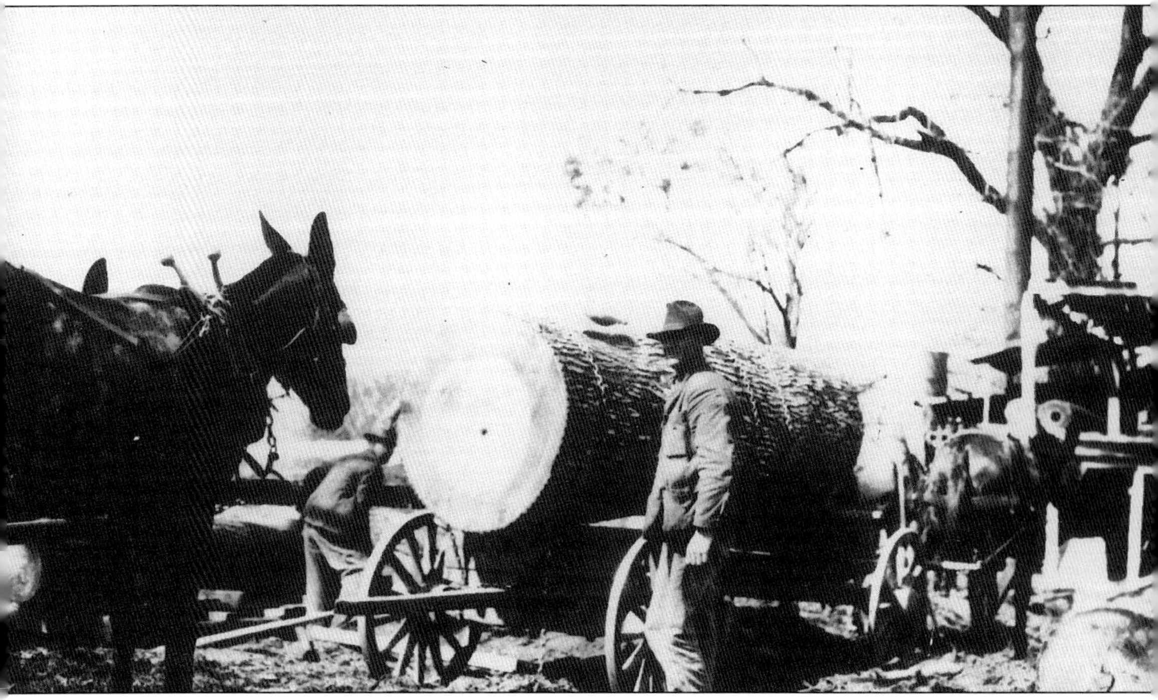

This photo image with man and mule waiting to unload was made of a sawmill at Cass. In 1914 there was a timber boom in the Ozark Mountains. The logs and lumber were transported by means of horse and mule over deeply rutted trails. When the Civilian Conservation Corps first began to clear the forest they cut virgin timber similar to the log shown, and even larger. Note how small the man and mule appear in comparison to the log. (Sadler H. Burrow Collection.)

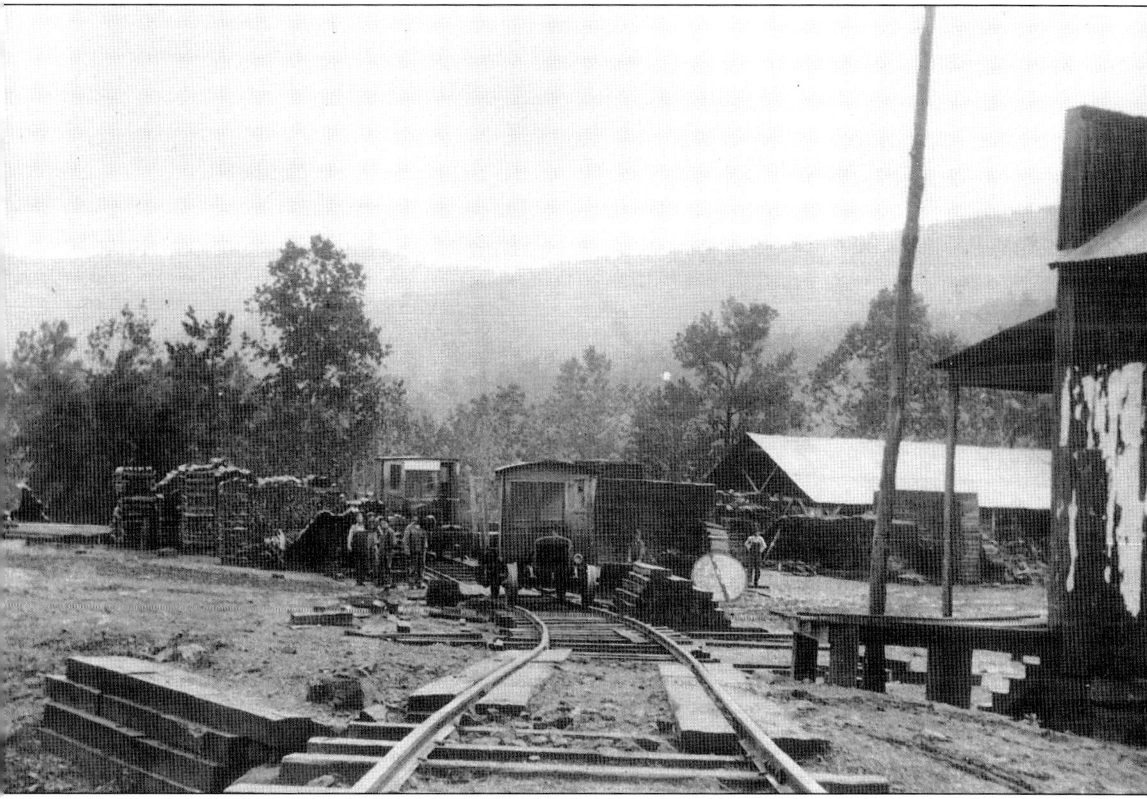

Shown is the Cass-Combs and Eastern Railway Train, and logging camp. This short-line railroad, from Fayetteville to Cass, was built in 1914, using mule teams, picks, shovels, axes, and saws. It hauled passengers and logs across wooden bridges that spanned four gorges. One wooden framework was 110 feet high, and one bridge sloped 9 feet lower at the north end than at the south. Due to sharp curves the train ran out on a spur and back to the main line in four locations. (U.S. Forest Service, Russellville.)

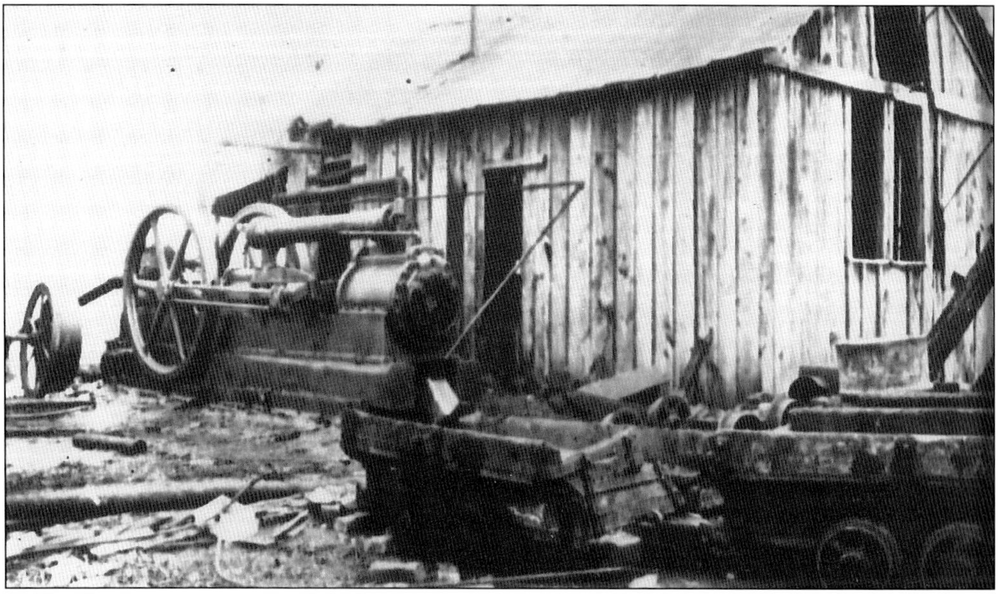

During the first five years of service the Cass-Combs Railroad had two small steam locomotives, six regular flatcars, two boxcars, and two passenger cars. During the final five years, the company used an old streetcar with power furnished by two tractor engines. The engine shown was utilized in some way to move the train. In 1921 the Arkansas Tax Commission estimated the railroad to be worth $37,480. When Highway 23 was built through Cass, it became unprofitable to run the train. (Sadler H. Burrow Collection.)

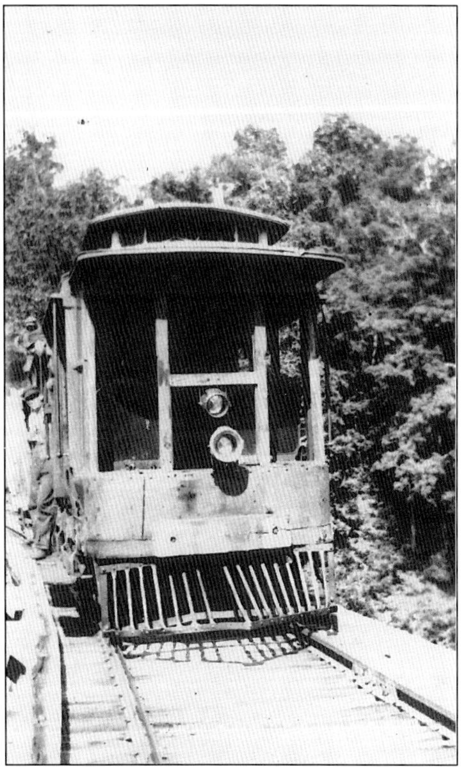

The Cass-Combs Railroad caboose is shown in the early 1920s. The two towns were only ten miles apart as the crow flies, yet were connected by 17 miles of track. In later years passenger service was provided by means of the caboose only. When the owners began to lose money, the track was not maintained and became unsafe. Sadly, the colorful little railroad ceased to operate and the steels were pulled in 1924. (Sadler H. Burrow Collection.)

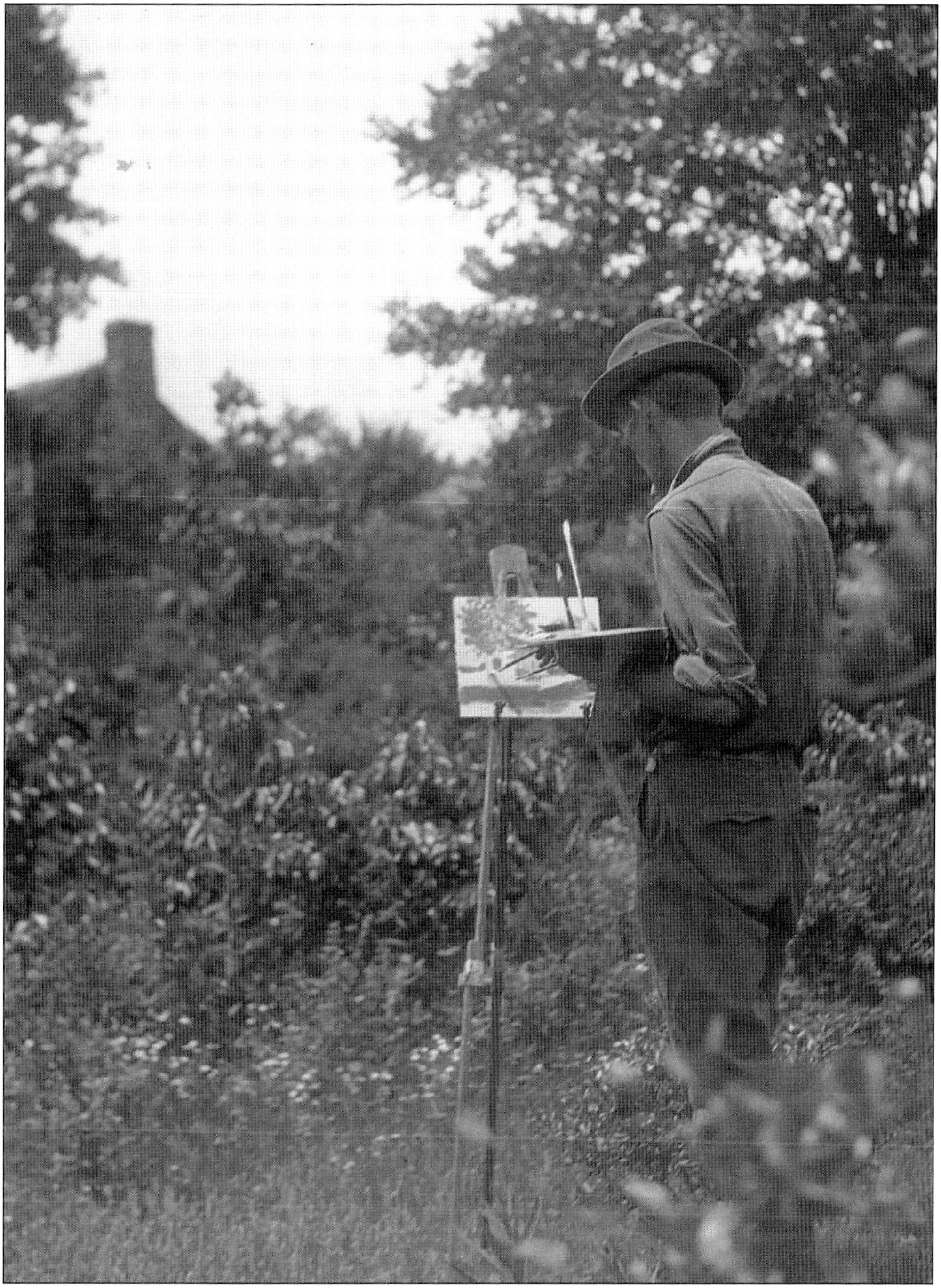

Artist Olin Travis is shown painting a picturesque scene at Cass in the late 1920s. The Travis Art Camp artist retreat was often used by folks as a Sunday afternoon outing. Travis's primitive painting style has enjoyed a revival in recent times. Cass, in the Ozark National Forest, is one of the most impressive valleys in mid-America. Rugged trails, the spectacular Mulberry River, and the scenic Highway System can be beautifully interpreted through an artist's palette. (Sadler H. Burrow Collection.)

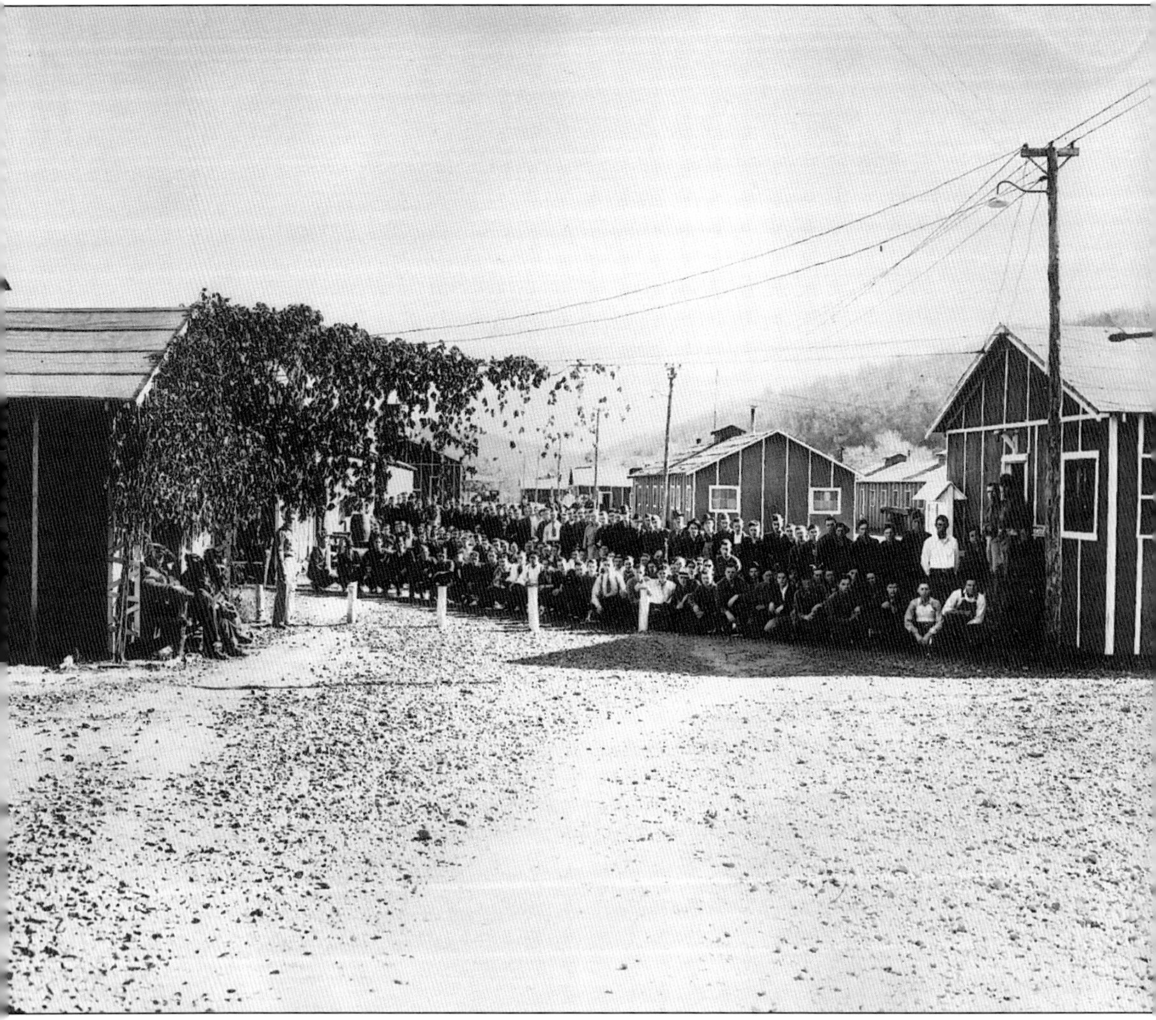

Shown are staff and recruits of the Cass Civilian Conservation Corps, formed by President Franklin Roosevelt in the 1930s. With the start of WW II the CCC camps closed, and recruits dispersed into the armed forces and defense industries. The Cass Job Corps of today trains students for the skills needed to obtain a job. Students may become chefs, carpenters, painters, welders, or office workers. (Sadler H. Burrow Collection.)

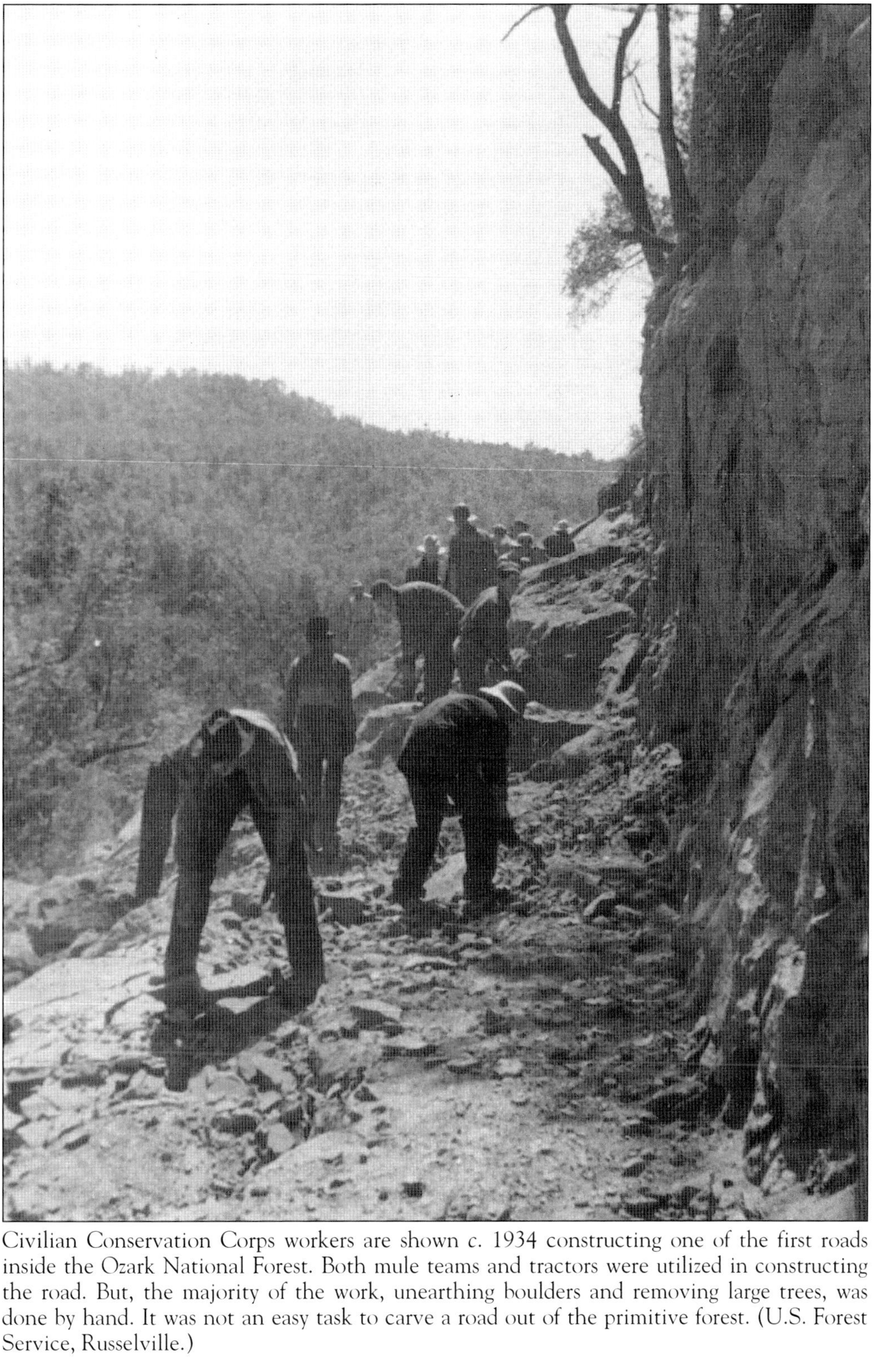

Civilian Conservation Corps workers are shown c. 1934 constructing one of the first roads inside the Ozark National Forest. Both mule teams and tractors were utilized in constructing the road. But, the majority of the work, unearthing boulders and removing large trees, was done by hand. It was not an easy task to carve a road out of the primitive forest. (U.S. Forest Service, Russelville.)

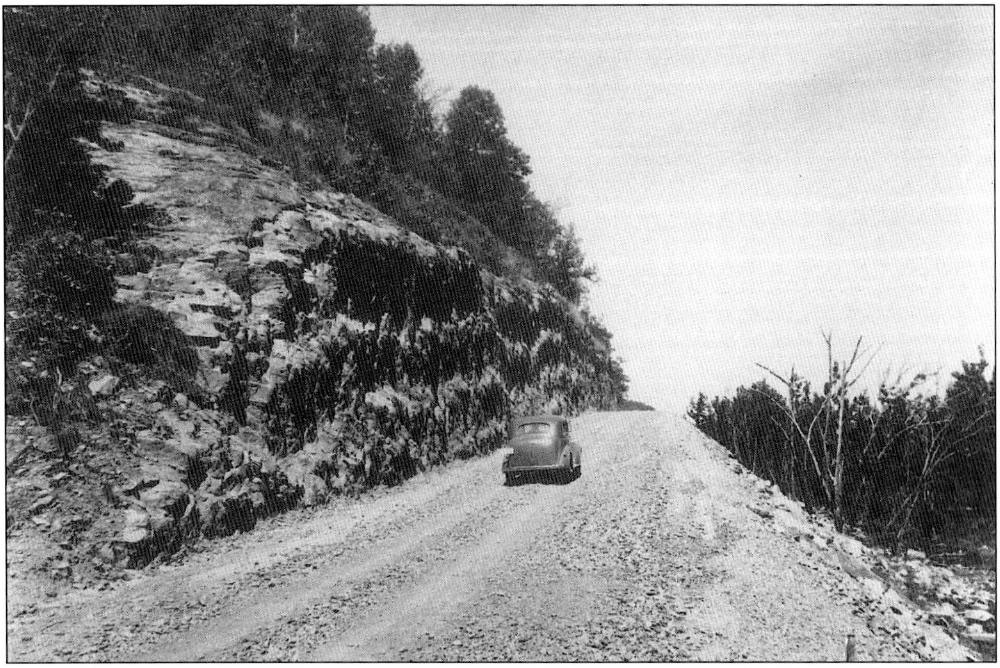

The car, shown c. 1935, travels along the Cass-Bidville Road soon after completion. The road was built by CCC recruits from the facility at Cass. All the fire look-out towers in Franklin County were eventually connected by all-weather roads. These roads were also constructed by the CCC boys under U.S. Forest supervision. The Cass facility of the CCC was the oldest camp in Arkansas, having been established in 1933. (U.S. Forest Service, Russellville.)

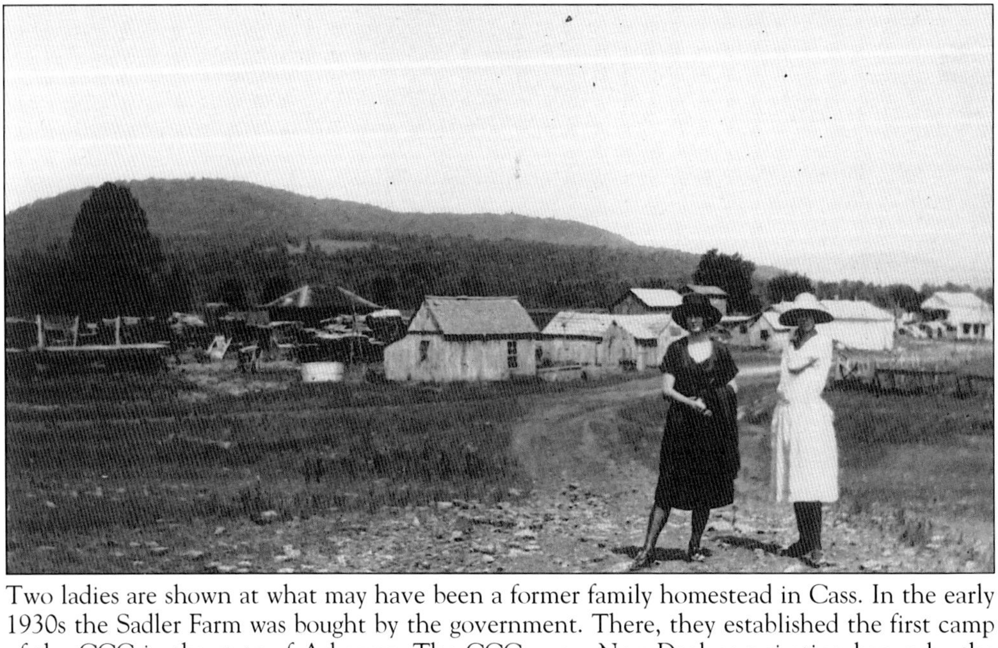

Two ladies are shown at what may have been a former family homestead in Cass. In the early 1930s the Sadler Farm was bought by the government. There, they established the first camp of the CCC in the state of Arkansas. The CCC was a New Deal organization begun by the Departments of Agriculture, and Interior, to provide work camps for unemployed young men. The old CCC camp is now the Cass Job Corps Center. (Sadler H. Burrow Collection.)

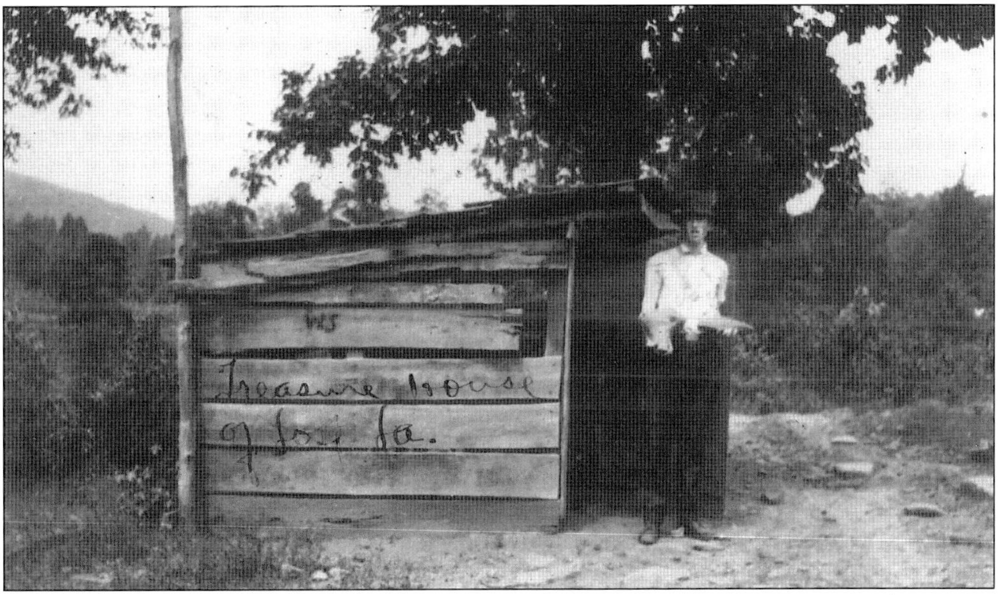

Shown is believed to be Dr. Tobe Hill, owner of the famous Lost Louisiana Mine. The writing on the photo image says "Treasure House." Hill is holding what appears to be the bone of a large cow or buffalo. According to legend Hernando DeSoto's men murdered the Aztec Indians mining gold in the region. The Conquistadors stored the gold deep in an excavated tunnel and left mysterious writings on the cliff face to guide them when they returned. They never came back. (Sadler H. Burrow Collection.)

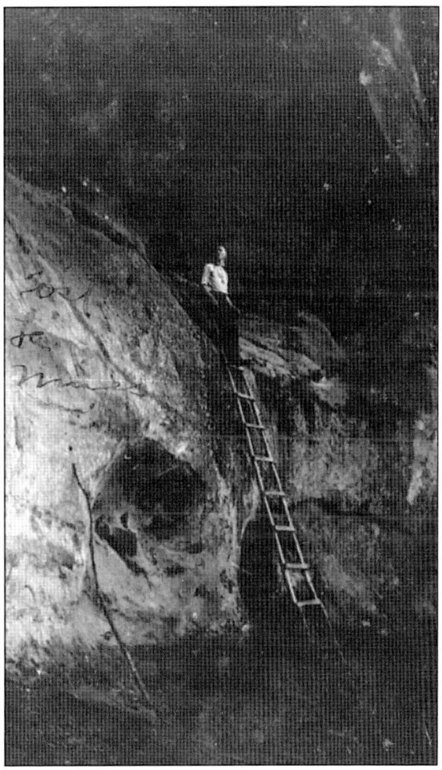

Pictured is what Dr. Tobe Hill and his Louisiana Mining Company associates believed was a Spanish Treasure Cave. In more recent times many of the curious still accept the treasure story. Some say they have seen the entrance to the "Doc Hill Mine." The reported entrance is said to be six feet square and penetrates the mountain to a depth of nearly 150 feet. Those who believe in the legend say the ancient writings tell the exact location of the treasure. As yet no one has interpreted them. (Sadler H. Burrow Collection.)

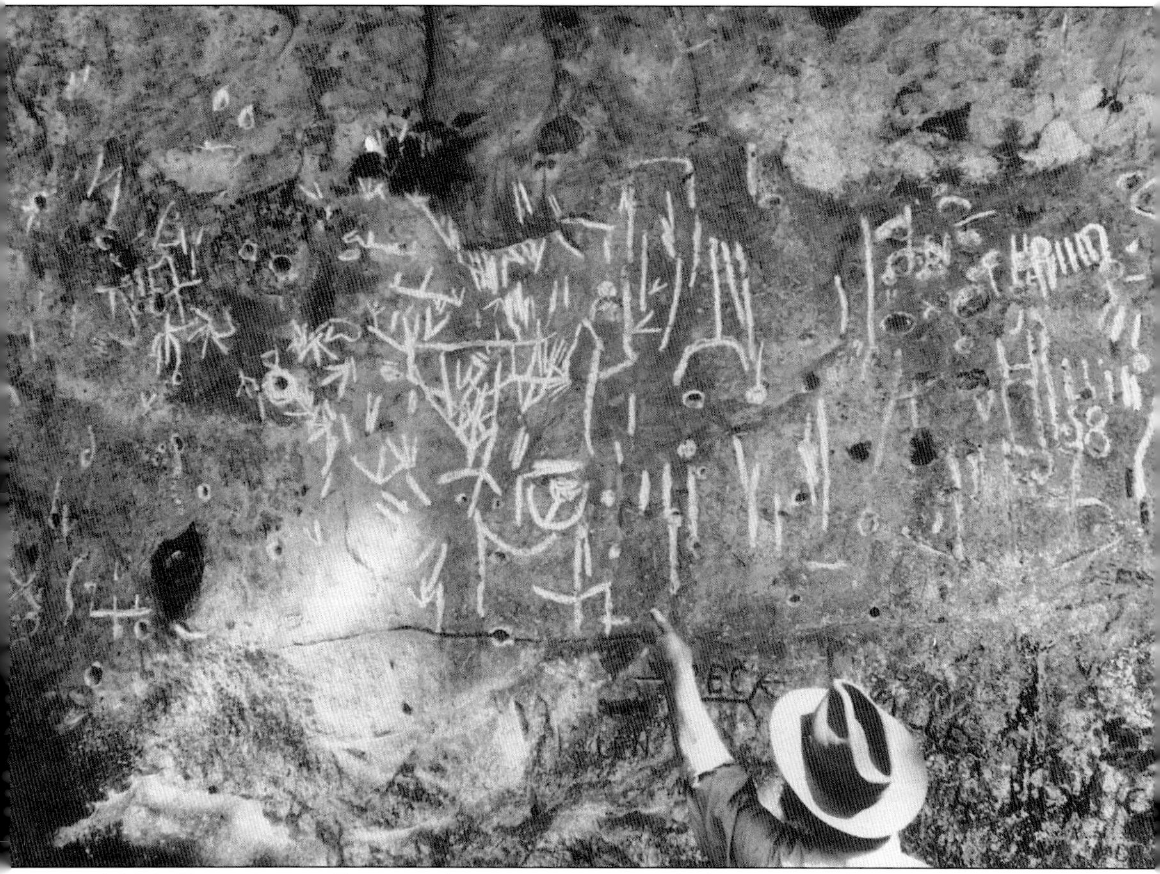

A U.S. Forest Service Ranger indicates ancient petroglyphs on the walls of a cave two miles from the Cass Job Corps Center, near the Mulberry River. Shafts and tunnels can still be seen where would-be treasure hunters searched for more than 30 years for a buried treasure of Spanish gold. Thousands of dollars were invested in the Lost Louisiana mining venture. All that investors ever found were these oddly marked rocks. Note the bullet holes in the wall near the writings. Early day vandalism of archeological sites is common. (U.S. Forest Service, Russellville.)